LAW, CRIME AND LAW ENFORCEMENT

AN EXAMINATION OF SENTENCING LEVELS AND MANDATORY MINIMUMS

LAW, CRIME AND LAW ENFORCEMENT

Additional books in this series can be found on Nova's website under the Series tab.

Additional E-books in this series can be found on Nova's website under the E-books tab.

LAW, CRIME AND LAW ENFORCEMENT

AN EXAMINATION OF SENTENCING LEVELS AND MANDATORY MINIMUMS

CATHERINE N. BATES
EDITOR

Nova Science Publishers, Inc.
New York

For permission to use material from this book please contact us:
Telephone 631-231-7269; Fax 631-231-8175
Web Site: http://www.novapublishers.com

LIBRARY OF CONGRESS CATALOGING-IN-PUBLICATION DATA

An examination of sentencing levels and mandatory minimums / editors,
Catherine N. Bates.
p. cm.
Includes index.
"CRS report for Congress prepared for members and committees of Congress."
ISBN 978-1-61209-563-9 (hardcover)
1. Sentences (Criminal procedure)--United States. 2. Mandatory sentences--United States. 3. Drugs of abuse--Law and legislation--United States--Criminal provisions. 4. Narcotic laws--United States. I. Bates, Catherine N. II. Library of Congress. Congressional Research Service. III. United States. Congress. House. Committee on the Judiciary. Subcommittee on Crime, Terrorism, and Homeland Security.
KF9685.A25 2011
345.73'0772--dc22

2011004002

Published by Nova Science Publishers, Inc. + New York

CONTENTS

PREFACE

Depending on how the class is defined, there are hundreds of federal mandatory minimum offenses, yet only a handful are prosecuted with any regularity. In October 2009, Congress instructed the United States Sentencing Commission to prepare a report on the mandatory minimum sentencing provisions under federal law. In early 2010, the Commission conducted a survey of federal district court judges regarding their views on mandatory minimum sentencing. A majority of those responding endorsed amendments to the safety valve and substantial assistance exceptions. This new book examines sentencing levels and mandatory minimums with regard to drug sentences and the safety valve, federal cocaine sentencing disparities and three-strike mandatory sentencing.

Chapter 1- Pursuant to the Anti-Drug Abuse Act of 1986, Congress established basic sentencing levels for crack cocaine offenses. Congress amended 21 U.S.C. § 841 to provide for a 100:1 ratio in the quantities of powder cocaine and crack cocaine that trigger a mandatory minimum penalty. As amended, 21 U.S.C. § 841(b)(1)(A) required a mandatory minimum 10-year term of imprisonment and a maximum life term of imprisonment for trafficking offenses involving 5 kilograms of cocaine or 50 grams of cocaine base. In addition, 21 U.S.C. § 841(b)(1)(B) established a mandatory 5-year term of imprisonment for offenses involving 500 grams of cocaine or 5 grams of cocaine base. 21 U.S.C. § 844(a) called for a 5-year mandatory minimum punishment for simple possession of crack cocaine. Although the Fair Sentencing Act of 2010 revises these penalties (as discussed below), there still remains a disparity in the threshold amount of powder cocaine and crack cocaine that triggers the mandatory minimums in 21 U.S.C. § 841.

Chapter 2- Section 924(c) requires the imposition of one of a series of mandatory minimum terms of imprisonment upon conviction for misconduct involving the firearm and the commission of a federal crime of violence or a federal drug trafficking offense. The terms vary according to the type of firearm used, the manner of the firearm's involvement, and whether the conviction involves a single, first-time offense.

Chapter 3- Federal law requires a sentencing judge to impose a minimum sentence of imprisonment following conviction for any of a number of federal offenses. Congress has created two exceptions. One is available in all cases when the prosecutor asserts that the defendant has provided substantial assistance in the criminal investigation or prosecution of another, 18 U.S.C. 3553(e). The other, commonly referred to as the safety value, is available, without the government's approval, for a handful of the more commonly prosecuted drug trafficking and unlawful possession offenses that carry minimum sentences, 18 U.S.C. 3553(f).

Chapter 4- The federal three strikes provision calls for a mandatory term of life imprisonment for defendants convicted of a serious violent felony who have two or more federal or state serious violent felony convictions or one or more of such felony conviction plus one or more federal or state serious drug conviction, 18 U.S.C. 3559(c). The qualifying violent felonies are those specifically enumerated within the section—murder, rape, violent robberies, extortion, among others—as well as unenumerated felonies, that is, any state and federal 10-year felony that involves the fact or risk of physical violence. The qualifying serious drug offenses are those punishable by imprisonment for 10 years or more under state or federal law. The section creates an exemption where defendants can prove that an otherwise qualifying conviction involved neither the fact nor risk of injury.

Chapter 5- The Armed Career Criminal Act (ACCA), 18 U.S.C. 924(e), requires imposition of a minimum 15-year term of imprisonment for recidivists convicted of unlawful possession of a firearm under 18 U.S.C. 922(g). Section 924(e) applies only to those defendants who have three prior state or federal convictions for violent felonies or serious drug offenses.

Violent felonies for purposes of section 924(e) are those that either (1) have an element of threat, attempt, or use of physical force against another or (2) that involve burglary, arson, or extortion, or some similar offense. Serious drug offenses are those punishable by imprisonment for 10 years or more.

Constitutional challenges to the application of section 924(e) have been generally unsuccessful, regardless of whether they were based on arguments of cruel and unusual punishment, double jeopardy, due process, grand jury indictment or jury trial rights, the right to bear arms, or limits on Congress's legislative authority.

Chapter 6- This is a chart of the maximum fines and terms of imprisonment that may be imposed as a consequence of conviction for violation of the federal Controlled Substances Act (CSA) and other drug supply and drug demand related laws.

It lists the penalties for: heroin, cocaine, crack, PCP, LSD, marihuana (marijuana), amphetamine, methamphetamine, listed (precursor) chemicals, paraphernalia, date rape drugs, rave drugs, designer drugs, ecstasy, drug kingpins, as well as the other substances including narcotics and opiates assigned to Schedule I, Schedule II, Schedule III, Schedule IV, and Schedule V of the Controlled Substances Act and the Controlled Substances Import and Export Act (Title II and Title III of the Comprehensive Drug Abuse and Control Act).

Chapter 7 – This statement was delivered as testimony on July 14, 2009. Judge Julie E. Carnes, Chair of the Criminal Law Committee on behalf of the Judicial Conference, before the United States House of Representatives, Committee on the Judiciary, Subcommittee on Crime, Terrorism and Homeland Security.

Chapter 8 - This is a statement of Julie Stewart, President, Families Against Mandatory Minimum, submitted to the Subcommittee on Crime, Terrorism, and Homeland Security, of the Committee on the Judiciary, United States House of Representatives.

Chapter 9 - This is a statement of Michael J. Sullivan, Partner, Ashcroft Sulliva, before the Subcommittee on Crime, terrorism, and Homeland Security, Committee on the Judiciary, United States House of Representatives.

Chapter 10 - This is a statement of National Border Patrol Council of the American Federation of Government Employees, before the Subcommittee on Crime, Terrorism and Homeland Security, Committee on the Judiciary, United States House of Representatives.

Chapter 11 - This is a statement of Grover G. Norquist, President, Americans for Tax Reform, Subcommittee on Crime, Terrorism, and Homeland Security, House Committee on the Judiciary.

Chapter 12 - This is a statement of Lanny A. Breuer, Assistant Attorney General, Criminal Division, United States Department of Justice, before the United States House of Representatives, Committee on the Judiciary, Subcommittee on Crime, Terrorism and Homeland Security.

Chapter 13 - This is a statement of Ricardo H. Hinojosa, Acting Chair, United States Sentencing Commission, before the House Committee on the Judiciary, Subcommittee on Crime, Terrorism, and Homeland Security.

Chapter 14 - This is a statement of Joseph I. Cassilly, State's Attorney Harford County, Bel Air, Maryland, and President, national District Attorneys Association, House Judiciary Committee, Subcommittee on Crime, Terrorism, and Homeland Security, United States House of Representatives.

Chapter 15 - This is a statement of Willie M. Aikens, before the Subcommittee on Crime, terrorism, and Homeland Security of the House Judiciary Committee.

Chapter 16 - This is a statement of Bob Bushman, Vice President, National Narcotic Officers' Associations' Coalition, before the Subcommittee on Crime, Terrorism, and Homeland Security, Committee on Judiciary, United States House of Representatives.

Chapter 17 - This is a statement of Veronica F. Coleman-Davis, former United States Attorney for the Western District of Tennessee, before the United States house of Representatives, Committee on the Judiciary, Subcommittee on Crime, Terrorism, and Homeland Security.

Chapter 18 - This is a statement of Marc Mauer, Executive Director, The Sentencing Project, prepared for the House Judiciary, Subcommittee on Crime, Terrorism, and Homeland Security.

In: An Examination of Sentencing Levels and Mandatory... ISBN: 978-1-61209-563-9
Editor: Catherine N. Bates

Chapter 1

FEDERAL COCAINE SENTENCING DISPARITY: SENTENCING GUIDELINES, JURISPRUDENCE, AND LEGISLATION

Brian T. Yeh

SUMMARY

Pursuant to the Anti-Drug Abuse Act of 1986, Congress established basic sentencing levels for crack cocaine offenses. Congress amended 21 U.S.C. § 841 to provide for a 100:1 ratio in the quantities of powder cocaine and crack cocaine that trigger a mandatory minimum penalty. As amended, 21 U.S.C. § 841(b)(1)(A) required a mandatory minimum 10-year term of imprisonment and a maximum life term of imprisonment for trafficking offenses involving 5 kilograms of cocaine or 50 grams of cocaine base. In addition, 21 U.S.C. § 841(b)(1)(B) established a mandatory 5-year term of imprisonment for offenses involving 500 grams of cocaine or 5 grams of cocaine base. 21 U.S.C. § 844(a) called for a 5-year mandatory minimum punishment for simple possession of crack cocaine. Although the Fair Sentencing Act of 2010 revises these penalties (as discussed below), there still remains a disparity in the threshold amount of powder cocaine and crack cocaine that triggers the mandatory minimums in 21 U.S.C. § 841.

Federal sentencing guidelines (the Guidelines) established by the U.S. Sentencing Commission reflect the statutory differential treatment of crack and powder cocaine offenders. Until 2005, the Guidelines were binding on federal courts: the judge had discretion to sentence a defendant, but only within the narrow sentencing range that the Guidelines provided. In its 2005 opinion *United States v. Booker*, the Supreme Court declared that the Guidelines must be considered advisory rather than mandatory, in order to comply with the Constitution. Instead of being bound by the Guidelines, sentencing courts must treat the federal guidelines as just one of a number of sentencing factors (which include the need to avoid undue sentencing disparity).

In the aftermath of *Booker*, some judges, who did not believe that crack cocaine is 100 times worse than powder cocaine, imposed lower sentences on crack cocaine offenders than the ones recommended by the Guidelines. In 2007, the Supreme Court in *Kimbrough v. United States* upheld this practice, ruling that a court *may* impose a below-the-Guidelines sentence based on its conclusion that the 100:1 ratio is greater than necessary or may foster unwarranted disparity.

Also in 2007, the Sentencing Commission revised the Guidelines by lowering the base offense level for crack cocaine offenses by two levels, thereby eliminating the 100:1 ratio for future sentencing guideline purposes (except at the point at which the statutory mandatory minimums are triggered). In addition, the Sentencing Commission decided to make these amendments retroactively applicable, thus allowing eligible crack cocaine offenders who were sentenced prior to November 1, 2007, to petition a federal judge to reduce their sentences. On June 17, 2010, the Supreme Court decided *Dillon v. United States*, in which it held that *Booker* does *not* apply in a sentence modification proceeding that is based on the retroactive crack cocaine amendment to the Guidelines; thus, district courts do not have the authority to further reduce a crack cocaine offender's sentence in such proceedings below the retroactive, amended Guidelines range.

The Fair Sentencing Act of 2010 (S. 1789) changes the *statutory* 100:1 ratio in crack/powder cocaine quantities that trigger the mandatory minimum penalties under 21 U.S.C. § 841(b)(1). President Obama signed the bill into law on August 3, 2010 (P.L. 111-220). S. 1789 reduces the statutory 100:1 ratio to 18:1, by increasing the threshold amount of crack cocaine to 28 grams (for the 5-year sentence) and 280 grams (for the 10-year sentence). S. 1789 also eliminates the 5-year mandatory minimum for simple possession of crack cocaine. Other bills introduced in the 111th Congress would completely eliminate the statutory disparity in cocaine sentencing, including H.R. 18, H.R. 265, H.R. 1459, H.R. 2178, and H.R. 3245. Another bill, H.R. 1466, would repeal all statutory mandatory minimums for drug offenses.

BACKGROUND

In its 2005 opinion *United States v. Booker*,[1] the U.S. Supreme Court declared that the once- binding federal sentencing guidelines (the Guidelines) set by the United States Sentencing Commission are now only advisory, in order to be compatible with the Sixth Amendment to the Constitution.[2] Until 2007, the Guidelines reflected a statutory scheme that made crack cocaine defendants subject to the same sentence as those defendants trafficking in 100 times more powder cocaine; thus, the sentences for crack cocaine offenses were three to over six times longer than those for offenses involving equivalent amounts of powder cocaine.[3] In the immediate aftermath of *Booker*, federal courts disagreed about whether the 100:1 ratio produces disparities that justify a sentence lower than that recommended by the Guidelines. The Supreme Court resolved that issue in its 2007 opinion *Kimbrough v. United States*, by holding that a federal court may impose a sentence below that called for under the Guidelines' then-existing 100:1 ratio, based on its conclusion that the ratio is greater than necessary or may foster unwarranted disparity.[4]

The pre-*Booker* era for federal sentencing began with the Sentencing Reform Act of 1984,[5] which established a sentencing system under the United States Sentencing Commission's federal sentencing guidelines.[6] The previous system tailored sentences to the individual defendants. Judges were given broad ranges within which they could, at their discretion, sentence a defendant.[7] The sentence was supposed to be based on the defendant's character as much as his conduct. Thereafter, the discretion given to the judge was passed on to the Parole Commission to determine how much of the judge's sentence the defendant ultimately served.[8] Under the Guidelines, the judge's role at sentencing was more uniform and unvaried.[9] The judge could inquire into a number of factors, including the defendant's conduct and criminal history. The judge then weighed each factor according to the Sentencing Commission's mandate and calculated an offense level for the defendant.[10] The judge had discretion to sentence the defendant but, with little ground for departure, only within the narrow sentencing range that the Guidelines provided for each offense level.[11] The Sentencing Reform Act also abolished the Parole Commission's role. [12]

Crack cocaine became prevalent in the mid-1980s and received widespread media attention following the death of the University of Maryland all-American basketball player, Len Bias, from the use of cocaine. [13] Crack cocaine was portrayed as a violence-inducing, highly addictive plague of inner cities, and this notoriety led to the quick passage of a federal sentencing law concerning crack cocaine in 1986.[14] This legislation created two mandatory sentencing ranges for drug offenses.[15] The lower bracket spanned periods of imprisonment ranging from a mandatory minimum of 5 years to a maximum of 40 years; the higher bracket spanned periods ranging from a mandatory minimum of 10 years to a maximum of life. [16] Congress prescribed the threshold quantities of both crack and powdered cocaine required to bring a particular offense within either bracket.[17] Despite the chemical identity of crack and powder cocaine, Congress set widely disparate threshold quantities for the two drugs, requiring 100 times more powder cocaine than crack cocaine to trigger inclusion in a particular range.[18] The rationale offered was that many considered crack much more addictive than powder cocaine, and they feared a wave of violent crimes spawned by drug users as well as the health threats to infants born to addicted mothers.[19] The Sentencing Commission also incorporated this ratio into the drug guidelines, although it later concluded that the 100:1 powder to crack ratio produces sentences that are greater than necessary to satisfy the purposes of punishment because it exaggerates the relative harmfulness of crack cocaine; the majority of crack offenders have low drug quantities, short criminal histories, and no history of violence. The Sentencing Commission also concluded that a ratio providing for sentences that are greater than necessary creates an unwarranted disparity, inappropriate uniformity, racial disparity, and disrespect for the law. [20]

Over the years, Congress has had second thoughts about the disparity in drug sentences. To achieve a more equitable balance, as part of the Violent Crime Control and Law Enforcement Act of 1994, Congress enacted a safety valve provision, which provided an avenue for lowering mandatory minimum sentences in a limited category of drug cases.[21] During the same year, Congress directed the Sentencing Commission to study the crack-to-powder ratio and submit recommendations relative to whether the ratio should be retained or modified.[22] The Sentencing Commission recommended revision of the 100:1 quantity ratio in 1995, finding the ratio to be unjustified by the small differences in the two forms of cocaine.[23] Congress rejected the recommendation of the Sentencing Commission and did not change the law.[24]

Two years later, the Sentencing Commission issued a follow-up report.[25] In this report, the commission reiterated its position that the 100:1 ratio was excessive.[26] It recommended that the 100:1 ratio be reduced to 5:1 by increasing the threshold quantities for offenses involving crack cocaine and decreasing the threshold quantities for offenses involving powder cocaine.[27] Again, Congress took no action and did not amend the law.

In 2001, the Senate Judiciary Committee asked the Sentencing Commission to revisit its position regarding the 100:1 ratio, and in the subsequent year, the Sentencing Commission issued its third report.[28] In this report, the commission again proposed narrowing the gap that separated crack cocaine offenses from powder cocaine because (1) the severe penalties for crack cocaine offenses seemed to fall mainly on low-level criminals and African Americans, (2) the dangers posed by crack could be satisfactorily addressed through sentencing enhancements that would apply neutrally to all drug offenses, and (3) recent data suggested that the penalties were disproportionate to the harms associated with the two drugs.[29] Unlike the previous report, the Commission did not recommend a reduction in the powder cocaine threshold. The Commission did recommend elimination of the 5-year mandatory minimum for simple possession of crack cocaine. Congress considered the substance of the Commission's 2002 report but took no action.

Judges have long been critical of the automatic prison terms, commonly referred to as mandatory minimum sentences, which were enacted pursuant to the Anti-Drug Abuse Act of 1986 in part to stem the drug trade.[30]

United States v. Booker

Prior to the Supreme Court's decision in *United States v. Booker*,[31] the case law was generally cognizant of the seriousness in the sentencing disparities between crack and powder cocaine but regularly deferred to Congress's policy judgments.[32] This undertaking led to a series of decisions that upheld the 100:1 ratio against a variety of challenges, which included the Equal Protection Clause[33] and the rule of lenity.[34] It was also decided that under the mandatory guidelines system that was popular before *Booker*, neither the Sentencing Commission's criticism of the 100:1 ratio nor its unacknowledged 1995 proposal to eliminate the differential provided a valid basis for leniency in the sentencing of crack cocaine offenders.[35]

In *Booker*, the Supreme Court consolidated two lower court cases and considered them in tandem, *United States v. Fanfan*[36] and *United States v. Booker*.[37] Booker was arrested after officers found in his duffle bag 92.5 grams of crack cocaine. He later gave a written statement to the police in which he admitted selling an additional 566 grams of crack cocaine. [38] A jury in the United States District Court for the Western District of Wisconsin found Booker guilty of two counts of possessing at least 50 grams of cocaine base with the intent to distribute it, in violation of 21 U.S.C. § 841 (b)(1)(A)(iii).[39] At sentencing, the judge found by a preponderance of the evidence that Booker had distributed 566 grams in addition to the 92.5 grams that the jury found; the judge also found that Booker had obstructed justice.[40] In the absence of the judge's additional findings, Booker would have only faced a maximum sentence of 262 months under the United States Sentencing Guidelines.[41] The judge, however sentenced Booker to 360 months, based on the Guidelines' treatment of the additional cocaine and the obstruction of justice.[42] The United States Court of Appeals for the Seventh Circuit affirmed the conviction but overturned the sentence.[43]

Narcotic agents arrested Fanfan when they discovered 1.25 kilograms of cocaine and 281.6 grams of cocaine base in his vehicle.[44] A jury in the District of Maine found that he possessed "500 or more grams" of cocaine with the intent to distribute, in violation of 21 U.S.C. § 846. At sentencing, the court determined that Fanfan was the "ring leader of a significant drug conspiracy," which, combined with his criminal history, resulted in a sentence of 188 to 235 months under the Guidelines. However, four days before the June 28, 2004, sentencing hearing, the Supreme Court decided *Blakely v. Washington*,[45] holding that as part of a state sentencing guideline system, a Washington state judge could not find an aggravating fact authorizing a higher sentence than the state statutes otherwise permitted. The sentencing judge in *Fanfan* considered the effect that *Blakely* may have on the federal sentencing Guidelines and recalculated the Guidelines based only on the possession of 500 grams and imposed the 78 month maximum for that range.

The Supreme Court granted certiorari in *Booker* and *Fanfan* in an effort to give some guidance to lower courts that had begun a variety of applications of the *Blakely* decision to federal prisoners. For example, in *Booker*, the Seventh Circuit found that the federal sentencing guidelines violate the Sixth Amendment in some situations.[46] The Fifth Circuit, on the other hand, concluded that *Blakely* did not apply to the Guidelines because to do so would create a separate "offense" for each possible sentence for a particular crime.[47] The Second Circuit, without resolving the issue, certified questions to the Supreme Court regarding the application of *Blakely* to federal sentences pursuant to the Guidelines.[48]

The Supreme Court issued a majority opinion in two parts. The first part, written by Justice Stevens for a 5-4 majority (Justices Scalia, Souter, Thomas, and Ginsburg) decided that the Guidelines violate the Sixth Amendment and are thus unconstitutional because they require a judge to increase a sentence above the maximum guideline range if the judge finds facts to justify an increase. They said a defendant's right to trial by jury is violated if a judge must impose a higher sentence than the sentence that the judge could have imposed based on the facts found by the jury.[49] Pursuant to 18 U.S.C. § 3553(b), the Guidelines were mandatory and thus create a statutory maximum for the purpose of *Apprendi v. New Jersey*, 530 U.S. 466 (2000), which had condemned mandatory judicial fact-finding for purposes of imposing a sentence beyond the statutory maximum.[50] The Court had applied *Apprendi*'s reasoning to a state sentencing guideline system in *Blakely v. Washington*, and the rationale applied with equal force to the federal guideline system in *Booker*.[51] Under the then current administration of the Guidelines, judges, rather than juries, were required to find sentence determining facts, and thus the practice was unconstitutional.

The second part, written by Justice Breyer for a different 5-4 majority (Justices Rehnquist, O'Connor, Kennedy, and Ginsburg) remedies this defect by holding that the Guidelines are advisory, thereby making it necessary for the courts to consider the Guidelines along with other traditional factors when deciding on a sentence, and also finding that the appellant courts may review sentences for "reasonableness." Driven by the Court's first holding, it "excises" (through severance and excision of two provisions) 18 U.S.C. § 3553(b)(1) and § 3742(e) from the Sentencing Reform Act and declares the Guidelines are now "advisory."[52] Pursuant to § 35 53(a), district judges need only to "consider" the Guideline range as one of many factors, including the need for the sentence to provide just punishment for the offense (§ 3553(a)(2)(A), to afford adequate deterrence to criminal conduct (§ 3553(a)(2)(B), to protect the public from further crimes of the defendant (§ 3553(a)(2)(C)), and to avoid unwarranted sentencing disparities among similarly situated defendants (§3553(a) (6)).[53] The Sentencing Reform Act, absent the mandate of § 3553(b)(1), authorizes the judge to apply his own perceptions of just punishment, deterrence, and protection of the public, even when these differ from the perceptions of the United States Sentencing Commission.[54] The Sentencing Reform Act continues to provide for appeals from sentencing decisions (regardless of whether the trial judge sentences are within or outside of the Guideline range) based on an "unreasonableness" standard (18 U.S.C. § § 3553(a)[55] and 3742(e)(3)).[56]

Booker and the Crack Defendant

After *Booker*, the federal courts wrestled with whether they may or must impose sentences below the Guidelines' ranges in crack cocaine cases in view of the United States Sentencing Commission's conclusions and recommendations, the facts and circumstances of the case, the history and characteristics of the defendant, and the command of 18 U.S.C. § 3553(a)(2)(6) to avoid unwarranted sentencing disparity. Typically, the federal courts follow a three-step sentencing procedure in which they determine "(1) the applicable advisory range under the Sentencing Guidelines; (2) whether, pursuant to the Sentencing Commission's policy statements, any departures from the advisory guideline range clearly apply; and (3) the appropriate sentence in light of the statutory factors to be considered in imposing a sentence."[57]

An appellate court held that the federal courts are not compelled to lower a sentence recommended by the Guidelines based on the sentencing differential for crack cocaine versus powder cocaine.[58] On the other hand, in more than a few cases, the application of *Booker* has led to lower sentences than those suggested by the 100:1 ratio ranges established in the Guidelines.[59]

In some cases, after considering the factors set forth in 18 U.S.C. § 3553(a), the courts found a different ratio, either 20:1 or 10:1, more compatible with the statutory command of 18 U.S.C. § 3553(a)(6) to weigh the need to avoid unwarranted disparities.[60]

The appellate courts were not so inclined to ignore the 100:1 ratio reflected in the then-existing Guidelines. For instance, the First Circuit held that the district court could not discard the guideline range and construct a new sentencing range,[61] but could take into account, on a case-bycase basis, "the nature of the contraband and/or the severity of a projected guideline sentence."[62] The First Circuit described the disparity as a "problem that has tormented enlightened observers ever since Congress promulgated the 100:1 ratio" and "share[d] the district court's concern about the fairness of maintaining the across-the-board sentencing gap associated with the 100:1 crackto-powder ratio."[63] But to recapitulate, said the First Circuit, "we hold that the district court erred ... when it constructed a new sentencing range based on the categorical substitution of a 20:1 crack-to-powder ratio for the 100:1 embedded in the sentencing guidelines."[64] A panel in the Fourth Circuit agreed:

> [t]he principal question ... is whether a district court in the post-*Booker* world can vary from the advisory sentencing range under the guidelines by substituting its own crack cocaine/powder cocaine ratio for the 100:1 crack cocaine/powder cocaine ratio chosen by Congress. For the reasons stated below, we conclude a court cannot.... [The] sentencing court must identify the individual aspects of the defendant's case that fit within the factors listed in

> 18 U.S.C. § 3553(a) and in reliance on those findings, impose a non-Guideline sentence that is reasonable ... in arriving at a reasonable sentence, the court simply must not rely on a factor that would result in a sentencing disparity that totally is at odds with the will of Congress.[65]

The Fourth Circuit decision formed the basis for its later unpublished opinion in *Kimbrough v. United States*.[66]

Kimbrough v. United States

Norfolk, VA, police arrested Derrick Kimbrough after they came upon him in the midst of what appeared to be a curbside drug sale. At the time, they discovered more than $1,900 in cash, 56 grams of crack cocaine, and more than 60 grams of powder cocaine in his car.[67] They also recovered a loaded hand gun for which Kimbrough was holding a full magazine clip.[68] Kimbrough subsequently pleaded guilty[69] to federal charges for trafficking in more than 50 grams of crack,[70] trafficking in cocaine powder,[71] conspiracy to traffic in crack,[72] and possession of a firearm during and in furtherance of a drug trafficking offense.[73] He faced mandatory minimum terms of imprisonment of 10 years on the crack trafficking charge and of 5 years on the gun charge.[74] The applicable sentencing guidelines called for a sentence of imprisonment in the range of 168 to 210 months on the drug charges with an additional 60 months on the gun charge (to be served consecutive to the drug charges for a range of imprisonment of 228 to 270 months).[75] Kimbrough's attorney apparently urged a departure from the Guideline's recommended sentence based on the Sentencing Commission's dissatisfaction with the 100:1 ratio, Kimbrough's military service, the absence of any prior felony conviction, his employment record, and the suggestion that federal involvement represented an instance of "sentence shopping" in what was otherwise a state case.[76]

Under the facts before it, the district court considered the sentence recommended by the Guidelines "ridiculous."[77] It sentenced Kimbrough to the statutory minimum of 180 months in prison (10 years on the drug charges and 5 years on the gun charge).[78] It did so in part because of the sentencing disparity for crack and powder cocaine.[79] However, the Fourth Circuit Court of Appeals vacated and remanded the sentence, consistent with its holding in *United States v. Eura*[80] that "a sentence that is outside the guidelines range is per se unreasonable when it is based on a disagreement with the sentencing disparity for crack and powder offenses."[81] On June 11, 2007, the Supreme Court agreed to consider whether the district court abused its discretion when it determined that in Kimbrough's case the sentencing range recommended by the Guidelines would be greater than necessary to serve the penological purposes described in 18 U.S.C. § 3553(a)(2) and should not be controlling in light of the instruction in 18 U.S.C. § 3553(a)(6) to consider the need to avoid unwarranted disparity among similarly situated defendants.[82]

On December 10, 2007, the Supreme Court reversed the Court of Appeals in a 7-2 ruling. Writing for the majority, Justice Ginsburg held that although a district judge must respectfully consider the Guidelines range as one factor (among many) in determining an appropriate sentence, the judge has discretion to depart from the Guidelines based on the disparity between the Guidelines' treatment of crack and powder cocaine offenses.[83] As the *Booker* decision had made clear that the Sentencing Guidelines—which include the cocaine Guidelines—are to be advisory only, the Fourth Circuit Court of Appeals had erred in holding the crack/powder disparity "effectively mandatory," the Court explained.[84] Furthermore, the Supreme Court concluded that the 180- month sentence imposed on Kimbrough is reasonable given the particular circumstance of Kimbrough's case and that the district judge did not abuse his discretion in finding that the crack/powder disparity is at odds with the objectives of sentencing set forth in 18 U.S.C. § 3553(a)(2).[85]

Spears v. United States

In a case that had been remanded by the Supreme Court for further consideration in light of *Kimbrough*, the Eighth Circuit Court of Appeals held in *United States v. Spears* that district courts "may not categorically reject the [crack-to-powder] ratio set forth by the Guidelines," and that "[n]othing in *Kimbrough* suggests the district court may substitute its own ratio for the ratio set forth in the Guidelines."[86] On January 21, 2009, the Supreme Court issued a per curiam opinion that summarily reversed the appellate court's decision on remand, finding that the judgment conflicted with *Kimbrough*.[87] The Court stated that "with respect to the crack cocaine Guidelines, a categorical disagreement with and variance from the Guidelines is not suspect" and reiterated that *Kimbrough* stands for the proposition that district courts have the "authority to vary from the crack cocaine Guidelines based on *policy* disagreement with them, and not simply based on an individualized determination that they yield an excessive sentence in a particular case."[88] The Supreme Court explained,

> As a logical matter, of course, rejection of the 100:1 ratio, explicitly approved by *Kimbrough*, necessarily implies adoption of some other ratio to govern the mine-run case. A sentencing judge who is given the power to reject the disparity created by the crack-topowder ratio must also possess the power to apply a different ratio which, in his judgment, corrects the disparity. Put simply, the ability to reduce a mine-run defendant's sentence necessarily permits adoption of a replacement ratio.[89]

In releasing the opinion in *Spears v. United States*, the Supreme Court sought to clarify its holding in *Kimbrough* that had been misinterpreted by not only the Eighth Circuit Court of Appeals, but the First and Third Circuits as well.[90] The Court speculated that if the Eighth Circuit's restrictive interpretation of *Kimbrough* was correct, one of two things would likely occur:

> Either district courts would treat the Guidelines' policy embodied in the crack-to-powder ratio as mandatory, believing that they are not entitled to vary based on "categorical" policy disagreements with the Guidelines, or they would continue to vary, masking their categorical policy disagreements as "individualized determinations." The latter is institutionalized subterfuge. The former contradicts our holding in *Kimbrough*. Neither is an acceptable sentencing practice.[91]

2007 Amendment of the Sentencing Guidelines

In May 2007, the United States Sentencing Commission submitted proposed amendments to the Guidelines (including those applicable in *Kimbrough*) that essentially did away with the 100:1 ratio for purposes of the Guidelines (except at the point at which the statutory mandatory minimums are triggered).[92] It also recommended that Congress raise the thresholds for the statutory mandatory minimums for trafficking in crack, thereby eliminating the statutory 100:1 ratio.[93] In making the decision to amend the Guidelines, the Commission sought to "somewhat alleviate" the "urgent and compelling ... problems associated with the 100-to-1 drug quantity ratio."[94] The Commission opined that the amendment was "only ... a partial remedy" and was "neither a permanent nor complete solution."[95]

In July 2007, the Commission proposed that the changes relating to what had been the 100:1 ratio in the Guidelines be made retroactively applicable to previously sentenced crack cocaine offenders.[96] On November 1, 2007, the amendments to the Guidelines including those relating to crack and the 100:1 ratio went into effect.[97] On December 11, 2007, the Sentencing Commission unanimously voted to apply the crack amendment retroactively.[98]

As noted earlier, the Controlled Substances Act makes trafficking in 5 to 50 grams of crack cocaine or 500 to 5,000 grams of cocaine powder punishable by imprisonment for not less than 5 years and not more than 40 years.[99] It makes trafficking more than 50 grams of crack or more than 5,000 grams of cocaine powder punishable by imprisonment for not less than 10 years and not more than life.[100] These sanctions, like most federal criminal penalties, are reflected in the Sentencing Guidelines. The Guidelines assign most federal crimes to an individual guideline which in turn assigns the offense an initial base sentencing level. Drug trafficking offenses, for example, have been assigned to section 2D 1.1, which sets the base offense level according to the amount of crack or powder cocaine involved in a particular case.[101] Levels are then added or subtracted on the basis of any aggravating or mitigating factors presented in a particular defendant's case. For example, a defendant's offense level may be decreased by two or four levels, if the offense involved a number of participants and the defendant's role in the offense was minor or minimal.[102] A defendant's final offense level and his criminal history (criminal record) govern the sentence recommended by the Guidelines.[103] The Guidelines assign sentencing ranges for each of the 43 possible final offense levels.[104] Each of the 43 has a series of six escalating sentencing ranges to mirror the extent of the defendant's criminal history.[105] For example, if a defendant has no prior criminal record and his final sentencing level is 26, the Guidelines recommend that the sentencing court impose a term of imprisonment somewhere between 63 and 78 months; at the other extreme, if a defendant has an extensive prior criminal record and his final sentencing level is the same 26, the Guidelines recommend a sentencing range of between 120 to 150 months.[106]

The drug quantity table that is part of the drug sentencing guideline, U.S.S.G. § 2D 1.1(c), assigns offenses to one of several steps with corresponding sentencing levels based on the kind and volume of the controlled substances involved in the offense.[107] For example, an offense involving 150 kilograms or more of powder cocaine is assigned a step (1) offense level of 38, while an offense involving less than 25 grams is assigned a step (14) offense level of 12.[108] Prior to the amendments effective on November 1, 2007, each of the steps reflected a 100:1 ratio between crack and powder cocaine; for instance, offenses involving either more than 150 kilograms of powder cocaine or more than 1.5 kilograms of crack cocaine were each assigned a step (1) offense level of 38.[109] In order to reduce the prospect of a Guideline result beneath the statutory minimums, the pre-amendment Guidelines assigned the 5-year-minimum-triggering 5 grams (crack)/500 grams (powder) offenses to U.S.S.G. § 2D1. 1(c), step (7), with an offense level of 26 which translated to a sentencing range of from 5 years and 3 months (63 months) to 6 years and 6 months (78 months).[110] It made a similar assignment for the 10-year mandatory minimum offenses involving 50 grams of crack or 5,000 grams of powder cocaine: level 32 with a sentencing range for first offenders of from 10 years and 1 month (121 months) to 12 years and 7 months (151 months).[111]

The Commission's amendments focused first on the assignment for crack offenses subject to a mandatory minimum. The Commission noted that its earlier assignment set the bottom of the two ranges higher than necessary to satisfy minimum sentencing requirements (5 years and 3 months in the case of 5 grams; 10 years and 1 month in the case of 50 grams).[112] Its amendments reassign those offenses to offense levels where the mandatory minimum fell within the middle of the ranges, that is, to offense level 24 (51 to 63 months for first offenders) and offense level 30 (97 to 121 months for first offenders) for 5- and 50-gram crack offenses, respectively.[113] They then provide a similar two-level reduction for crack offenses involving amounts above and beyond those that trigger the mandatory minimums.[114] The amendments, however, make no such changes in the offense levels to which powder cocaine offenses are assigned. As a consequence, the 100:1 ratio has disappeared from the Guidelines (although the statutory 100:1 ratio in the quantities of powder cocaine and crack cocaine that trigger the mandatory minimum penalties still remains).[115]

Retroactivity Decision

In July 2007, the Commission proposed that the amendment be made retroactively applicable to previously sentenced crack cocaine offenders.[116] After receiving public comment on the issue of retroactivity[117] and holding public hearings to consider the issue,[118] the Commission voted 7-0 in favor of retroactivity on December 11, 2007. While the Commission found "that the statutory purposes of sentencing are best served by retroactive application of the amendment," it emphasized that not all previously sentenced crack cocaine offenders will automatically receive a reduction in sentence—rather, federal sentencing judges will have the final authority to make that determination based on the merits of each case, after considering a variety of factors, including whether public safety would be endangered by early release of the prisoner.[119]

Case Law Applying the Retroactive Crack Cocaine Amendments

In general, a federal court "may not modify a term of imprisonment once it has been imposed."[120] However, there are limited exceptions to this general rule, including the following: a federal prisoner may petition a court to modify his original term of imprisonment if he was "sentenced to a term of imprisonment based on a sentencing range that has subsequently been lowered by the Sentencing Commission."[121] Such a modification is authorized "if such a reduction is consistent with" policy statements issued by the Sentencing

Commission supporting the reduction for previously sentenced offenders—in other words, if the Commission makes its Guideline amendments retroactively applicable. [122] The federal court is not required to approve a sentence reduction motion; rather, the statute provides that a court "may" reduce such imprisonment term. However, a court may *not* reduce a sentence below a statutory mandatory minimum. [123]

A federal court considering a so-called "§ 3582(c)(2)" motion has discretion to reduce the imprisonment sentence after considering the following statutory factors, set forth in 18 U.S.C. § 3553(a):

- the nature and circumstances of the offense and the history and characteristics of the defendant;
- the need for the sentence imposed: (A) to reflect the seriousness of the offense, to promote respect for the law, and to provide just punishment for the offense; (B) to afford adequate deterrence to criminal conduct; (C) to protect the public from further crimes of the defendant; and (D) to provide the defendant with educational or vocational training, medical care, or other correctional treatment in the most effective manner;
- the sentencing range established by the Commission;
- any pertinent policy statement issued by the Commission regarding application of the guidelines;
- the need to avoid unwarranted sentence disparities among defendants with similar records who have been found guilty of similar conduct; and
- the need to provide restitution to any victims of the offense. [124]

The Sentencing Commission's policy statement governing reduction of terms of imprisonment based on amended Guidelines ranges is Sentencing Guidelines § 1B1.10.[125] The policy statement explains that "proceedings under 18 U.S.C. § 3582(c)(2) and this policy statement do not constitute a full resentencing of the defendant."[126] The policy statement also provides that a "court shall not reduce the defendant's term of imprisonment ... to a term that is less than the minimum of the amended guideline range."[127]

In the wake of the Sentencing Commission's crack cocaine amendment retroactivity decision, the federal courts began considering § 3582(c)(2) motions filed by crack offenders to obtain reductions in their sentences. [128] In the month of March 2008, when the retroactivity decision became effective, more than 3,000 prisoners nationwide had their sentences reduced; 1,000 of these inmates were released immediately.[129] As of May 2010, a nationwide total of 15,778 motions have been granted, with an average decrease of 26 months from the prisoners' original sentence (a 17% decrease), while 8,280 petitions have been denied. [130]

Several issues have arisen during these cases, including whether prisoners who request sentence reductions are entitled to have court-appointed lawyers to represent them in court, whether crack offenders who were sentenced as career-offenders are eligible for sentence reductions, and whether courts may reduce a sentence below the bottom end of the amended Guideline range (a power that would be available to a court assuming that *Booker* applies to § 3582(c)(2) proceedings). Many of the § 3582(c)(2) motions have been filed by defendants pro se, although often with some assistance by the local federal public defender office. A panel from the Fifth Circuit Court of Appeals declined to decide whether a § 3582(c)(2) motion triggers a statutory or constitutional right to an attorney, but rather used its discretionary authority to appoint the prisoner an attorney "in the interest of justice."[131] Other federal courts have rejected the argument that a prisoner has a constitutional right to assistance of counsel in pursuing a § 3582(c)(2) motion for a sentence reduction.[132]

Another question facing the courts was whether defendants who were convicted of crack cocaine offenses but sentenced as career offenders[133] could benefit from the amended crack cocaine sentencing guidelines. Courts of appeals that have considered the issue have ruled that they cannot.[134] An opinion from the Eleventh Circuit Court of Appeals is typical of these decisions:

> Where a retroactively applicable guideline amendment reduces a defendant's base offense level, but does not alter the sentencing range upon which his or her sentence was based, § 3582(c)(2) does not authorize a reduction in sentence. Here, although Amendment 706 [the crack cocaine amendment] would reduce the base offense levels applicable to the defendants, it would not affect their guideline ranges because they were sentenced as career offenders under [U.S. Sentencing Guidelines] § 4B1.1.[135]

Dillon v. United States

Federal courts have also addressed whether *Booker* applies to § 3582(c)(2) proceedings (which would determine whether district courts have the authority to impose a sentence that is even lower than the minimum of the amended Sentencing Guideline range). Ten courts of appeals have held that while *Booker* applies to original sentencing proceedings, "in which a district court must make a host of guideline application decisions in arriving at a defendant's applicable guideline range and then ultimately impose a sentence after reviewing the § 3553(a) factors," *Booker* does *not* apply to sentence modification proceedings under § 3582(c)(2) because such proceedings are "much more narrow in scope."[136] One federal appellate court offered the following reasoning to justify its decision not to apply *Booker* to § 3582(c)(2) proceedings:

> Nowhere in *Booker* did the Supreme Court mention §3582(c)(2). Because §3582(c)(2) proceedings may only reduce a defendant's sentence and not increase it, the constitutional holding in *Booker* does not apply to §3582(c)(2). ... Additionally, the remedial holding in *Booker* invalidated only 18 U.S.C. §3553(b)(1), which made the Sentencing Guidelines mandatory for full sentencings, and §3742(e), which directed appellate courts to apply a de novo standard of review to departures from the Guidelines. Therefore, *Booker* applies to full sentencing hearings –whether in an initial sentencing or in a resentencing where the original sentence is vacated for error, but not to sentence modification proceedings under §3582(c)(2).[137]

In disagreement with all of the other circuit courts of appeals, the Ninth Circuit Court of Appeals found that *Booker* renders the Guidelines advisory in a § 3582(c)(2) proceeding, and thus a district court may reduce a sentence below the amended guideline range.[138]

To resolve this circuit split and offer a definitive answer to this question, the Supreme Court granted certiorari in *Dillon v. United States*, a Third Circuit Court of Appeals case that had held that *Booker* does not apply to the size of a sentence reduction that may be granted under § 3582(c)(2).[139] The defendant in the case, Percy Dillon, was convicted in 1993 of several felony offenses involving cocaine and was sentenced to the bottom of the then-applicable Guidelines range, 322 months. At his sentencing, the district court judge commented that "I personally don't believe that you should be serving 322 months[, b]ut I feel I am bound by those Guidelines.... I don't say to you that these penalties are fair. I don't think they are fair. I think they are entirely too high for the crime you have committed."[140]

After the Sentencing Commission's decision to make the amendments to the crack cocaine Guidelines retroactive in December 2007, Dillon filed a pro se motion for a sentence reduction pursuant to § 3582(c)(2). The district court reduced Dillon's sentence to 270 months (the term at the bottom of the revised Guidelines range), although Dillon desired an even greater reduction, below the bottom of the amended Guidelines range, in light of *Booker* and the institutional rehabilitation and educational and community-outreach achievements that he has accomplished while incarcerated. On appeal, the Third Circuit opined that "[i]f *Booker* did apply in proceedings pursuant to § 3582, Dillon would likely be an ideal candidate for a non-Guidelines sentence," but ultimately upheld the district court's conclusion that it lacked the authority to further reduce his sentence because the Sentencing Commission's applicable policy statement (Sentencing Guidelines § 1B1 .10) is binding on the district court pursuant to 18 U.S.C. 3582(c)(2).[141]

In his briefs submitted to the Supreme Court, Dillon argued that *Booker* extends to resentencings conducted under § 3582(c)(2) and criticized the Sentencing Commission's policy statement (Sentencing Guidelines § 1B1 .10) that binds district courts to the Guidelines sentencing range during resentencings under § 3582(c)(2). The policy statement, he asserted, "attempts to resurrect the mandatory Guidelines system *Booker* invalidated."[142] In its brief on the merits, the United States argued that *Booker* only applies "when a court engages in a plenary sentencing."[143] A § 3582(c)(2) proceeding, however, "provides a one-way ratchet to lower a defendant's otherwise- final sentence" in a way that "does not implicate the Sixth Amendment rule applied in *Booker*" because the court may not increase a defendant's sentence based on judicially found facts.[144] Furthermore, the United States warned the Supreme Court of the consequences of applying *Booker* to § 3582(c)(2) proceedings:

> [E]very retroactive Guidelines amendment would carry the potential to reopen thousands of sentences of imprisonment under the statutory sentencing factors set out in Section 3 553(a). Petitioner's proposed rule not only would undermine principles of finality that are essential to the operation of the criminal justice system, but also would inevitably affect the Sentencing Commission's calculus in deciding whether to make its Guidelines amendments retroactive in the first place. That result would diminish Section 3582(c)(2)'s value as a mechanism for the exercise of leniency.[145]

On June 17, 2010, the Supreme Court issued its opinion in *Dillon*, in which it sided with the position of the United States. In a 7-1 decision authored by Justice Sonia Sotomayor, the Court ruled that *Booker* did not apply to § 3582(c)(2) proceedings.[146] Justice Sotomayor observed that while *Booker* had invalidated two provisions of the Sentencing Reform Act (SRA) of 1984, the decision "left intact other provisions of the SRA including those giving the Commission authority to revise the Guidelines ... and to determine when and to what extent a revision will be retroactive."[147] This authority vested by Congress in the Sentencing Commission reflects the "substantial role" that Congress envisioned for the Commission with respect to sentence- modification proceedings.[148]

Furthermore, she noted that the statutory text of § 3582(c)(2) undercuts Dillon's characterization of the sentence-modification proceedings as "plenary resentencing proceedings"; rather, the section provides a limited opportunity for a court to "modify a term of imprisonment" by reducing an otherwise final sentence under certain narrow circumstances specified by the Commission.[149] "A court's power under § 3582(c)(2) thus depends in the first instance on the Commission's decision not just to amend the Guidelines but to make the amendment retroactive."[150] A court is also bound by the Commission's determination of the extent to which a prisoner's term of imprisonment may be reduced.[151] Justice Sotomayor described § 3582(c)(2) as not a constitutionally required proceeding, but rather "a congressional act of lenity intended to give prisoners the benefit of later enacted adjustments to the judgments reflected in the Guidelines."[152] She explained that § 3582(c)(2) does not implicate the Sixth Amendment right vindicated in *Booker* because any facts that may be found by a judge in a § 3582(c)(2) proceeding would not increase the range of punishment—rather, it would only affect the judge's exercise of discretion within a particular amended Guidelines range.[153] Thus, Dillon's constitutional rights were not violated by the district court that considered a reduction only within the amended range.

In lone dissent, Justice Stevens argued that *Booker* should apply to § 3582(c)(2) proceedings. He accused the Court of being "unfaithful" to *Booker* in treating the Commission's policy statements "as a mandatory command rather than an advisory recommendation."[154] He also regarded the Court's decision to allow "the Commission to exercise a barely constrained form of lawmaking authority" as "manifestly unjust" and "on dubious constitutional footing."[155] While accepting that *Booker* explicitly severed only two specific statutory sections of the Sentencing Reform Act, Justice Stevens believed that a fair reading of *Booker* requires the elimination of *all* mandatory features of the Guidelines.[156] He surmised that "the Court's decision today may reflect a concern that a contrary holding would discourage the Commission from issuing retroactive amendments to the Guidelines, owing to a fear of burdening the district courts"; however, he urged that such concern "should not influence our assessment of the legal question" before the Court.[157] He opined that "Dillon's continued imprisonment is a truly sad example of what I have come to view as an exceptionally, and often mindlessly, harsh federal punishment scheme."[158]

LEGISLATION IN THE 111TH CONGRESS

Several bills have been introduced concerning cocaine sentencing; to date, the Congress has passed one into law: S. 1789 (Fair Sentencing Act of 2010). Introduced by Senator Richard Durbin, S. 1789 will, among other things, increase the threshold amount of crack cocaine necessary to trigger the mandatory minimum penalties to 28 grams (from 5 grams for the current 5-year sentence) and 280 grams (from 50 grams for the current 10-year sentence).[159] This change will reduce the statutory 100:1 ratio to 18:1. The bill also eliminates the 5-year mandatory minimum for simple possession of crack cocaine.[160] The bill goes beyond crack cocaine sentencing issues by increasing criminal fine amounts available for major drug traffickers[161] and also directing the U.S. Sentencing Commission to amend the Sentencing Guidelines to ensure that the Guidelines provide an additional penalty increase of at least two offense levels if the defendant used violence, made a credible threat to use violence, or directed the use of violence during a drug trafficking offense. [162] The Sentencing Commission is also required to study and submit to Congress within five years a report concerning the impact of the changes in federal sentencing law made by the Fair Sentencing Act of 2010.[163] On March 17, 2010, the Senate passed S. 1789 by unanimous consent. On July 28, 2010, the House considered S. 1789 under suspension of the rules and passed it by voice vote. President Obama signed the bill into law on August 3, 2010 (P.L. 111-220). The Congressional Budget Office has estimated that implementation of S. 1789 will generate $42 million in savings to the federal prison system over the 2011-2015 period.[164]

Representative Roscoe Bartlett introduced H.R. 18 (Powder-Crack Cocaine Penalty Equalization Act of 2009), which would equalize the triggering quantity for the mandatory minimum sentences for cocaine offenses at the crack cocaine levels (5 grams of powder cocaine would result in a 5- year sentence and 50 grams a 10-year sentence). Currently, it takes 100 times those quantities to trigger the 5- and 10-year mandatory minimum sentences for powder cocaine.

Representative Sheila Jackson-Lee introduced H.R. 265 (Drug Sentencing Reform and Cocaine Kingpin Trafficking Act of 2009), which would eliminate the statutory 100:1 ratio in cocaine cases by raising the crack cocaine threshold to 500 grams and 5 kilograms for the 5- and 10-year mandatory minimums, respectively. It would call upon the Sentencing Commission to reexamine the weight given aggravating and mitigating factors in drug trafficking cases. It also would eliminate the 5-year mandatory minimum for simple possession of crack cocaine. In addition, the bill would increase fines for significant drug trafficking offenses, authorize funding for prison- and jail-based drug treatment programs, and authorize increased resources for the Departments of Justice, Treasury, and Homeland Security.

Representative Bobby Scott introduced H.R. 1459 (Fairness in Cocaine Sentencing Act of 2009), which would amend the Controlled Substances Act and the Controlled Substances Import and Export Act regarding cocaine penalties. The bill would treat 50 grams of crack the same as 50 grams of other forms of cocaine, 5 grams of crack the same as 5 grams of other forms of cocaine, and would eliminate all mandatory minimum penalties relating to cocaine offenses. The bill also would reestablish the possibility of probation, suspended sentence, or parole for cocaine offenders. Representative Scott also has introduced H.R. 3245 (Fairness in Cocaine Sentencing Act of 2009), which would make fewer changes to the drug laws; the bill would eliminate references to "cocaine base" from the Controlled Substances Act and the Controlled Substances Import and Export Act (meaning that these laws would treat all forms of cocaine the same for sentencing purposes) and would eliminate the mandatory minimum for simple possession of crack cocaine.

Representative Maxine Waters introduced H.R. 1466 (Major Drug Trafficking Prosecution Act of 2009), which would, among other things, eliminate all mandatory minimum sentences for drug trafficking and possession offenses, and permit courts to place drug offenders on probation or suspend their sentences. The bill also would require the Attorney General to provide written approval before the commencement of a federal prosecution for an offense involving less than 500 grams of powder or crack cocaine.

Representative Charles Rangel introduced H.R. 2178 (Crack-Cocaine Equitable Sentencing Act of 2009), which would amend the Controlled Substances Act and the Controlled Substances Import and Export Act to treat 50 grams of crack the same as 50 grams of other forms of cocaine; 5 grams of crack the same as 5 grams of other forms of cocaine, and eliminate the 5-year mandatory minimum for simple possession of crack cocaine.

Past Congresses have considered legislation relating to cocaine sentencing; some of these bills had called for a 1:1 drug quantity ratio between crack and powder cocaine,[165] while other bills would have changed the statutory ratio to 20:1.[166]

APPENDIX. DRUG QUANTITY TABLE (BEFORE AND AFTER AMENDMENT)

Controlled Substance and Quantity	Base Offense Level
150 KG or more of Cocaine	Level 38
~~1.5~~ 4.5 KG or more of Cocaine Base	
At least 50 KG but not less than 150 KG of Cocaine	Level 36
At least ~~500~~ 1.5 G but not less than ~~1.5~~ 4.5 KG of Cocaine Base	
At least 15 KG but not less than 50 KG of Cocaine	Level 34
At least ~~150~~ 500 G not less than 500 G ~~1.5~~ KG of Cocaine Base	
At least 5 KG but not less than 15 KG of Cocaine	Level 32
At least ~~50~~ 150 G not less than ~~150~~ 500 G of Cocaine Base	
At least 3.5 KG but not less than 5 KG of Cocaine	Level 30
At least ~~35~~ 50 G not less than ~~50~~ 150 G of Cocaine Base	
At least 2 KG but not less than 3.5 KG of Cocaine	Level 28
At least ~~20~~ 35 G not less than ~~35~~ 50 G of Cocaine Base	
At least 500 G but not less than 2 KG of Cocaine	Level 26
At least ~~5~~ 20 G not less than ~~20~~ 35 G of Cocaine Base	
At least 400 G but not less than 500 G of Cocaine	Level 24
At least 4 5 G not less than ~~5~~ 20 G of Cocaine Base	
At least 300 G but not less than 400 G of Cocaine	Level 22
At least ~~3~~ 4 G not less than 4 5 G of Cocaine Base	
At least 200 G but not less than 300 G of Cocaine	Level 20
At least ~~2~~ 3 G not less than ~~3~~ 4 G of Cocaine Base	
At least 100 G but not less than 200 G of Cocaine	Level 18
At least ~~1~~ 2 G not less than ~~2~~ 3 G of Cocaine Base	
At least 50 G but not less than 100 G of Cocaine	Level 16
At least ~~500 MG~~ 1 G not less than ~~1~~ 2 G of Cocaine Base	
At least 25 G but not less than 50 G of Cocaine	Level 14
At least ~~250~~ 500 MG not less than ~~500 MG~~ 1 G of Cocaine Base	
At least 25 G of Cocaine	Level 12
At least ~~250~~ 500 MG of Cocaine Base	

ACKNOWLEDGMENTS

This report was originally prepared by Paul Starett Wallace Jr., Specialist in American Public Law, CRS.

End Notes

[1] 543 U.S. 220 (2005).

[2] *Id.* at 245-46.

[3] E.g., U.S.S.G. § 2D1. 1(c)(1)(November 1, 2006)(both 150 kilograms of powder cocaine and 1.5 kilograms of cocaine base were assigned a base offense level of 38); the same ratio continued throughout § 2D 1.1(C) for lesser amounts and lower base offense levels). Amendments that became effective on November 1, 2007, adjusted the ratios, U.S.S.G. § 2D1. 1(c)(1) (November 1, 2007).

[4] 552 U.S. 85 (2007).

[5] Sentencing Reform Act of 1984, 28 U.S.C. § 991(b)(1) (1988).

[6] 23 U.S.C. § 995(a)(20) (1988).

[7] 28 U.S.C. § 995(b) (1988).

[8] 28 U.S.C. § 995(a)(9-10) (1988).

[9] 28 U.S.C. § 994(w) (1988).

[10] 28 U.S.C. § 991(a)(1) (1988).

[11] See 18 U.S.C. § 3553(b) (the statute specifies what departures are allowable in cases where "there exist an aggravating or mitigating circumstance of a kind, or to a degree not adequately taken into consideration by the Sentencing Commission in formulating the guidelines").

[12] P.L. 98-473, § 218(a)(5), 98 Stat. 2027 (1984).

[13] Keith Harriston and Sally Jenkins, *Maryland Basketball Star Len Bias Is Dead at 22; Evidence of Cocaine Reported Found*, WASH. POST, June 20, 1986, at A-1.

[14] The sentencing differential for crack and powder cocaine offenses had its origin in the Anti-Drug Abuse Act of 1986, P.L. 99-570, 100 Stat. 3207 (1986) (codified in pertinent part at 21 U.S.C. § 841). The act speaks of "cocaine base," not crack. See 21 U.S.C. § 841(b)(1)(A)(iii). The guidelines, however, define cocaine base to mean crack cocaine. See United States Sentencing Guidelines (U.S.S.G.) § 2D1. 1, n.D (November 1, 2007).

[15] See id. § 1002 (codified at 21 U.S.C. § 841(b)(1)).

[16] See *Id.*

[17] See *Id.*

[18] See *Id.* Congress set the threshold quantities for the lower range at 500 grams of powder cocaine and 5 grams of cocaine base and the threshold quantities for the higher range at 5 kilograms and 50 grams, respectively. Thus, for sentencing purposes, Congress treated 1 unit of crack cocaine on the same level as 100 units of powder cocaine. Relative to the difference between crack and powder cocaine—powder cocaine is derived from coca paste, which is in turn derived from the leaves of the coca plant—crack cocaine is made by taking cocaine powder and cooking it with baking soda and water until it forms a hard substance. These "rocks" can then be broken into pieces and sold in small quantities. Each gram of powder cocaine produces approximately .89 grams of crack. United States Sentencing Commission, *Cocaine and Federal Sentencing Policy* (May 2002).

[19] See United States Sentencing Commission, *Special Report to Congress: Cocaine and Federal Sentencing Policy*, at 117-118 (1995).

[20] See United States Sentencing Commission, *Cocaine and Federal Sentencing Policy,* Executive Summary, at v-viii (May 2002).

[21] See 18 U.S.C. § 3553 (f); see also United States v. Matos, 328 F.3d 34, 38-42 (1st Cir. 2003) (a description of the operation of the safety valve).

[22] See Violent Crime Control and Law Enforcement Act of 1994, P.L. 103-322, § 280006, 108 Stat. 1796, 2097 (1994).

[23] See Notice of Submission to Congress of Amendments to the Sentencing Guidelines, 60 *Fed. Reg.* 25,075-25,076 (May 10, 1995).

[24] See P.L. 104-38, § 1, 109 Stat. 334, 334 (1995).

[25] See U.S. Sentencing Commission, *Cocaine and Federal Sentencing Policy* (1997) (1997 Report).

[26] *Id.* at 2.

[27] *Id.* at 2, 5, 9.

[28] See United States Sentencing Commission, *Cocaine and Federal Sentencing Policy* (2002), at 2-3 (2002 Report).

[29] *Id.* at v-viii.

[30] Lynette Clemetson, *Judges Look to New Congress for Changes in Mandatory Sentencing Laws,* N.Y. TIMES, January 9, 2007, at A12.

[31] 543 U.S. 220 (2005).

[32] See, e.g., United States v. Eirby, 262 F.3d 31, 41 (1st Cir. 2001); United States v. Singleterry, 29 F.3d 733, 741 (1st Cir. 1994) ; United States v. Anderson, 82 F.3d 436, 440-41 (D.C. Cir. 1996); United States v. Dumas, 64 F.3d 1427, 1429-430 (9th Cir. 1995).

[33] See, e.g., United States v. Graciani, 61 F.3d 70, 74-75 (1st Cir. 1995) ; United States v. Bingham, 81 F.3d 617, 630- 31 (6th Cir. 1996); United States v. Thomas, 86 F.3d 647, 655 (7th Cir. 1966).

[34] See, e.g., United States v. Manzueta, 167 F.3d 92, 94 (1st Cir. 1999); United States v. Herron, 97 F.3d 234, 238-39 (8th Cir. 1996); United States v. Canales, 91 F.3d 363, 367-69 (2d Cir. 1996).

[35] See United States v. Andrade, 94 F.3d 9, 14-15 (1st Cir. 1996); United States v. Sanchez, 81 F.3d 9, 11 (1st Cir. 1996); United States v. Booker, 73 F.3d 706, 710 (7th Cir. 1996); United States v. Alton, 60 F.3d 1065, 1070-71 (3d Cir. 1995); United States v. Haynes, 985 F.2d 65, 70 (2d Cir. 1993)(each discussing the possibility of a downward departure under U.S.S.G. § 5K2.0). See generally, CRS Report 97-743, *Federal Cocaine Sentencing: Legal Issues*, by Paul Starett Wallace Jr.

[36] 2004 WL 1723114 (D. Me. June 28, 2004), *cert. granted*, 542 U.S. 956 (2004).

[37] 375 F.3d 508 (7th Cir. 2004), *cert. granted*, 542 U.S. 956 (2004).

[38] *Id.*

[39] *Id.*

[40] *Id.*

[41] *Id.* at 510.

[42] *Id.*

[43] *Id.* at 515.

[44] United States v. Fanfan, 2004 WL 1723114 (D. Me. June 28 2004).

[45] 542 U.S. 296 (2004).

[46] United States v. Booker, 375 F.3d 508, 509 (7th Cir. 2004), *judgment of the Court of Appeals aff'd and remanded; judgment of the District Court vacated and remanded*, 543 U.S. 160 (2005).

[47] United States v. Pineiro, 377 F.3d 464 (5th Cir. 2004).

[48] United States v. Penaranda, 375 F.3d 238 (2d Cir. 2004).

[49] For example, the then-effective Guidelines required a defendant convicted by a jury of possession with intent to distribute five grams of crack cocaine to be sentenced within a guideline range of 63 to 78 months. Prior to *Booker*, the Guidelines required a judge to increase the sentence beyond that prescribed range if the judge found additional facts (e.g., the presence of a gun, additional drug quantities, or a leadership role in the illegal activity). Each of these factual findings required a new higher sentencing range. The Court said a judge may not go over the sentence at the top of the Guideline range authorized by the jury—in this case 78 months—unless the jury finds the necessary facts for the higher range or the defendant admits to them.

[50] 543 U.S. at 221. *Apprendi* held that "[o]ther than the fact of a prior conviction, any fact that increases the penalty for a crime beyond the prescribed statutory maximum must be submitted to a jury and proved beyond a reasonable doubt." 530 U.S. at 490.

[51] *Id.* at 244.

[52] *Id.* at 246-247.

[53] *Id.* at 260.

[54] *Id.* at 234.

[55] The primary directive in Section 3553(a) is for sentencing courts to "impose a sentence sufficient, but not greater than necessary, to comply with the purposes set forth in paragraph 2." Section 3553(a)(2) states that such purposes are (A) to reflect the seriousness of the offense, to promote respect for the law, and to provide just punishment for the offense; (B) to afford adequate deterrence to criminal conduct; (C) to protect the public from further crimes of the defendant; and (D) to provide the defendant with needed educational or vocational training, medical care, or other correctional treatment in the most effective manner.

In determining the minimally sufficient sentence, § 3553(a) further directs sentencing courts to consider the following factors: (A) "the nature and circumstances of the offense and the history and characteristics of the defendant" (§ 3553(a)(1)); (B) the penological needs to be served by the sentence (§ 3553(2)); (C) "the kinds of sentences available" (§ 3553(a)(3)); (D) "the need to avoid unwarranted sentence disparities among defendants with similar records who have been found guilty of similar conduct" (§ 3553(a)(6)); and (E) "the need to provide restitution to any victims of the offense." (§ 3553(a)(7)).

[56] 543 U.S. at 261.

[57] United States v. Beamon, 373 F. Supp.2d 878 (E.D. Wis. 2005).

[58] United States v. Gipson, 425 F.3d 335, 337 (7th Cir. 2005).

[59] See United States v. Nellum, 2005 WL 300073 (N.D. Ind. February 3, 2005); United States v. Clay, 2005 WL 1076243 (E.D. Tenn. 2005); United States v. Williams, 372 F. Supp.2d 1335 (M.D. Fla. 2005); Simon v. United States, 361 F. Supp.2d 35 (S.D.N.Y. 2005); United States v. Moreland, 366 F. Supp.2d 416 (S.D.W.Va. 2005), vac'd in part, 437 F.3d 424 (4th Cir. 2006).

[60] See United States v. Smith, 359 F. Supp.2d 771 (E.D. Wis. 2005) (substituting a 20:1 ratio for the 100:1 ratio used in the Guidelines); United States v. Leroy, 373 F.Supp.2d 887 (E.D. Wis. 2005) (20:1 ratio); United States v. Castillo, 2005 WL 1214280 (S.D.N.Y. May 20, 2005) (20:1 ratio); United States v. Perry, 389 F.Supp.2d 278 (D.R.I. 2005) (20:1 ratio); United States v. Fisher, 451 F.Supp.2d 553 (S.D.N.Y. October 11, 2005) (10:1 ratio).

[61] United States v. Pho, 433 F.3d 53, 64-65 (1st Cir. 2006).

[62] *Id.* at 65.

[63] *Id.*

[64] *Id.* at 64.

[65] United States v. Eura, 440 F.3d 625, 627, 634 (4th Cir. 2006). Among some of the district courts, United States v. Doe, 412 F. Supp.2d 87 (D.D.C. 2006), it was also observed that sentencing courts lack the authority to impose a sentence below the applicable Guidelines range solely based on perceived disparities attributable to the crack cocaine/powder cocaine sentencing differential; see also United States v. Tabor, 365 F. Supp.2d 1052 (D.Neb. 2005) (No need for a departure, said the court, under pre-*Booker* theory, and no reason to vary or deviate from the crack cocaine Guidelines based on defendant's possession with intent to distribute 50 or more grams of crack cocaine, thereby making him eligible imprisonment for 10 years to life under 21 U.S.C. § 841(b)(1)(A)); United States v. Valencia-Aguirre, 409 F.Supp.2d 1358 (M.D. Fla. 2006).

[66] 174 Fed.Appx. 798 (4th Cir. May 9, 2006), cert. granted, 127 S.Ct. 2933 (2007).

[67] Brief for the United States at 10-11, Kimbrough v. United States, No. 06-6330 (2007)(U.S. Brief).

[68] *Id.* at 11.

[69] *Kimbrough,* 174 Fed.Appx. at 798.

[70] 21 U.S.C. § 841(a),(b)(1)(A)(iii).

[71] 21 U.S.C. § 841(a),(b)(1)(C).

[72] 21 U.S.C. §§ 846, 841(a),(b)(1)(A)(iii).

[73] 18 U.S.C. § 924(c)(1)(A)(i).

[74] 21 U.S.C. § 841(b)(1)(A), 18 U.S.C. § 924(c)(1)(A)(i).

[75] *Kimbrough*, 174 Fed.Appx. at 798-99.

[76] Brief of Petitioner at 9-10, Kimbrough v. United States, No. 06-6330 (2007)(Petitioner's Brief). As for the sentence shopping contention, drug trafficking is a crime under federal law and the laws of each of the states. Consequently, most drug offenses can be tried in either state or federal court. In *United States v. Armstrong*, 517 U.S. 456 (1996), the defendant argued unsuccessfully that the Constitution precluded an alleged practice under which minority crack defendants were being federally prosecuted, while similarly situated white defendants faced only less severe state prosecution. There the Court observed that a selective prosecution claimant "must demonstrate that the federal prosecution policy had a discriminatory effect and that it was motivated by a discriminatory purpose. To establish a discriminatory effect in a race case, the claimant must show that similarly situated individuals of a different race were not prosecuted." *Id.* at 465. Federal crack prosecutions have apparently been particularly prevalent in the Fourth Circuit, see e.g., "Retroactivity for crack sentence cuts debated," *The National Law Journal* at 4 (October 22, 2007)(citing Sentencing Commission statistics indicating that should the Commission's recent crack cocaine amendments be made retroactive the Fourth Circuit would have almost twice as many eligible prisoners as the next highest Circuit and over nine times as many as the largest Circuit). Nevertheless, this hardly demonstrates selective prosecution. Moreover, since state sentencing practices differ from state to state, requiring compatibility of federal and state sentencing patterns within a given state would be at odds with the Guidelines' underlying premise of uniform, nationwide federal sentencing practices.

[77] Petitioner's Brief at 11.

[78] *Kimbrough*, 174 Fed.Appx. at 799.

[79] *Id.* The district court apparently cited Kimbrough's military and employment records, the fact he had no prior felony convictions, and "the court specifically relied upon the fact that 'the Sentencing Commission has recognized that crack cocaine has not caused the damage that the Justice Department alleges it has and on its recognition of the disproportionate and unjust effect that crack cocaine guidelines have in sentencing.'" Petitioner's Brief at 11 (internal citations omitted).

[80] 440 F.3d 625 (4th Cir. 2006).

[81] *Kimbrough*, 174 Fed.Appx. at 799.

[82] Kimbrough v. United States, cert. granted, 127 S.Ct. 2933 (2007).

[83] Kimbrough v. United States, 552 U.S. 85, 90 (2007). In an opinion issued on the same day as *Kimbrough,* the Supreme Court in *Gall v. United States,* 552 U.S. 38, 49 (2007) opined that while district courts must treat the Guidelines as the "starting point and the initial benchmark," they are not the only consideration. Furthermore, the Court rejected the need for requiring district judges to demonstrate that "extraordinary" circumstances justify a sentence outside the Guidelines range. *Id.* at 47.

[84] *Kimbrough,* 552 U.S. at 91.

[85] *Id.* at 111.

[86] United States v. Spears, 533 F.3d 715, 717 (8th Cir. 2008).

[87] Spears v. United States, 555 U.S. ___, 2009 U.S. LEXIS 864, No. 08-572 1 (Jan. 21, 2009). Justice Kennedy would have granted the petition for certiorari. Justice Thomas dissented without opinion. Chief Justice Roberts wrote a dissenting opinion, joined by Justice Alito, in which he agreed that "there are cogent arguments that the Eighth Circuit's decision was contrary to" *Kimbrough,* but he did not feel that "any error is so apparent as to warrant the bitter medicine of summary reversal." *Id.* at *12 (Roberts, C.J., dissenting). He also commented: "*Apprendi, Booker, Rita, Gall,* and *Kimbrough* have given the lower courts a good deal to digest over a relatively short period. We should give them some time to address the nuances of these precedents before adding new ones. As has been said, a plant cannot grow if you constantly yank it out of the ground to see if the roots are healthy." *Id.* at *15.

[88] *Id.* at *5. (emphasis in original)

[89] *Id.* at *7.

[90] *Id.* at *11 (citing United States v. Russell, 537 F.3d 6, 11 (1st Cir. 2008); United States v. Gunter, 527 F.3d 282, 286 (3rd Cir. 2008)).

[91] *Id.* at *8.

[92] 72 *Fed. Reg.* 28558 (May 21, 2007). A change in the statutory 100:1 ratio found in 21 U.S.C. § 841(b)(1) would require congressional action.

[93] United States Sentencing Commission, *Report to Congress: Cocaine and Federal Sentencing Policy,* at 8 (May 2007), available on November 13, 2007, at http://www.ussc.gov/r_congress

[94] *Id.* at 9; 72 *Fed. Reg.* 28558, 28572-573 (May 21, 2007).

[95] United States Sentencing Commission, *Report to Congress: Cocaine and Federal Sentencing Policy,* at 10 (May 2007).

[96] 72 *Fed. Reg.* 41794 (July 31, 2007). Proposed Guideline amendments submitted to Congress on or before May 1 become effective on the following November 1, unless modified or disapproved by Act of Congress. 28 U.S.C. § 994(p). A federal court may modify a sentence it has imposed to reflect a subsequently reduced sentencing range, to the extent the modification is consistent with Sentencing Commission policy statements. 18 U.S.C. § 3582(c)(2).

[97] UNITED STATES SENTENCING COMMISSION, GUIDELINES MANUAL (November 1, 2007), available on November 13, 2003 at http://www.ussc.gov/2007guid/GL2007.pdf.

[98] U.S. Sentencing Commission, *News Release: U.S. Sentencing Commission Votes Unanimously to Apply Amendment Retroactively for Crack Cocaine Offenses,* Dec. 11, 2007, *available at* http://www.ussc.gov/PRESS/rel121107.htm.

[99] 21 U.S.C. 841(b)(1)(B)(ii), (iii).

[100] 21 U.S.C. 841(b)(1)(A)(ii), (iii).

[101] U.S.S.G. § 2D1. 1(c)(Drug Quantity Table) (November 1, 2007).

[102] U.S.S.G. § 3B1.2 (November 1, 2007).

[103] U.S.S.G. § 1B1.1 (November 1, 2007).

[104] U.S.S.G. ch.5A (Sentencing Table) (November 1, 2007).

[105] *Id.*

[106] *Id.* A defendant's criminal history score is separately calculated, U.S.S.G. ch.4, and scores correspond to 1 of the 6 sentencing ranges assigned to each final offense level. In the case of offense level 26, for instance, the sentencing range for a defendant with an extensive criminal record (13 or more criminal history points) is 120 to 150 months rather than the 63 to 78 months for a first time offender. *Id*

[107] U.S.S.G. § 2D1. 1(c) (November 1, 2007).

[108] *Id.*

[109] U.S.S.G. § 2D1. 1(c)(1) (November 1, 2006).

[110] U.S.S.G. § 2D1. 1(c), ch.5A (Sentencing Table) (November 1, 2006).

[111] *Id.*

[112] "The drug quantity thresholds in the Drug Quantity Table are set so as to provide base offense levels corresponding to guideline ranges that are above the statutory mandatory minimum penalties. Accordingly, offenses involving 5 grams or more of crack cocaine were assigned a base offense level (level 26) corresponding to a sentencing guideline range of 63 to 78 months from a defendant in criminal History Category I (a guideline range that exceeds the five-year statutory minimum for such offenses by at least three months.... " United States Sentencing Commission, *Amendments to the Sentencing Guidelines*, at 66 (May 11, 2007)(emphasis in the original); 72 *Fed. Reg.* 28573 (May 21, 2007).

[113] "This amendment modifies the drug quantity thresholds in the Drug Quantity Table so as to assign, for crack cocaine offenses, base offense levels corresponding to guideline ranges that *include* the statutory mandatory minimum penalties. Accordingly, pursuant to the amendment, 5 grams of cocaine base are assigned a base offense level of 24 (51 to 63 months at Criminal History Category I, which includes the five-year (60 month) statutory minimum for such offenses).... " United States Sentencing Commission, *Amendments to the Sentencing Guidelines*, at 66 (May 11, 2007)(emphasis in the original); 72 *Fed. Reg.* 28573 (May 21, 2007).

[114] *Id.*

[115] The existing ratio in the Guidelines varies from step to step, ranging from 25:1 to 80:1. The changes that the amendment made to the Drug Quantity Table are appended below.

[116] 72 *Fed. Reg.* 41,794 (July 31, 2007).

[117] Opinions were received from a variety of parties, including the judiciary, the executive branch, interested organizations, members of the defense bar, and individual citizens. These public comment letters are available at http://www.ussc.gov/pubcom_Retro/PC200711.htm.

[118] A transcript of the public hearing, held by the Commission on November 13, 2007, is available at http://www.ussc.gov/hearings/11_13_07/Transcript111307.pdf.

[119] U.S. Sentencing Commission, *News Release: U.S. Sentencing Commission Votes Unanimously to Apply Amendment Retroactively for Crack Cocaine Offenses,* Dec. 11, 2007, *available at* http://www.ussc.gov/PRESS/rel121107.htm.

[120] 18 U.S.C. § 3582(c)(2).

[121] *Id.*

[122] *Id.*

[123] *Kimbrough,* 522 U.S. at 108 ("[A]s to crack cocaine sentences in particular, we note [that] district courts are constrained by the mandatory minimums Congress prescribed in the 1986 Act.").

[124] 18 U.S.C. § 3553(a).

[125] UNITED STATES SENTENCING COMMISSION, GUIDELINES MANUAL § 1B1.10 (November 1, 2009), *available at* http://www.ussc.gov/2009guid/1b1_10.htm.

[126] U.S.S.G. § 1B1.10(a)(3) (November 1, 2009).

[127] U.S.S.G. § 1B1. 10(b)(2)(A) (November 1, 2009).

[128] Darryl Fears, *Government Starts Cutting Sentences Of Crack Inmates,* WASH. POST, Mar. 5, 2008, at A02.

[129] *Crack Cocaine: Resentencing Goes Smoothly,* THE THIRD BRANCH, Vol. 40, No. 5 (May 2008), *available at* http://www.uscourts.gov/ttb/2008-05/article02.cfm.

[130] U.S. Sentencing Commission, *Preliminary Crack Cocaine Retroactivity Data Report,* (May 2010 Data), *available at* http://www.ussc.gov/USSC_Crack_Retroactivity_Report_2010_May.pdf.

[131] United States v. Robinson, 542 F.3d 1045 (5th Cir. 2008).

[132] See, e.g., United States v. Olden, 2008 U.S. App. LEXIS 22191 (10th Cir. 2008); United States v. Legree, 205 F.3d 724, 730 (4th Cir. 2000); United States v. Townsend, 98 F.3d 510, 512-13 (9th Cir. 1996); United States v. Tidwell, 178 F.3d 946 (7th Cir. 1999); United States v. Whitebird, 55 F.3d 1007 (5th Cir. 1995); United States v. Reddick, 53 F.3d 462 (2d Cir. 1995); United States v. Webb, 565 F.3d 789 (11th Cir. 2009).

[133] A defendant is a career offender if (1) the defendant was at least 18 years old at the time the defendant committed the instant offense of conviction; (2) the instant offense of conviction is a felony that is either a crime of violence or a controlled substance offense; and (3) the defendant has at least two prior felony convictions of either a crime of violence or a controlled substance offense. U.S. Sentencing Guidelines § 4B 1.1.

[134] United States v. Thomas, 524 F.3d 889 (8th Cir. 2008); United States v. Sharkey, 543 F.3d 1236 (10th Cir. 2008); United States v. Moore, 541 F.3d 1323 (11th Cir. 2008); United States v. Caraballo, 552 F.3d 6 (1st Cir. 2008).

[135] *Moore,* 541 F.3d at 1330.

[136] United States v. Rhodes, 549 F.3d 833, 840 (10th Cir. 2008); *see also* United States v. Fanfan, 558 F.3d 105 (1st Cir. 2009); United States v. Savoy, 567 F.3d 71 (2d Cir. 2009); United States v. Dillon, 572 F.3d 146 (3d Cir. 2009), *cert. granted,* 130 S. Ct. 797 (2009); United States v. Dunphy, 551 F.3d 247 (4th Cir. 2009); United States v. Doublin, 572 F.3d 235 (5th Cir. 2009); United States v. Washington, 584 F.3d 693 (6th Cir. 2009); United States v. Cunningham, 554 F.3d 703 (7th Cir. 2009); United States v. Starks, 551 F.3d 839 (8th Cir. 2009); United States v. Melvin, 556 F.3d 1190 (11th Cir. 2009).

[137] United States v. Doe, 564 F.3d 305, 313 (3d Cir. 2009) (internal citations and quotations omitted).

[138] United States v. Hicks, 472 F.3d 1167, 1169 (9th Cir. 2007) ("Because *Booker* abolished the mandatory application of the Sentencing Guidelines in all contexts, and because reliance on its holding is not inconsistent with any applicable policy statement, we reverse the district court and hold that *Booker* applies to § 3582(c)(2) proceedings.").

[139] United States v. Dillon, 572 F.3d 146 (3d Cir. 2009), *cert. granted*, 130 S. Ct. 797 (2009).

[140] *Dillon*, 572 F.3d at 148.

[141] *Id.* at 147, 149.

[142] Brief of Petitioner at 32-33, Dillon v. United States, No. 09-6338 (2010)(Petitioner's Brief).

[143] Brief of Respondent at 14, Dillon v. United States, No. 09-6338 (2010)(Respondent's Brief).

[144] *Id.*

[145] *Id.* at 15.

[146] Dillon v. United States, No. 09-6338, slip op. at 1-2 (560 U.S. ___, June 17, 2010). Justice Alito recused himself from the case.

[147] *Id.* at *3 (citations omitted).

[148] *Id.* at *8.

[149] *Id.* at *7-8.

[150] *Id.* at *8.
[151] *Id.,* citing 28 U.S.C.§ 994(u).
[152] *Id.* at *11.
[153] *Id.*
[154] Dillon v. United States, No. 09-6338, slip op. at 3 (560 U.S. ___, June 17, 2010) (Stevens, J., dissenting).
[155] *Id.*
[156] *Id.* at *8.
[157] *Id.* at *16-17.
[158] *Id.* at *20.
[159] S. 1789, §2.
[160] *Id.* §3.
[161] *Id.* §4.
[162] *Id.* §5.
[163] *Id.* §10.
[164] Congressional Budget Office Cost Estimate, available at http://www.cbo.gov/ftpdocs/114xx/doc11413/s1789.pdf.
[165] See, e.g., H.R. 2456, 109th Cong., 1st Sess. (Crack-Cocaine Equitable Sentencing Act of 2005); H.R. 79, 1 10th Cong., 1st Sess. (Powder-Crack Cocaine Penalty Equalization Act of 2007); H.R. 460, 1 10th Cong., 1st Sess. (Crack- Cocaine Equitable Sentencing Act of 2007); S. 1711, 1 10th Cong., 1st Sess. (Drug Sentencing Reform and Cocaine Kingpin Trafficking Act of 2007).
[166] S. 1383, 1 10th Cong., 1st Sess. (Drug Sentencing Reform Act of 2007); S. 1685, 110th Cong., 1st Sess. (Fairness in Drug Sentencing Act of 2007).

In: An Examination of Sentencing Levels and Mandatory... ISBN: 978-1-61209-563-9
Editor: Catherine N. Bates

Chapter 2

FEDERAL MANDATORY MINIMUM SENTENCING: THE 18 U.S.C. 924(C) TACK-ON IN CASES INVOLVING DRUGS OR VIOLENCE

Charles Doyle

SUMMARY

Section 924(c) requires the imposition of one of a series of mandatory minimum terms of imprisonment upon conviction for misconduct involving the firearm and the commission of a federal crime of violence or a federal drug trafficking offense. The terms vary according to the type of firearm used, the manner of the firearm's involvement, and whether the conviction involves a single, first-time offense.

If a machine gun, silencer, short barreled rifle, short barreled shotgun, or body armor is involved, the offense is punished more severely. If the firearm is brandished or discharged, the offense is punished more severely. Multiple violations are likewise punished more severely. The mandatory minimum terms range from imprisonment for five years to imprisonment for life; in each case the maximum term is life imprisonment.

Liability extends to co-conspirators and to those who aid or abet in the commission of a violation of the section.

Constitutional changes based on the Eighth Amendment's cruel and unusual punishments clause, on the Sixth Amendment's right to jury trial, on the Fifth Amendment's double jeopardy clause, and on the Tenth Amendment have been largely unsuccessful.

INTRODUCTION

Federal law attaches one of several mandatory minimum terms of imprisonment whenever a firearm is used or possessed during and in relation to a federal crime of violence or drug trafficking, 18 U.S.C. 924(c). Section 924(c) has been the subject of repeated Supreme Court litigation[1] and regular congressional amendment since its inception in 1968.[2]

Congress recently instructed the United States Sentencing Commission to report to it on the operation of federal mandatory minimum sentencing statutes.[3] Although some of the witnesses at the Commission's hearing were critical, more than 60% of the judges who responded to the Commission's survey felt that the mandatory minimum sentencing provisions of section 924(c) were appropriate.[4]

This is a brief overview of the current state of the law.

BACKGROUND

In its current form, section 924(c) imposes one of several different minimum sentences when a firearm is used or possessed in furtherance of another federal crime of violence or of drug trafficking. The minimums, imposed in addition to the sentence imposed for the underlying crime of violence or drug trafficking, vary depending upon the circumstances:

- imprisonment for not less than five years, unless one of higher mandatory minimums below applies;
- imprisonment for not less than seven years, if a firearm is brandished;
- imprisonment for not less than 10 years, if a firearm is discharged;
- imprisonment for not less than 10 years, if a firearm is a short-barreled rifle or shotgun or is a semi-automatic weapon;
- imprisonment for not less than 15 years, if the offense involves the armor piercing ammunition;
- imprisonment for not less than 25 years, if the offender has a prior conviction for violation of section 924(c);
- imprisonment for not less than 30 years, if the firearm is a machine gun or destructive device or is equipped with a silencer; and
- imprisonment for life, if the offender has a prior conviction for violation of section 924(c) and if the firearm is a machine gun or destructive device or is equipped with a silencer.

The mandatory minimum sentences were added to section 924 as a floor amendment to the Gun Control Act of 1968.[5] The amendment, as introduced, called for a 10-year minimum of imprisonment to be imposed when a firearm was used in the commission of various state and federal crimes of violence.[6] A substitute amendment reduced the minimums from 10 years to one year for a first offense, and from 25 years to five years of subsequent offenses.[7] It limited its application to federal felonies, but also barred a sentencing court from imposing the sanction as a concurrent sentence, from suspending the sentence, or from imposing a probationary sentence.[8] The impact was somewhat mitigated by a 1971 amendment which reduced the minimum for second and subsequent offenses from five years to two years.[9] Moreover, until the Sentencing Reform Act of 1984 eliminated parole, a federal offender was eligible for parole after serving the lesser of one-third of his sentence or 10 years.[10]

The Sentencing Reform Act also rewrote section 924(c) limiting its application to firearms-related federal crimes of violence, but changing its mandatory minimums to a flat five-year term of imprisonment for first offenders and a flat 10-year term for a second or subsequent conviction.[11]

Section 104 of the Firearms Owners Protection Act expanded the predicate offenses to include drug trafficking as well as crimes of violence and added a flat 10-year minimum for cases involving machine guns or silencers (a flat 20-years for a second or subsequent offense)[12] – which two years later Congress increased to flat sentences of 30 years and life imprisonment, respectively.[13]

After adding the shot-barreled firearms and destructive device provisions in 1990,[14] Congress rewrote section 924(c) in 1998, which with little change is how we now find it.[15]

FIREARM

A "firearm" for purposes of section 924 includes not only guns ("weapons ... which will or [are]designed to or may readily be converted to expel a projectile by the action of an explosive"), but silencers and explosives as well.[16] It does not, however, include toys or imitations.[17]

USED, CARRIED, OR POSSESSED IN FURTHERANCE

Originally, section 924(c) condemned only "use" of a firearm in connection with certain federal offenses.[18] Then, the Supreme Court pointed out in *Bailey* that the word "use" demands more than simple possession.[19] Congress amended the section thereafter to outlaw not only use during and in relation to a predicate offense, but possession "in furtherance" of a predicate offense as well.[20]

Possession in Furtherance

The "in furtherance" element compels the government to show some nexus between possession of a firearm and a predicate offense, that is, to show that the firearm furthered, advanced, moved forward, promoted, or in some way facilitated the predicate offense.[21] This requires more than proof of the presence of a firearm in the same location as the predicate offense. [22] Most circuits have identified specific factors that commonly allow a court to distinguish guilty possession from innocent "possession at the scene," particularly in a drug case, i.e., "type of drug activity [or violent crime] that is being conducted, accessibility of the firearm, the type of the weapon, whether the weapon is stolen, the status of the possession (legitimate or illegal), whether the gun is loaded, proximity to the drugs or drug profits, and the time and circumstances under which the gun is found."[23]

Although the Supreme Court has made it clear that acquiring a firearm in an illegal drug transaction does not constitute "use" in violation of the section 924(c),[24] several of the circuits have found that such acquisition may constitute "possession in furtherance."[25] Possession of a firearm in furtherance of a crime of violence also falls within the "in furtherance" branch of section 924(c), but crime of violence cases are most often prosecuted under the "use or carry" branch.

Use or Carriage During and Relation to

The "use" outlawed in the use or carriage branch of section 924(c) requires that a firearm be actively employed during and in relation to a predicate offense, i.e., either a crime of violence or a drug trafficking offense.[26] A defendant "uses" a firearm during or in relation to a drug trafficking offense when he uses it to acquire drugs in a drug deal,[27] or when he uses it as collateral in a drug deal,[28] but not when he accepts a firearm in exchange for drugs in a drug deal.[29] The "carry[ing]" that the section outlaws encompasses instances when a firearm is carried on the defendant's person as well as when it is simply readily accessible in vehicle during and in relation to a predicate offense. [30]

A firearm is used or carried "during or in relation" to a predicate offense when it has "some purpose or effect with respect" to the predicate offense; "its presence or involvement cannot be the result of accident or coincidence."[31] The government must show that the availability of the firearm played an integral role in the predicate offense. [32]

PREDICATE OFFENSES

The firearm enhancements of section 924(c) only come into play when related to the commission of either a federal crime of violence or a federal drug trafficking offense. The existence of a predicate offense is an element of a section 924(c) violation that must be established beyond a reasonable doubt, but the defendant need neither be charged nor convicted of the underlying predicate offense. [33]

Crimes of Violence

A crime qualifies as a crime of violence under section 9 24(c), if it is a federal felony, and if it satisfies either of two tests, i.e. (1) if it "has as an element the use, attempted use, or threatened use of physical force against the person or property of another," or (2) if it "by its nature, involves a substantial risk that physical force against the person or property of another may be used in the course of committing the offense."[34]

The courts have recognized a number of surprising, and not so surprising, crimes as section 924(c) predicate offenses, e.g.,

- Bank robbery (18 U.S.C. 2113)[35]
- Attempted bank robbery (18 U.S.C. 2113)[36]
- Kidnapping (18 U.S.C. 1201)[37]
- Carjacking (18 U.S.C. 2119)[38]
- Attempted seduction of a minor by computer (18 U.S.C. 2422(b)[39]

- Deprivation of civil rights under color of law resulting in injury or involving a dangerous weapon (statutory sentencing factors)(1 8 U.S.C. 242) [40]
- Interfering with fair housing rights (42 U.S.C. 3631)[41]
- Conspiracy to commit crimes that are violent crimes[42]
- Conspiracy to oppress the enjoyment of civil rights (18 U.S.C. 241)[43]
- Hobbs Act conspiracy (robbery or extortion)[44]
- Conspiracy to assault in aid of racketeering (18 U.S.C. 1959)[45]
- Conspiracy to violate the Neutrality Act (18 U.S.C. 9 60)[46]
- Conspiracy to provide material support to a terrorist organization (18 U.S.C. 2339B)[47]
- Conspiracy to commit RICO offenses (18 U.S.C. 1962) with predicates which are violent crimes.[48]

The Supreme Court has addressed several other aspects of section 924(c), but it has yet to decide what constitutes a crime of violence for purposes of the section. In *Leocal v. Ashcroft*, 543 U.S. 1 (2004), however, it had occasion to examine the question under 18 U.S.C. 16 which defines crimes of violence in virtually the same terms.[49] There, it reasoned that the wording of the definition precluded its application to the crime of driving under the influence and causing injury. When the statute speaks of the element involving the "*use* ... of physical force against the person or property another" – as both sections 16 and 924(c)(3) do – it means "a higher degree of intent than negligent or merely accidental conduct."[50] When, like sections 16 and 924(c)(3), it speaks of a "risk that physical force against the person or property of another may be used in the course of committing the offense," it means the "risk that the use of physical force against another might be *required* in committing the offense," not the risk that physical force might inadvertently or negligently visited upon another.[51] "The ordinary meaning of this term [(the use physical force)].... 'calls to mind a tradition of crimes that involve the possibility of more closely related, *active* violence'").[52]

One appellate court has used the *Leocal* tests to reconcile the conflicting views in other circuits and decide that firearm possession offenses are not crimes of violence for purposes of section 924(c).[53]

Federal Drug Offenses

The drug trafficking predicates include any felony violation of the Controlled Substances Act, the Controlled Substances Import and Export Act, or the Maritime Drug Law Enforcement Act.[54]

Sentencing Factors: Discharged and Brandished

The basic five-year mandatory minimum penalty for using, carrying, or possessing a firearm in the course of a predicate offense becomes a seven-year mandatory minimum if a firearm was brandished during the course of the offense and becomes a 10-year mandatory minimum if a firearm was discharged during the course of the offense.[55] The discharge provision applies even if the firearm is discharged inadvertently.[56] Whether a firearm is discharged or brandished is not an element of a separate offense, but a sentencing factor for the underlying use, carriage, or possession offense.[57] As a consequence, it need not be presented to the jury and proven beyond a reasonable doubt. It may instead may be decided by the trial court under a preponderance of the evidence standard.[58]

A firearm is brandished for these purposes when (1) it is displayed or its presence made known (2) in order to intimidate another.[59] Intimidation is a necessary feature of brandishing, but it is no less present when the fear is induced by using the gun as a club rather than merely displaying it.[60]

Elements of a Separate Crime: Short Barrels, Semiautomatics, Machine Guns, and Bombs

For some time, section 924(c) consisted of a single long paragraph. When Congress added the "possession in furtherance" language, it parsed the section. Now, the general, brandish, and discharge mandatory penalties provisions appear in one part, 18 U.S.C. 924(c)(1)(A)(i), (ii), and (iii).[61] The provisions for offenses involving a short-barreled rifle or shotgun, a semiautomatic assault weapon, a silencer, a machinegun, or explosives appear in a second part, 18 U.S.C. 924(c)(1)(B)(i) and (ii).[62] The provisions for second and consequent convictions appear in a third part, 18 U.S.C. 924(c)(1) (C)(i) and (ii).[63]

Prior to the division, the Supreme Court had identified as an element of a separate offense (rather than a sentencing factor) the question of whether a machinegun was the firearm used during and in relation to a predicate offense.[64] Thereafter, it concluded that the division was a matter of style rather than substance. Thus, the answer remains the same – use of a short-barreled rifle, semiautomatic assault weapon, silencer, machine gun, or bomb is not a sentencing factor, but an element of a separate offense to be charged and proved to the jury beyond a reasonable doubt.[65] The question of whether a second or subsequent conviction has occurred, however, remains a sentencing factor.[66]

Other Sentencing Considerations

The penalties under section 924(c) were once flat sentences, e.g., the penalty for use of a firearm during the course of a predicate offense was a five-year term of imprisonment.[67] Now, they are simply mandatory minimums, each carrying an unspecified maximum term of life imprisonment.[68]

A court may not avoid the mandatory minimums called for in section 924(c)(1) by imposing a probationary sentence,[69] or by ordering that a 924(c)(1) minimum mandatory sentence be served concurrently with some other sentence.[70] Nor may a court mute the impact of a mandatory minimum sentence by artificially reducing the sentence for the predicate offense.[71]

If a criminal episode involves more than one predicate offense, more than one violation of section 924(c) may be punished.[72] Moreover, the second or subsequent convictions which trigger enhanced mandatory minimum penalties need not be the product of separate trials, but may be part of the same verdict. Thus, a defendant charged and convicted in a single trial on several counts may be subject to multiple, consecutive, mandatory minimum terms of imprisonment.[73]

A number of defendants have sought refuge in the clause of section 924(c) which introduces the section's mandatory minimum penalties with an exception: "[e]xcept to the extent that a greater minimum sentence is otherwise provided by this subsection or by any other provision of law." Defendants have argued that the mandatory minimums of section 924(c) become inapplicable, if they are subject to a higher mandatory minimum under the predicate drug trafficking offense under the Armed Career Criminal Act (18 U.S.C. 924(e)), or some other provision of law. Two circuits consider the argument compelling.[74] The others have construed the clause to mean that the standard five-year minimum applies except in cases where the facts trigger one of section 924(c)'s higher minimums.[75]

Section 924(c) applies overseas to the extent that there is extraterritorial jurisdiction over the predicate offense. [76]

ARMOR PIERCING AMMUNITION

Section 924(c) has a separate provision which outlaws predicate crime-related use, carriage, or possession of armor piercing ammunition, 18 U.S.C. 924(c)(5).[77] The provision, added in 2005, greatly resembles a pre-existing provision in 18 U.S.C. 929.[78] There are two significant differences. Section 924(c)(5) carries a 15-year mandatory minimum with special provisions if a death results from the commission of the offense. Section 929 carries a five-year mandatory minimum with no mention of death-resulting offenses. Yet, section 929 specifically excludes the possibility of probation or concurrent sentencing; while section 924(c)(5) makes no mention of either. Neither provision appears to have been prosecuted with any regularity.

SECTION 924(C) AND THE SENTENCING GUIDELINES

The mandatory minimums of section 924(c) each carry a maximum of life imprisonment. A defendant's sentencing between the minimum and maximum is a matter that begins with the Sentencing Guidelines. The Sentencing Guidelines were once binding on federal district courts.[79] They are now advisory, but remain the starting point for all federal sentencing.[80] Section 2K2.4 of the Guidelines declares that unless the defendant qualifies as a career offender, the sentence for a violation of section 924(c) shall be the minimum called for there. The offense level adjustments in chapter 3 (victim vulnerability, role in the offense, abuse of trust/use of special skill, multiple counts, acceptable of responsibility) do not apply in such cases.[81]

In the case of career offenders, section 4B1.1(c) of the Guidelines is the operable provisions.[82] A career offender for these purposes is a defendant who has at least two prior state or federal felony convictions for a crime of violence or a drug trafficking offense. [83] The Guideline sentence for a career offender convicted of violating section 924(c) varies according to whether he is convicted of section 924(c) alone and whether the court awards an acceptance of responsibility reduction (the adjustment under chapter 3 are otherwise inapplicable).

A career offender convicted of 924(c) alone is subject to a sentencing range of either: (1) 262-327 (months)(if given a 3 level responsibility reduction); (2) 292-365 (months) (if given a 2 level responsibility reduction); or (3) 360 (months)-life) (if given no responsibility reduction).[84] If the defendant is convicted of other offenses in addition to section 924(c), his Guidelines sentence is the greater of (1) the Guideline sentence for those offenses with the 924(c) mandatory minimum tacked on, or (2) the Guideline sentence for a violation of 924(c) alone.[85]

The Guidelines themselves supply an example of how this last situation might play out:

> The defendant is convicted of one count of violating 18 U.S.C. § 924(c) for possessing a firearm in furtherance of a drug trafficking offense (5 year mandatory minimum), and one count of violating 21 U.S.C. § 841(b)(1)(B) [(e.g., trafficking in 5-50 grams of crack cocaine)] (5 year mandatory minimum, 40 year statutory maximum). Applying subsection (c)(2)(A), the court determines that the drug count (without regard to the 18 U.S.C. § 924(c) count) qualifies the defendant as a career offender under §4B1 .1(a). Under §4B1 .1(a), the otherwise applicable guideline range for the drug count is 188-235 months (using offense level 34 (because the statutory maximum for the drug count is 40 years), minus 3 levels for acceptance of responsibility, and criminal history category VI). The court adds 60 months (the minimum required by 18 U.S.C. § 924(c)) to the minimum and the maximum of that range, resulting in a guideline range of 248-295 months. Applying subsection (c)(2)(B) [(the Guideline sentence for conviction of § 924(c) alone)], the court then determines the career offender guideline range from the table in subsection (c)(3) is 262-327 months. The range with the greatest minimum, 262-327 months, is used to impose the sentence in accordance with §5G1.2(e). U.S.S.G. §4B1.1, cmt, app. n.3(E).

After the court has determined the sentencing range under the Guidelines, it determines the defendant's sentence, taking into account the results of the Guidelines' calculation and the other factors referred to 18 U.S.C. 3553(a).[86]

AIDING, ABETTING, AND CONSPIRACY

As a general rule, conspirators are liable for any foreseeable crimes committed by any of their coconspirators in furtherance of the conspiracy.[87] The rule applies when a defendant's coconspirator has committed a violation of section 924(c).[88]

Under federal law, moreover, anyone who commands, counsels, aids, or abets the commission of a federal offense by another is punishable as though he had committed the crime himself, 18 U.S.C. 2.[89] Here too, the general proposition applies to section 924(c). "[A] defendant is liable of aiding and abetting the use of a firearm during a crime of violence if he (1) knows his cohort used a firearm in the underlying crime, and (2) knowingly and actively participates in that underlying crime."[90]

CONSTITUTIONAL CONSIDERATIONS

Defendants have challenged the constitutionality of section 924(c) and its application on a number of grounds including contentions that (1) the sentence imposed constituted a cruel and unusual punishment in violation of the Eighth Amendment; (2) the procedure used to implement its provisions was contrary to the Sixth Amendment right to trial by jury, and to the Fifth Amendment right to grand jury indictment; (3) imposition of the sanctions violated the prohibition against double jeopardy; and (4) Congress lacked the legislative authority to enact the section.

Cruel and Unusual Punishment

The Eighth Amendment provides in its entirety that "[e]xcessive bail shall not be required, nor excessive fines imposed, nor cruel and unusual punishments inflicted," U.S. Const. Amend. VIII. Until very recently, there has been little consensus on the Supreme Court regarding the most appropriate test to determine whether punishment in a noncapital case is cruel and unusual. That may have changed in *Graham v. Florida*, 130 S.Ct. 2011 (2010), when a majority of the court referred to one test for "length of term-of-years" cases and another for "categorical cases."

Contemporary Eighth Amendment jurisprudence begins with *Furman v. Georgia*.[91] There, a divided Supreme Court held that the Eighth Amendment, applicable to the states through the Fourteenth Amendment, precluded imposition of the death penalty under the procedures then common in most jurisdictions.[92] Thereafter, the Court's treatment Eighth Amendment questions followed two paths – one for capital punishment cases and another for imprisonment cases. In the first of the imprisonment cases, *Rummel v. Estelle*, the Court rejected an Eighth Amendment challenge from a prisoner who had been sentenced under a state repeat offender statute to life imprisonment for the fraudulent use of the credit card.[93] Yet, three years later in *Solem v. Helm*, the Court found contrary to Eighth Amendment proscriptions a state repeat offender statute which carried a mandatory term of life imprisonment.[94] The Court considered Helm's punishment far more severe than Rummel's, because Helm was ineligible for parole while Rummel would have been eligible in 12 years.[95]

The Court in *Solem* identified three factors to be considered in the Eighth Amendment assessment of punishment in a noncapital case: "(i) the gravity of the offense and the harshness of the penalty; (ii) the sentences imposed on the criminals in the same jurisdiction [for other crimes]; and (iii) the sentences imposed for commission of the same crime in other jurisdictions."[96]

Then in *Harmelin v. Michigan*, a splintered Court rejected the Eighth Amendment challenge of a first time offender who had been sentenced to life imprisonment without parole following conviction on serious drug charges.[97] Two distinct theories converged to form the judgment of the Court. Two members of the Court, Justice Scalia and Chief Justice Rehnquist, rejected Harmelin's argument that his sentence was disproportionate to his crime because they saw no proportionality requirement in the Eighth Amendment noncapital cases.[98] Three others, Justices Kennedy, O'Connor, and Souter, found the gravity of

Harmelin's offense sufficient to satisfy the first factor of the *Solem* test and to dispense with the need to consider the other factors.[99]

The Court remained divided when it took up the next Eighth Amendment challenge to recidivist sentencing in *Ewing v. California*.[100] Three members of the Court, Chief Justice Rehnquist and Justices Kennedy and O'Connor, concluded that a sentence of imprisonment of from 25 years to life for a three-time offender convicted of theft was not unconstitutionally disproportionate.[101] Two others, Justices Scalia and Thomas, concurred in the judgment because neither believed that the Eighth Amendment proscribes disproportionate sentences.[102]

Most recently in *Graham v. Florida*, the Court found cruel and unusual the sentence of life imprisonment without parole imposed upon a child for a nonhomicide offense.[103] It did so on the basis of an Eighth Amendment "categorical" test heretofore used only in capital cases.[104] As an aside, a majority of the Court endorsed the view that "[t]he approach in cases such as *Harmelin* and *Ewing* is suited for considering a gross proportionality challenge to a particular defendant's sentence."[105] This coincides with the position taken in the lower federal appellate courts faced with Eighth Amendment challenges to sentences under section 924(c) – a sentence of imprisonment is not unconstitutionally cruel and unusual except in those rare cases where it is grossly disproportionate to the offense of conviction.[106]

Apprendi, Harris, and Booker

The creation, construction, and remodeling of section 924(c) occurred within the shadow of a Supreme Court debate over which sentence-impacting factors may be decided by the trial court by a preponderance of the evidence and which the Constitution requires to be charged and proven to a jury beyond a reasonable doubt. The Constitution declares that "[n]o person shall be held to answer for a capital, or otherwise infamous crime, unless on ... indictment of a Grand Jury ... nor be deprived of life, liberty, or property, without due process of law," and that '[i]n all criminal prosecutions, the accused shall enjoy the right to a ... trial, by ... jury." U.S. Const. Amends. V, VI.

The seeds of the jury versus judge debate were sown in the *In re Winship* case, where the Court announced that due process "protects the accused against conviction except upon proof beyond a reasonable doubt *of every fact necessary to constitute the crime with which he is charged*."[107] Moreover, the Court explained soon thereafter, due process does not permit a transfer of this burden from the prosecution to the accused; a defendant may not be convicted upon his failure to disprove one of the elements of the crime of conviction.[108] Once the prosecution has proven each of the elements of the crime charged to the satisfaction of the jury, however, due process does permit imposition of a mandatory minimum sentence based on the existence of a sentencing factor, such as brandishing a firearm, proven to a judge, rather than the jury, by a preponderance of the evidence, rather than beyond a reasonable doubt.[109]

The tension between elements and sentencing factors became apparent in *Almendarez-Torres*. There a majority of the Court found no constitutional impediment to a statutory scheme that raised the maximum penalty for an immigration offense from two years to 20 years if the court found by a preponderance of the evidence that a defendant had previously been convicted of an aggravated felony.[110] Logical though it may have been in light of the

Court's precedents, several members of the Court became uneasy with the "tail wagging the dog" implications of *Almendarez-Torres*. To avoid constitutional complications, the Court began to strain to construe as elements statutory components that might otherwise be characterized as sentencing factors.[111] Then, the Court shifted and announced in *Apprendi* that the Constitution required that "[o]ther than the fact of a prior conviction, any fact that increases the penalty for a crime prescribed statutory maximum must be submitted to the jury and proved beyond a reasonable doubt."[112] *Harris* followed, where the Court faced the question of the application of *Apprendi* to section 924(c). It concluded that provisions that increased the minimum punishment to which the defendant was exposed did not intrude upon the principles that gave birth to the *Apprendi* rule.[113]

But, *Harris* was decided before the application of the *Apprendi* rule to the federal Sentencing Guidelines. As originally cast, the Guidelines were mandatory and replete with sentencing factors under which a sentencing court was required to increase the sentence imposed upon an individual defendant.[114] This the *Apprendi* rule could not abide.[115] Yet in *Booker*, the Court made clear that it was not the presence of sentencing factors, but their binding nature, which offended.[116] If the presence of a particular factor did not require a sentencing increase, it did not implicate the constitutional considerations which gave rise of the *Apprendi* rule. So, the Court in *Booker* struck down the statutory provisions that made the Guidelines mandatory.[117] Although the Supreme Court has not spoken on the question, the lower federal appellate courts writing after *Booker* have concluded, either implicitly or explicitly, that *Harris* still controls: the *Apprendi* rule does not preclude the imposition of statutory mandatory minimums based on facts found by the court rather than the jury.[118]

Double Jeopardy

The Fifth Amendment declares that "No person shall be ... subject for the same offence to be twice put in jeopardy of life or limb.... "[119] The double jeopardy clause protects against both successive prosecutions and successive punishments for the same offense. [120] The initial test for whether a defendant has been twice tried or punished for the same offense or two different offenses is whether each of the two purported offenses requires proof that the other does not. [121] Thus, without violating the double jeopardy clause, an individual may be convicted and sentenced for two violations of section 924(c), if each has a different predicate offense. [122] On the other hand, there is no consensus over whether a single predicate offense may support conviction and sentencing for two or more violations of section 924(c).[123] Moreover, the conviction for a serious offense will ordinarily preclude prosecution or punishment for a lesser included offense, since the lesser offense consists of only elements found in the more serious offense. [124] For example, a defendant may not be convicted and punished for both a violation of section 924(c)(use of a firearm in furtherance of a robbery) and of section 924(j)(use of the same firearm in the same robbery resulting in death). [125]

Commerce Clause Authority

The Constitution gives Congress the power to regulate commerce among the states and between the United States and other nations.[126] It also bestows on Congress the authority to enact such legislation as it considered necessary and proper to carry into execution those other powers which the Constitution vests in Congress, the Government of the United States, or any of its Departments or officers.[127] At the same time, the Constitution reserves to the states and the people those powers which it has not otherwise conveyed.[128] On occasion, the Supreme Court has held that a particular statute was too far removed from Congress's commerce clause power to make the statute constitutionally viable.[129] Defendants have sometimes seized upon these cases to assert that section 924(c) lies beyond Congress's legislative reach. The courts have yet to be convinced.[130]

APPENDIX. 18 U.S.C. 924(C)(TEXT)

(c)(1)(A) Except to the extent that a greater minimum sentence is otherwise provided by this subsection or by any other provision of law, any person who, during and in relation to any crime of violence or drug trafficking crime (including a crime of violence or drug trafficking crime that provides for an enhanced punishment if committed by the use of a deadly or dangerous weapon or device) for which the person may be prosecuted in a court of the United States, uses or carries a firearm, or who, in furtherance of any such crime, possesses a firearm, shall, in addition to the punishment provided for such crime of violence or drug trafficking crime –

(i) be sentenced to a term of imprisonment of not less than 5 years;

(ii) if the firearm is brandished, be sentenced to a term of imprisonment of not less than 7 years; and

(iii) if the firearm is discharged, be sentenced to a term of imprisonment of not less than 10 years.

(B) If the firearm possessed by a person convicted of a violation of this subsection -

(i) is a short-barreled rifle, short-barreled shotgun, or semiautomatic assault weapon, the person shall be sentenced to a term of imprisonment of not less than 10 years; or

(ii) is a machinegun or a destructive device, or is equipped with a firearm silencer or firearm muffler, the person shall be sentenced to a term of imprisonment of not less than 30 years.

(C) In the case of a second or subsequent conviction under this subsection, the person shall -

(i) be sentenced to a term of imprisonment of not less than 25 years; and

(ii) if the firearm involved is a machinegun or a destructive device, or is equipped with a firearm silencer or firearm muffler, be sentenced to imprisonment for life.

(D) Notwithstanding any other provision of law -

(i) a court shall not place on probation any person convicted of a violation of this subsection; and

(ii) no term of imprisonment imposed on a person under this subsection shall run concurrently with any other term of imprisonment imposed on the person, including any term of imprisonment imposed for the crime of violence or drug trafficking crime during which the firearm was used, carried, or possessed.

(2) For purposes of this subsection, the term "drug trafficking crime" means any felony punishable under the Controlled Substances Act (21 U.S.C. 801 et seq.), the Controlled Substances Import and Export Act (21 U.S.C. 951 et seq.), or chapter 705 of title 46.

(3) For purposes of this subsection the term "crime of violence" means an offense that is a felony and -

(A) has as an element the use, attempted use, or threatened use of physical force against the person or property of another, or

(B) that by its nature, involves a substantial risk that physical force against the person or property of another may be used in the course of committing the offense.

(4) For purposes of this subsection, the term "brandish" means, with respect to a firearm, to display all or part of the firearm, or otherwise make the presence of the firearm known to another person, in order to intimidate that person, regardless of whether the firearm is directly visible to that person.

(5) Except to the extent that a greater minimum sentence is otherwise provided under this subsection, or by any other provision of law, any person who, during and in relation to any crime of violence or drug trafficking crime (including a crime of violence or drug trafficking crime that provides for an enhanced punishment if committed by the use of a deadly or dangerous weapon or device) for which the person may be prosecuted in a court of the United States, uses or carries

armor piercing ammunition, or who, in furtherance of any such crime, possesses armor piercing ammunition, shall, in addition to the punishment provided for such crime of violence or drug trafficking crime or conviction under this section -

(A) be sentenced to a term of imprisonment of not less than 15 years; and

(B) if death results from the use of such ammunition -

(i) if the killing is murder (as defined in section 1111), be punished by death or sentenced to a term of imprisonment for any term of years or for life; and

(ii) if the killing is manslaughter (as defined in section 1112), be punished as provided in section 1112.

End Notes

[1] See *United States v. O'Brien*, 130 S.Ct. 2169, 2172 (2010)("The Court must interpret, once again, §924(c) of Title 18 of the United States Code"). Earlier cases included *Dean v . United States*, 129 S.Ct. 1849 (2009); *Watson v. United States*, 552 U.S. 74 (2007); *Harris v. United States*, 536 U.S. 545 (2002); *Castillo v. United States*, 530 U.S. 120 (2000); *Mascarello v. United States*, 524 U.S. 125 (1998); *United States v. Gonzales*, 520 U.S. 1 (1997); *Bailey v. United States,* 516 U.S. 137 (1995); *Smith v. United States*, 508 U.S. 223 (1993); *Deal v. United States*, 508 U.S. 129 (1993).

[2] Substantive amendments to section 924(c) are discussed in the following section.

[3] Section 4713, P.L. 111-84, 123 Stat. 2843 (2009).

[4] United States Sentencing Commission, *Results of Survey of United States District Judges: January 2010 through March 2010, Question 1. Mandatory Minimums* (June 2010), available at http://www.ussc.gov/Judge_Survey/2010/JudgeSurvey_201006.pdf.

[5] P.L. 90-618, 82 Stat. 1223 (1968).

[6] 114 *Cong. Rec.* 22229 (1968)(amendment offered by Rep. Casey). The original amendment would have also established a 25-year minimum for second and subsequent offenses, *Id.*

[7] 114 *Cong. Rec.* 222231 (1968)(substitute amendment offered by Rep. Poff).

[8] *Id.* Further modifications were offered during the course of the debate, but the language enacted was in large measure that of the Poff substitute, see 114 *Cong. Rec.* 22229-22248 (1968); H.Rept. 90-1956, at 12, 31-32 (1968)(confining the concurrent, suspended, and probationary sentencing provisions to second and subsequent violations), and 82 Stat. 1223 (1968), 18 U.S.C. 924(c)(1970 ed.).

[9] Section 13, P.L. 91-644, 84 Stat. 1889 (1971), 18 U.S.C. 924(c) (1976 ed.).

[10] 18 U.S.C. 4205 (1976 ed.).

[11] Section 1005, P.L. 98-473, 98 Stat. 2138 (1984), 18 U.S.C. 924(c) (1982 ed.)(Supp. II).

[12] P.L. 99-308, 100 Stat. 457 (1986), 18 U.S.C. 924(c) (1976 ed.)(Supp. IV).

[13] Section 6460, P.L. 100-690, 102 Stat. 4373 (1988), 18 U.S.C. 924(c) (1988 ed.).

[14] Section 1101, P.L. 101-647, 104 Stat. 4829 (1990), 18 U.S.C. 924(c) (1988 ed.)(Supp. II).

[15] Section 1, P.L. 105-386, 112 Stat. 3469 (1998), 18 U.S.C. 924(c) (2000 ed.). The armor piercing ammunition provisions were added in 2005, Section 6(b), P.L. 109-92, 119 Stat. 2102 (2005), 18 U.S.C. 924(c).

[16] 18 U.S.C. 921(a)(3), (4) ("(3) The term 'firearm' means (A) any weapon (including a starter gun) which will or is designed to or may readily be converted to expel a projectile by the action of an explosive; ... (C) any firearm muffler or firearm silencer; or (D) any destructive device.... (4) The term 'destructive device' means - (A) any explosive, incendiary, or poison gas - (i) bomb, (ii) grenade, (iii) rocket having a propellant charge of more than four ounces, (iv) missile having an explosive or incendiary charge of more than one-quarter ounce, (v) mine, or (vi) device similar to any of the devices described in the preceding clauses.... "); *United States v. York*, 600 F.3d 347, 354 (5th Cir. 2010)(Molotov cocktail constitutes a "firearm" for purposes of section 924(c)).

[17] *United States v. Garrido*, 596 F.3d 613, 617 (9th Cir. 2010)("Possession of a toy or replica gun cannot sustain a conviction under §924(c)"); *United States v. Roberson*, 459 F.3d 39, 47 (1st Cir. 2006).

[18] 18 U.S.C. 924(c)(1970 ed.).

[19] *Bailey v. United States*, 516 U.S. 137, 143 (1995)(emphasis in the original)(Section 924(c) "requires evidence sufficient to show an *active employment* of the firearm by the defendant, a use that makes the firearm an operative factor in relation to the predicate offense.... '[U]se' must connote more than mere possession of a firearm by a person who commits a drug offense").

[20] 18 U.S.C. 924(c)(2000 ed.). *United States v. Gurka*, 605 F.3d 40, 43 (1st Cir. 2010).

[21] *United States v. Huddleston*, 593 F.3d 596, 602 (7th Cir. 2010); *United States v. Parish*, 606 F.3d 480, 490 (8th Cir. 2010); *United States v. Pena*, 586 F.3d 105, 113 (1st Cir. 2009); *United States v. Jeffers*, 570 F.3d 557, 565 (4th Cir. 2009); *United States v. London*, 568 F.3d 553, 559 (5th Cir. 2009); *United States v. Lopez-Garcia*, 565 F.3d 1306, 1322 (11th Cir. 2009).

[22] *United States v. Huddleston*, 593 F.3d 596, 602 (7th Cir. 2010); *United States v. Villa*, 589 F.3d 1334, 1341 (10th Cir. 2009); *United States v. Pena*, 586 F.3d 105, 113 (1st Cir. 2009); *United States v. Penney*, 576 F.3d 297, 315 (1st Cir. 2009).

[23] *United States v. Huddleston*, 593 F.3d 596, 602 (7th Cir. 2010); *United States v. Villa*, 589 F.3d 1334, 1341 (10th Cir. 2009); *United States v. London*, 568 F.3d 553, 559 (5th Cir. 2009); *United States v. Lopez-Garcia*, 565 F.3d 1306, 1322 (1 1th Cir. 2009); *United States v. Perry*, 560 F.3d 246, 254 (4th Cir. 2009); *United States v. Iglesias*, 535 F.3d 150, 157 (3d Cir. 2008); see also *United States v. Chavez*, 549 F.3d 119, 130 (2d Cir. 2008)(noting after quoting the factors that, "while no conviction would lie for a drug dealer's innocent possession of a firearm, ... a drug dealer may be punished under §924(c)(1)(A) where the charged weapon is readily accessible to protect drugs, drug proceeds, or the drug dealer himself"); but see *United States v. Hector*, 474 F.3d 1150, 1157 (9th Cir. 2007)(internal citations omitted)("Although the Fifth Circuit has developed a non-exclusive list of factors ... we have concluded that this approach is not particularly helpful in close cases.... In our most recent case addressing the 'in furtherance question," we reiterated the importance of the factual inquiry. We declined once again to adopt a checklist approach to deciding this issue and held that it is the totality of the circumstances, coupled with a health dose of a jury's common sense when evaluating the facts in evidence, which will determine whether the evidence suffices to support a conviction").

[24] *Watson v. United States*, 552 U.S. 74 (2007).

[25] *United States v. Gurka*, 605 F.3d 40, 44 (1st Cir. 2010)("We join the three circuits holding *Watson* does not affect the prong of 18 U.S.C. §924(c)(1)(A) concerned with 'possession in furtherance'), citing in accord *United States v. Doody*, 600 F.3d 752,755-56 (7th Cir. 2010); *United States v. Gardner*, 602 F.3d 97, 103 (2d Cir. 2010); *United States v. Mahan*, 586 F.3d 1185, 1189 (9th Cir. 2009).

[26] *Bailey v. United States*, 516 U.S. 137, 143 (1995); *United States v. Haynes*, 582 F.3d 686, 704 (7th Cir. 2009)); *United States v. Combs*, 369 F.3d 925, 932 (6th Cir. 2004).

[27] *Smith v. United States*, 508 U.S. 223, 228 (1993); *Bailey v. United States*, 516 U.S. 137, 148 (1995).

[28] *United States v. Cox*, 324 F.3d 77, 82 (2d Cir. 2003).

[29] *Watson v. United States*, 552 U.S. at 78.

[30] *Muscarello v. United States*, 524 U.S. 125, 126 (1998)("The question before us is whether the phrase 'carries a firearm' is limited to the carrying of firearms on the person. We hold that it is not so limited. Rather, it also applies to a person who knowingly possesses and carries a firearm in a vehicle, including locked in a glove compartment or trunk of a car, which the person accompanies"); *United States v. Franklin*, 561 F.3d 398, 403 (5th Cir. 2009); *United States v. Winder*, 557 F.3d 1129, 1138-139 (10th Cir. 2009); *United States v. Robinson*, 390 F.3d 853, 878 (6th Cir. 2005); *United States v. Williams*, 344 F.3d 365, 370 (3d Cir. 2003).

[31] *United States v. Mashek*, 606 F.3d 922, 930 (8th Cir. 2010), quoting *Smith v. United States*, 508 U.S. 223, 238 (1993); *United States v. Roberson*, 459 F.3d 39, 48 (1st Cir. 2006); *United States v. Combs*, 369 F.3d 925, 933 (6th Cir. 2004); *United States v. Williams*, 344 F.3d 365, 371 (3d Cir. 2003).

[32] *United States v. Burkley*, 513 F.3d 1183, 1189-190 (10th Cir,. 2008)("A firearm is carried during and in relation to the underlying crime when the defendant avails himself of the weapon and ... the weapon plays an integral role in the underlying offense.... Thus, the government must prove that the defendant intended the firearm to be available for use in the offense").

[33] *United States v. Kuehne*, 547 F.3d 667, 680 (6th Cir. 2009).

[34] 18 U.S.C. 924(c)(3).

[35] *United States v. Andrews*, 442 F.3d 996, 1002 (7th Cir. 2006); *United States v. Bandy*, 239 F.3d 802, 805 (6th Cir. 2001); *United States v. Wright*, 215 F.3d 1020, 1028 (9th Cir. 2000).

[36] *United States v. Jones*, 418 F.3d 726, 729 (7th Cir. 2005); *United States v. Green*, 115 F.3d 1479, 1486-487 (10th Cir. 1997).

[37] *United States v. Green*, 521 F.3d 929, 932-33 (8th Cir. 2008); *United States v. Sandoval*, 347 F.3d 627, 633-34 (7th Cir. 2003).

[38] *United States v. Frye*, 489 F.3d 201, 208-209 (5th Cir. 2007); *United States v. Moore*, 43 F.3d 568, 572-73 (1 1th Cir. 1995).

[39] *United States v. Munro*, 394 F.3d 865, 870-71 (10th Cir. 2005).

[40] *United States v. Acosta*, 470 F.3d 132, 135-36 (2d Cir. 2006), citing *United States v. Williams*, 343 F.3d 423, 434 (5th Cir. 2003).

[41] *United States v. Pospisil*, 186 F.3d 1023, 1031 (8th Cir. 1999).

[42] *United States v. Brown*, 200 F.3d 700, 706 (10th Cir. 1999)(conspiracy to carjack (18 U.S.C. 21 19)("Both the government and Mr. Brown acknowledge that several courts have held that conspiracy to commit a federal crime of violence is a crime of violence for purposes of §924(c). See e.g., *United States v. Elder*, 88 F.3d 127, 129 (2d Cir. 1996)(Hobbs Act conspiracy to commit robbery); *Untied States v. Harper*, 33 F.3d 1143, 1149 n.5 (9th Cir. 1994)(conspiracy to commit bank robbery").

[43] *United States v. Acosta*, 470 F.3d 132, 136-37 (2d Cir. 2006), citing *United States v. Greer*, 939 F.2d 1076, 1099 (5th Cir. 1991).

[44] *United States v. Turner*, 501 F.3d 59, 67-68 (1st Cir. 2007); *United States v. Taylor*, 176 F.3d 331, 337-38 (6th Cir. 1999); *United States v. Phan*, 121 F.3d 149, 152-53 (4th Cir. 1997); *United States v. Mendez*, 992 F.2d 1488, 1491-492 (7th Cir. 2005).

[45] *United States v. Desena*, 287 F.3d 170, 181 (2d Cir. 2002).

[46] *United States v. Khan*, 461 F.3d 477, 489-90 (4th Cir. 2006).

[47] *United States v. Khan*, 461 F.3d 477, 490 (4th Cir. 2006).

[48] *United States v. Ayala*, 601 F.3d 256, 266-67 (4th Cir. 2010)(RICO conspiracy with 18 U.S.C. 1959 predicates), quoting *United States v. Elder*, 88 F.3d 127, 129 (2d Cir. 1996)("[A] conspiracy 'is itself a crime of violence when its objectives are violent crimes'"); *United States v. Ivezaj*, 568 F.3d 88, 95-96 (2d Cir. 2009)(RICO conspiracy with loan sharking and extortionate predicates); *United States v. Juvenile Male*, 118 F.3d 1344, 1350 (9th Cir. 1997)(RICO conspiracy with Hobbs Act predicates).

[49] 18 U.S.C. 16 ("The term 'crime of violence' means - (a) an offense that has as an element the use, attempted use, or threatened use of physical force against the person or property of another, or (b) any other offense that is a felony and that, by its nature, involves a substantial risk that physical force against the person or property of another may be used in the course of committing the offense").

[50] *Leocal v. Ashcroft*, 543 U.S. 1, 9 (2004)(emphasis added).

[51] *Id.* at 10 (emphasis added)(quoting, *United States v. Doe*, 960 F.2d 221, 225 (1st Cir. 1992) ("The reckless disregard in §16 relates not to the general conduct or to the possibility that harm will result form a person's conduct, but to the risk that the use of physical force against another might be *required* in committing a crime.... The ordinary meaning of this term.... 'calls to mind a tradition of crimes that involve the possibility of more closely related, *active* violence'").

[52] *Id.*

[53] *United States v. Serafin*, 562 F.3d 1105, 1107-1116 (10th Cir. 2009)("[T]he danger from an unregistered short-barreled rifle is inherent to its use, not merely in its possession. Although Searfin clearly disregarded the law by possessing an illegal short-barreled rifle, we must confine the scope of §924(c)(3)(B) to active, violent crimes which pose a substantial risk that force may be used during the course of the offense"), citing among others *United States v. Hull*, 456 F.3d 133, 140 (3d Cir. 2006) (possession of an unregistered pipe bomb [included within the definition of firearm in 18 U.S.C. 921(a)(3), (4)] was not a crime of violence under 18 U.S.C. 16); *Henry v. Bureau of Immigration & Customs Enforcement*, 493 F.3d 303, 309 (3d Cir. 2007)(possession of an unregistered pipe bomb with the intent to use was a crime of violence under section 16); *United States v. Jennings*, 195 F.3d 795, 798 (5th Cir. 1999)(possession of a pipe bomb [without reference to intent] was a crime of violence under section 16); *United States v. Diaz-Diaz*, 327 F.3d 410, 413-14 (5th Cir. 2003)(possession of an unregistered short-barreled firearm was not a crime of violence under section 16; "apparently reversing its contrary holding in *United States v. Rivas-Palacios*, 244 F.3d 396 (5th Cir. 2001)").

[54] 18 U.S.C. 924(c)(2), referring to 21 U.S.C. 801-904; 21 U.S.C. 951-971; and 46 U.S.C. 70501-70507; respectively.

[55] 18 U.S.C. 924(c)(1)(A)(ii), (iii).

[56] *Dean v. United States*, 129 S.Ct. 1849, 1853 (2009).

[57] *Id.*; *Harris v. United States,* 536 U.S. 545, 556 (2002); *United States v. Bowen*, 527 F.3d 1065, 1072 (10th Cir. 2008); *United States v. Johnson*, 507 F.3d 793, 798 n.6 (2d Cir. 2007).

[58] *Harris v. United States,* 536 U.S. at 556; *United States v. Benford*, 574 F.3d 1228, 1233-234 (9th Cir. 2009); *United States v. Thompson*, 515 F.3d 556, 563064 (6th Cir. 2008); *United States v. Griffin*, 493 F.3d 856, 864 (7th Cir. 2007).

[59] 18 U.S.C. 924(c)(4)("For purposes of this subsection, the term 'brandish' means, with respect to a firearm, to display all or part of the firearm, or otherwise make the presence of the firearm known to another person, in order to intimidate that person, regardless of whether the firearm is directly visible to that person"); *United States v. Carter*, 560 F.3d 1107, 1114 (9th Cir. 2009).

[60] *United States v. Bowen*, 527 F.3d at 1075 (10th Cir. 2008).

[61] 18 U.S.C. 924(c)(1)(emphasis added)("(A) Except to the extent that a greater minimum sentence is otherwise provided by this subsection or by any other provision of law, any person who, during and in relation to any crime of violence or drug trafficking crime (including a crime of violence or drug trafficking crime that provides for an enhanced punishment if committed by the use of a deadly or dangerous weapon or device) for which the person may be prosecuted in a court of the United States, uses or carries a firearm, or who, in furtherance of any such crime, possesses a firearm, shall, in addition to the punishment provided for such crime of violence or drug trafficking crime - *(i) be sentenced to a term of imprisonment of not less than 5 years; (ii) if the firearm is brandished, be sentenced to a term of imprisonment of not less than 7 years; and (iii) if the firearm is discharged, be sentenced to a term of imprisonment of not less than 10 years....* ").

[62] 18 U.S.C. 924(c)(1)(" ... (B) If the firearm possessed by a person convicted of a violation of this subsection - (i) is a short-barreled rifle, short-barreled shotgun, or semiautomatic assault weapon, the person shall be sentenced to a term of imprisonment of not less than 10 years; or (ii) is a machinegun or a destructive device, or is equipped with a firearm silencer or firearm muffler, the person shall be sentenced to a term of imprisonment of not less than 30 years.... ").

[63] 18 U.S.C. 924(c)(1)(" ... (C) In the case of a second or subsequent conviction under this subsection, the person shall - (i) be sentenced to a term of imprisonment of not less than 25 years; and (ii) if the firearm involved is a machinegun or a destructive device, or is equipped with a firearm silencer or firearm muffler, be sentenced to imprisonment for life").

[64] *Castillo v. United States*, 530 U.S. 120, 121 (2000).

[65] *United States v . O'Brien*, 130 U.S. 2169, 2180 (2010).

[66] *United States v. Rivera-Rivera,* 555 F.3d 277, 291 (1st Cir. 2009); *United States v. Mejia*, 545 F.3d 179, 207-208 (2d Cir. 2008).

[67] 18 U.S.C. 924(c)(1976 ed.).

[68] *United States v. Shabazz*, 564 F.3d 280, 289 (3d Cir. 2009), citing in accord *United States v. Johnson*, 507 F.3d 793, 798 (2d Cir. 2007); *United States v. Dare*, 425 F.3d 634, 642 (9th Cir. 2005); *United States v. Avery*, 295 F.3d 1158, 1170 (10th Cir. 2002); *United States v. Cristobal*, 293 F.3d 134, 147 (4th Cir. 2002); *United States v. Sandoval*, 241 F.3d 549, 551 (7th Cir. 2001); *United States v. Pounds*, 230 F.3d 1317, 1319 (1 1th Cir. 2000); *United States v. Silas*, 227 F.3d 244, 246 (5th Cir. 2000).

[69] 18 U.S.C. 924(c)(1)(D)(i).

[70] 18 U.S.C. 924(c)(1)(D)(ii).

[71] *United States v. Chavez*, 549 F.3d 119, 135 (2d Cir. 2008); *United States v. Hatcher*, 501 F.3d 931, 933 (8th Cir. 2007); *United States v. Franklin*, 499 F.3d 578, 584-85 (6th Cir. 2007); *United States v. Roberson*, 474 F.3d 432, 436 (7th Cir. 2007).

[72] *United States v. Sandstrom*, 594 F.3d 634, 658 (8th Cir. 2010)(" ... [M]ultiple underlying offenses support multiple §924(c) convictions"); *United States v. Catalan-Roman*, 585 F.3d 453, 472 (1st Cir. 2009); *United States v. Penny*, 576 F.3d 297, 316 (6th Cir. 2009)("[W]hen two separate predicate offenses for triggering §924(c)(1) are charged and proved, a defendant may be convicted and sentenced for two separate crimes, even if both offenses were committed in the course of the same event"); *United States v. Looney*, 532 F.3d 392, 396 (5th Cir. 2008).

[73] *Deal v. United States*, 508 U.S. 129, 132 (1993); *United States v. Phaknikone*, 605 F.3d 1099, 1101, 1111-112 (11th Cir. 2010)(the defendant was charged with, and convicted for, a string of 15 armed bank robberies for which he received a sentenced of 2005 months (167 years); the court observed that, "Phaknikone also argues that, because each count under section 924 was charged in a single indictment, the district court erroneously applied the higher mandatory minimum of 25 years of imprisonment for second or subsequent conviction, 18 U.S.C. §924(c)(1)(C), to six of his seven convictions. We long ago rejected this argument"); *United States v. Beltran-Moreno*, 556 F.3d 913, 915 (9th Cir. 2009)("In this case, the defendants pled guilty to various drug offenses that, taken together, imposed a mandatory minimum sentence of ten years. They also pled guilty to two §9254(c) charges, the first of which required a mandatory minimum sentence of five years and the second of which required an additional sentenced of twenty-five years. Because the statute does not allow any of these sentences to run concurrently, the mandatory minimum sentence for both defendants is forty years in prison"); *United States v. Watkins*, 509 F.3d 277, 282 (6th Cir. 2007) ("Finally, the district court sentenced Watkins to an additional 7 years for brandishing a firearm during the first robbery, in violation of 18 U.S.C. §924(c), and to 25 years for each count of using or brandishing a firearm during the other five robberies. The length of the firearm sentences are predetermined by §924(c)(1)(C)(i). Pursuant to §924(c)(1(D)(ii), the court then ordered that each of the §924(c) gun convictions run consecutively to the underlying offenses").

[74] *United States v. Almany*, 598 F.3d 238, 241-42 (6th Cir. 2010); *United States v. Whitley*, 529 F.3d 150, 153-56 (2d Cir. 2008).

[75] *United States v. Villa*, 589 F.3d 1334, 1342-343 (10th Cir. 2009)("The phrase 'except to the extent hat a greater minim sentence is otherwise provided by this subsection or by another other provision of law ... connotes a comparison between alternative minimum sentences for a violation of §924(c), not between sentences for separate violations of §924(c) and another statute"), citing in accord *United States v. Segarra*, 582 F.3d 1269 (1 1th Cir. 2009); *United States v. Abbott*, 574 F.3d 203 (3d Cir. 2009); *United States v. Easter*, 553 F.3d 519 (7th Cir. 2009); *United States v. Parker*, 549 F.3d 5 (1st Cir. 2008); *United States v. Jolivette*, 257 F.3d 581 (6th Cir. 2002); *United States v. Studifinl*, 240 F.3d 415 (4th Cir. 2001); *United States v. Alaniz*, 235 F.3d 386 (8th Cir. 2000).

[76] *United States v. Belfast*, 611 F.3d 783, 813-15 (11th Cir. 2010)(upholding a section 924(c) conviction on the grounds that the predicate crime of violence (18 U.S.C. 2340A) had extraterritorial application).

[77] 18 U.S.C. 924(c)(5)("Except to the extent that a greater minimum sentence is otherwise provided under this subsection, or by any other provision of law, any person who, during and in relation to any crime of violence or drug trafficking crime (including a crime of violence or drug trafficking crime that provides for an enhanced punishment if committed by the use of a deadly or dangerous weapon or device) for which the person may be prosecuted in a court of the United States, uses or carries armor piercing ammunition, or who, in furtherance of any such crime, possesses armor piercing ammunition, shall, in addition to the punishment provided for such crime of violence or drug trafficking crime or conviction under this section - (A) be sentenced to a term of imprisonment of not less than 15 years; and (B) if death results from the use of such ammunition - (i) if the killing is murder (as defined in section 1111), be punished by death or sentenced to a term of imprisonment for

any term of years or for life; and (ii) if the killing is manslaughter (as defined in section 1112), be punished as provided in section 1112").

[78] 18 U.S.C. 929("(a)(1) Whoever, during and in relation to the commission of a crime of violence or drug trafficking crime (including a crime of violence or drug trafficking crime which provides for an enhanced punishment if committed by the use of a deadly or dangerous weapon or device) for which he may be prosecuted in a court of the United States, uses or carries a firearm and is in possession of armor piercing ammunition capable of being fired in that firearm, shall, in addition to the punishment provided for the commission of such crime of violence or drug trafficking crime be sentenced to a term of imprisonment for not less than five years. (2) For purposes of this subsection, the term "drug trafficking crime" means any felony punishable under the Controlled Substances Act (21 U.S.C. 801 et seq.), the Controlled Substances Import and Export Act (21 U.S.C. 951 et seq.), or chapter 705 of title 46.

"(b) Notwithstanding any other provision of law, the court shall not suspend the sentence of any person convicted of a violation of this section, nor place the person on probation, nor shall the terms of imprisonment run concurrently with any other terms of imprisonment, including that imposed for the crime in which the armor piercing ammunition was used or possessed").

[79] 18 U.S.C. 3553(b)(1) (2000 ed.).

[80] *United States v. Booker*, 543 U.S. 220, 245 (2005); *Gall v. United States*, 552 U.S. 38, 49-50 (2007)("[A] district court should begin all sentencing proceedings by correctly calculating the applicable Guidelines range.... [A]fter giving both parties an opportunity to argue for whatever sentence they deem appropriate, the district judge should then consider all of the §3553(a) factors to determine whether they support the sentence requested by a party").

[82] U.S.S.G. §4B1.1(c).

[83] U.S.S.G. §§4B1. 1(c), 4B1.2(b), (c); *United States v. McFalls*, 592 F.3d 707, 712-17 (6th Cir. 2010).

[84] U.S.S.G §4B1. 1(a), (c)(1), (c)(3); *United States v. Shabazz*, 564 F.3d 280, 288-89 (3d Cir. 2009).

[85] U.S.S.G §4B1. 1(a), (c)(2), (c)(3).

[86] 18 U.S.C. 3553(a)("The court shall impose a sentence sufficient, but not greater than necessary, to comply with the purposes set forth in paragraph (2) of this subsection. The court, in determining the particular sentence to be imposed, shall consider - (1) the nature and circumstances of the offense and the history and characteristics of the defendant; (2) the need for the sentence imposed - (A) to reflect the seriousness of the offense, to promote respect for the law, and to provide just punishment for the offense; (B) to afford adequate deterrence to criminal conduct; (C) to protect the public from further crimes of the defendant; and (D) to provide the defendant with needed educational or vocational training, medical care, or other correctional treatment in the most effective manner; (3) the kinds of sentences available; (4) the kinds of sentence and the sentencing range established for - (A) the applicable category of offense committed by the applicable category of defendant as set forth in the guidelines (i) issued by the Sentencing Commission pursuant to section 994(a)(1) of title 28, United States Code, subject to any amendments made to such guidelines by act of Congress (regardless of whether such amendments have yet to be incorporated by the Sentencing Commission into amendments issued under section 994(p) of title 28); and (ii) that, except as provided in section 3742(g), are in effect on the date the defendant is sentenced; or (B) in the case of a violation of probation or supervised release, the applicable guidelines or policy statements issued by the Sentencing Commission pursuant to section 994(a)(3) of title 28, United States Code, taking into account any amendments made to such guidelines or policy statements by act of Congress (regardless of whether such amendments have yet to be incorporated by the Sentencing Commission into amendments issued under section 994(p) of title 28); (5) any pertinent policy statement - (A) issued by the Sentencing Commission pursuant to section 994(a)(2) of title 28, United States Code, subject to any amendments made to such policy statement by act of Congress (regardless of whether such amendments have yet to be incorporated by the Sentencing Commission into amendments issued under section 994(p) of title 28); and (B) that, except as provided in section 3742(g), is in effect on the date the defendant is sentenced. (6) the need to avoid unwarranted sentence disparities among defendants with similar records who have been found guilty of similar conduct; and (7) the need to provide restitution to any victims of the offense").

[87] *Pinkerton v. United States*, 328 U.S. 640, 646 (1946); *Salinas v. United States*, 522 U.S. 52, 63 (1997).

[88] *United States v. Carter*, 560 F.3d 1107, 1113 (9th Cir. 2009)("There is no dispute that Carter himself did not use a firearm during the robbery. The question, accordingly, is whether it could be reasonably foreseen as a necessary or natural consequence of the unlawful agreement that one of Carter's coconspirators would use a firearm during the robbery"); *United States v. Haynes*, 582 F.3d 686, 707-708 (7th Cir. 2009); *United States v. Merlino,* 592 F.3d 22, 29 (1st Cir. 2010); *United States v. Ashley*, 606 F.3d 135, 142-43 (4th Cir. 2010).

[89] *United States v. Bowen,* 527 F.3d 1065, 1078 (10th Cir. 2008)(internal citations omitted)("[A]iding and abetting liability allows a jury to hold an aider and abettor responsible for a substantive offense to the same extent as a principal, even though his act was not the cause of the substantive harm. Acts committed in furtherance of the commission of a crime by another constitute 'abetting'.... To be liable for aiding and abetting, a defendant must (1) willfully associate himself with the criminal venture, and (2) seek to make the venture succeed through some action of his own ... One need not participate in an important aspect of a crime to be liable as an

aider and abettor; participation of 'relatively slight moment' is sufficient. Even mere 'words or gestures of encouragement' constitute affirmative acts capable of rendering one liable under this theory").

[90] *Id.* See also *United States v. Gomez*, 580 F.3d 94, 104 (2 Cir. 2009); *United States v. Figueroa-Cartagena*, 612 F.3d 69, 83-4 (1st Cir. 2010)("The indictment alleged that she aided and abetted Alberto and Gabriel in their use and carriage of a firearm during the carjacking. To secure a conviction on that count, the government had to prove that Neliza knew to a practical certainty that her confederates would carry or use a firearm and that she willingly took some step to facilitate the carrying or use"); cf., *United States v. Ashley*, 606 F.3d at 142-43.

[91] 408 U.S. 238 (1972).

[92] Each of the nine Justices wrote a separate opinion in *Furman*, six offering various reasons for support of the per curiam opinion for the Court and three in dissent.

[93] 445 U.S. 263, 265 (1980). Rummel had two earlier theft convictions involving relative modest amounts, i.e., a forged check for $28.36 and a scam involving $120.75; the credit card conviction involved $80 in goods and services, *id.* at 265-66.

[94] 463 U.S. 277, 303 (1983). Helm, convicted for uttering a "no account" check for $100, had six prior "nonviolent" felony convictions, *id.* at 279-80

[95] *Id.* at 303.

[96] *Id.* at 292.

[97] 501 U.S. 957 (1991).

[98] *Id.* at 994.

[99] *Id.* at 1004.

[100] 538 U.S. 11 (2003).

[101] *Id.* at 30-3 1.

[102] *Id.* at 31, 32.

[103] 130 S.Ct. 2011, 2034 (2010).

[104] *Id.* at 2022-23.

[105] *Id.* at 2022.

[106] *United States v. Wiest*, 596 F.3d 906, (8th Cir. 2010)("This court has adopted Justice Kennedy's analysis in *Harmelin* to determine whether a sentence is 'grossly disproportionate' to a crime and thus violates the Eighth Amendment ... Although this court has not directly addressed whether consecutive sentences under §924(c) violate the Eighth Amendment, other circuits uphold similar sentences under §924(c) ... No circuit has held that consecutive sentences under §924(c) violate the Eighth Amendment. Wiest's sentence was not grossly disproportionate to the crime committed, and does not violate the Eighth Amendment"), citing *United States v. Walker*, 473 F.3d 71, 79-84 (3d Cir. 2007); *United States v. Khan*, 461 F.3d 477, 494-95 (4th Cir. 2006); *United States v. Angelos*, 433 F.3d 738, 750-53 (10th Cir. 2006); *United States v. Beverly*, 369 F.3d 516, 536-38 (6th Cir. 2004); *United States v. Arrington*, 159 F.3d 1069, 1073 (7th Cir. 1998); see also *United States v. Looney*, 532 F.3d 392, 396-97 (5th Cir. 2008).

[107] *In re Winship*, 397 U.S. 358, 364 (1970)(emphasis added).

[108] For instance, a state may not require an accused to prove that he acted without malice aforethought (e.g., in the heat of passion), when malice aforethought is an element of the crime with which he is charged, *Mullaney v. Wilbur*, 421 U.S. 684, 698-701 (1975).

[109] *McMillan v. Pennsylvania*, 477 U.S. 79, 93 (1986).

[110] *Almendarez-Torres v. United States,* 523 U.S. 224, 226,-27 (1998).

[111] *United States v. Jones*, 526 U.S. 227, 239 (1999).

[112] *Apprendi v. New Jersey*, 526 U.S. 466, 490 (2000).

[113] *Harris v. United States*, 536 U.S. 545, 568 (2002).

[114] 18 U.S.C. 3553(b)(1)(2000 ed.); *United States Sentencing Commission Manual* (2003 ed.).

[115] *United States v. Booker*, 543 U.S. 220, 243-44 (2005).

[116] *United States v. Booker*, 543 U.S. at 245 ("We answer the question of remedy by finding the provision of the federal sentencing statute that makes the Guidelines mandatory, 18 U.S.C.A. §3553(b)(1)(Supp. 24004), incompatible with today's constitutional holding").

[117] *United States v. Booker*, 543 U.S. at 259.

[118] *United States v. Payne*, 591 F.3d 46, 68 (2d Cir. 2010); *United States v. Motley*, 587 F.3d 1153, 1158-159 (D.C.Cir. 2009); *United States v. Washington*, 584 F.3d 693, 700 (6th Cir. 2009); *United States v. Bucci*, 582 F.3d 108, 118 n.8 (1st Cir. 2009*); United States v. Strahan,* 565 F.3d 1047, 1053 (7th Cir. 2009); *United States v. Shabazz*, 564 F.3d 280, 288 (3d Cir. 2009); *United States v. Dunphy*, 551 F.3d 247, 253 n.3 (4th Cir. 2009); *United States v. A.B.*, 529 F.3d 1275, 1282 (10th Cir. 2008*); United States v. Freemont*, 513 F.3d 884, 890 (8th Cir. 2008).

[119] U.S. Const. Amend. V.

[120] *United States v. Dixon*, 509 U.S. 688, 696 (1993); *United States v. Mahdi*, 598 F.3d 883, 887 (D.C.Cir. 2010); *United States v. Hall*, 551 F.3d 257, 266 (4th Cir. 2009).

[121] *Blockburger v. Untied States*, 284 U.S. 299, 304 (1932); *United States v. Mahdi*, 598 F.3d at 888; *United States v. Sandstrom*, 594 F.3d 634, 654 (8th Cir. 2010); *United States v. Beltran-Moreno*, 556 F.3d 913, 916 (9th Cir. 2009).

[122] *United States v. Sandstrom*, 594 F.3d at 658); *United States v. Catalan-Roman*, 585 F.3d 453, 472 (1st Cir. 2009); *United States v. Penny*, 576 F.3d 297, 316 (6th Cir. 2009); *United States v. Looney*, 532 F.3d 392, 396 (5th Cir. 2008).

[123] *United States v. Diaz*, 592 F.3d 467, 470-75 (3d Cir. 2010), citing in accord United States v. Rodriguez, 525 F.3d 85, 1119 (1st Cir. 2008); *United States v. Batiste*, 309 F.3d 274, 279 (5th Cir. 2002); United States v. Anderson, 59 F.3d 1323, 1326-327 (D.C. Cir. 1995); *United States v. Cappas*, 29 F.3d 1187, 1195 (7th Cir. 1994); *United States v. Taylor*, 13 F.3d 986, 992-994 (6th Cir. 1994); *United States v. Lindsay*, 985 F.2d 666, 676 (2d Cir. 1993); *United States v. Hamilton*, 953 F.2d 1344, 1346 (1 1th Cir. 1992); *United States v. Smith*, 924 F.2d 889, 894-95 (9th Cir. 1991); *United States v. Henning*, 906 F.3d 1392, 1399 (10th Cir. 1990), and to the contrary, *United States v. Lucas*, 932 F.2d 1210, 1222-223 (8th Cir. 1991); *United States v. Camps*, 32 F.3d 108-109 (4th Cir. 1994).

[124] *Rutledge v. United States*, 517 U.S. 292, 306-307 (1996); *United States. Sand*strom, 594 F.3d at 654; *United States v. Catalan-Roman*, 585 F.3d 453, 472 (1st Cir. 2009).

[125] *United States v. Catalan-Roman*, 585 F.3d at 472.

[126] U.S. Const. Art. I, §8, cl. 3.

[127] U.S. Const. Art. I, §8, ch. 18.

[128] U.S. Const. Amend. X.

[129] *United States v. Morrison*, 529 U.S. 598, 612-13 (2000), quoting *United States v. Lopez*, 514 U.S. 549, 564 (1995)("We rejected these ... arguments because they would permit Congress to 'regulate not only all violent crime, but all activities that might lead to violent crime, regardless of how tenuously they related to interstate commerce'"); but consider *United States v. Comstock*, 130 S.Ct. 1949 (2010).

[130] *United States v. Belfast*, 611 F.3d 783, 815(1 1th Cir. 2010); *United States v. Lynch*, 367 F.3d 1148, 1158 (9th Cir. 2004); *United States v. Miller*, 283 F.3d 907, 913-14 (8th Cir. 2002).

In: An Examination of Sentencing Levels and Mandatory… ISBN: 978-1-61209-563-9
Editor: Catherine N. Bates

Chapter 3

FEDERAL MANDATORY MINIMUM SENTENCES: THE SAFETY VALVE AND SUBSTANTIAL ASSISTANCE EXCEPTIONS

Charles Doyle

SUMMARY

Federal law requires a sentencing judge to impose a minimum sentence of imprisonment following conviction for any of a number of federal offenses. Congress has created two exceptions. One is available in all cases when the prosecutor asserts that the defendant has provided substantial assistance in the criminal investigation or prosecution of another, 18 U.S.C. 3553(e). The other, commonly referred to as the safety value, is available, without the government's approval, for a handful of the more commonly prosecuted drug trafficking and unlawful possession offenses that carry minimum sentences, 18 U.S.C. 3553(f).

Qualification for the substantial assistance exception is ordinarily only possible upon the motion of the government. In rare cases, the court may compel the government to file such a motion when the defendant can establish that the refusal to do so was based on constitutionally invalid considerations, or was in derogation of a plea bargain obligation or was the product of bad faith.

Qualification for the safety valve exception requires a defendant to satisfy five criteria. His past criminal record must be minimal; he must not have been a leader, organizer, or supervisor in the commission of the offense; he must not have used violence in the commission or the offense, and the offense must not have resulted in serious injury; and prior to sentencing, he must tell the government all that he knows of the offense and any related misconduct.

Congress has instructed the United States Sentencing Commission to report on the operation of federal mandatory minimum sentencing provisions. A majority of the Federal judges responding to a Commission survey agree that the two exceptions should be expanded. A number of Commission hearing witnesses have also urged that the provisions be amended.

INTRODUCTION

Depending on how the class is defined, there are hundreds of federal mandatory minimum offenses.[1] Yet only a handful are prosecuted with any regularity, including under 21 U.S.C. 841 (trafficking in controlled substances), 844 (possession of controlled substances), and 960 (smuggling controlled substances). Congress has provided two escape hatches under which a court may sentence a defendant below the statutory mandatory minimum. One, 18 U.S.C. 3553(e), is available only on the motion of the prosecutor based on the defendant's substantial assistance to the government and without regard to the offense charged. The second, 18 U.S.C. 3553(f), requires neither substantial assistance nor the prosecutor's endorsement, but is limited to the mandatory minimum sentences required in five sections of the federal drug law.

In October, 2009, Congress instructed the United States Sentencing Commission to prepare a report on the mandatory minimum sentencing provisions under federal law.[2] In early 2010, the Commission conducted a survey of federal district court judges regarding their views on mandatory minimum sentencing. A majority of those responding endorsed amendments to the safety valve and substantial assistance exceptions.[3] The Commission also held a public hearing at which several witnesses urged adjustments in the safety valve and substantial assistance provisions.[4]

SUBSTANTIAL ASSISTANCE

Background

The substantial assistance provisions, 18 U.S.C. 3553(e), passed with little fanfare in the twilight of the 99th Congress as part of the massive Anti-Drug Abuse Act of 1986, legislation which established or increased a number of mandatory minimum sentencing provisions.[5] The section continues in its original form virtually unchanged:

> (e) Limited Authority To Impose a Sentence Below a Statutory Minimum. - Upon motion of the Government, the court shall have the authority to impose a sentence below a level established by statute as a minimum sentence so as to reflect a defendant's substantial assistance in the investigation or prosecution of another person who has committed an offense. Such sentence shall be imposed in accordance with the guidelines and policy statements issued by the Sentencing Commission pursuant to section 994 of title 28, United States Code.[6]

The section passed between the date authorizing the Sentencing Guidelines and the date they became effective. Rather than replicate the language of section 3553(e), the Guidelines contain an overlapping section which authorizes a sentencing court to depart from the minimum sentence called for by the Guidelines, U.S.S.G. §5K1.1.[7]

"Upon the Motion of the Government"

As a general rule, a defendant is entitled to a sentence below an otherwise applicable statutory minimum under the provisions of section 3553(e) only if the government agrees.[8] The courts have acknowledged that due process or equal protection or other constitutional guarantees may provide a narrow exception. "Thus, a defendant would be entitled to relief if a prosecutor refused to file a substantial-assistance motion, say, because of the defendant's race or religion."[9] A defendant is entitled to relief if the Government's refusal constitutes a breach of its plea agreement. [10] A defendant is also "entitled to relief if the prosecutor's refusal to move was not rationally related to any legitimate Government end."[11] Some courts have suggested that a defendant is entitled to relief if the prosecution refuses to move under circumstances that "shock the conscience of the court," or that demonstrate bad faith, or for reasons unrelated to substantial assistance. [12] A majority of the judges who answered the Sentencing Commission's survey agreed that relief under section 3553(e) should be available even in the absence of motion from the prosecutor.[13]

A motion under section 3553(e) for a sentence beneath the mandatory minimum and a motion under U.S.S.G. §5K1.1 for a sentence beneath the applicable Sentencing Guideline range are not the same. Thus, a motion under section 5K1.1 will ordinarily not be construed as a motion under section 3553(e).[14]

"To Reflect a Defendant's Substantial Assistance"

Any sentence imposed below the statutory minimum by virtue of section 3553(e) must be based on the extent of the defendant's assistance; it may not reflect considerations unrelated to such assistance. [15] It has been suggested that a court may use the section 5K1 .1 factors for that determination, i.e., "(1) the court's evaluation of the significance and usefulness of the defendant's assistance, taking into consideration the government's evaluation of the assistance rendered; (2) the truthfulness, completeness, and reliability of any information or testimony provided by the defendant; (3) the nature and extent of the defendant's assistance; (4) any injury suffered, or any danger or risk of injury to the defendant or his family resulting from his assistance; [and] (5) the timeliness of the defendant's assistance," U.S.S.G. §5K1.1(a).[16]

The substantial assistance exception makes possible convictions that might otherwise be unattainable. Yet, it may also lead to "inverted sentencing," i.e., a situation in which "the more serious the defendant's crimes, the lower the sentence – because the greater his wrongs, the more information and assistance he had to offer to a prosecutor;" while in contrast the exception is of no avail to the peripheral offender who can provide no substantial assistance.[17] Perhaps for this reason, most of the judges who responded to the Sentencing Commission survey agreed that a sentencing court should not be limited to assistance-related factors and should be allowed use the generally permissible sentencing factors when calculating a sentence under section 3553(e).[18]

Booker

Defendants, seeking relief on the basis of substantial assistance have often and unsuccessfully sought to claim benefits under the *Booker* line of cases. In *United States v. Booker*, the Supreme Court affirmed that "[a]ny fact (other than a prior conviction) which is necessary to support a sentence exceeding the maximum authorized by the facts established by a plea of guilty or a jury verdict must be admitted by the defendant or proved to a jury beyond a reasonable doubt."[19] Since this constitutional command would doom *mandatory* sentencing guidelines, the Court found unconstitutional that portion of the Sentencing Reform Act which purported to make the Sentencing Guidelines mandatory.[20]

The fact that the Guidelines are advisory hardly renders them irrelevant, as the Court's decision in *Gall* makes clear:

> [A] district court should begin all sentencing proceedings by correctly calculating the applicable Guidelines range. . . The Guidelines are not the only consideration, however, Accordingly, after giving both parties an opportunity to argue for whatever sentence they deem appropriate, the district judge should then consider all of the §3553(a) factors to determine whether they support the sentence requested by a party. . . . If he decides that an outside-Guidelines sentence is warranted, he must consider the extent of the deviation and ensure that the justification is sufficiently compelling to support he degree of the variance.[21]

Nevertheless, as the Fifth Circuit recently observed, "[D]istrict courts [may] impose a sentence of imprisonment below a statutory minimum only if: (1) the government so moves pursuant to 18 U.S.C. §3553(e), asserting the defendant's substantial assistance to the government; or (2) the defendant meets the 'safety valve' criteria, set forth in 18 U.S.C. 3553(f). Otherwise post-*Booker* sentencing courts lack discretion to depart below relevant statutory minimums."[22]

SAFETY VALVE

Background

Congress enacted section 3553(f), after it became concerned that the mandatory minimum sentencing provisions could resulted in equally severe penalties for both the more and the less culpable offenders.[23] The section permits a sentencing court to impose a shorter term of imprisonment for the covered controlled substance offenses, if the defendant satisfies five criteria:

Notwithstanding any other provision of law, in the case of an offense under section 401, 404, or 406 of the Controlled Substances Act (21 U.S.C. 841, 844, 846) or section 1010 or 1013 of the Controlled Substances Import and Export Act (21 U.S.C. 960, 963), the court shall impose a sentence pursuant to guidelines promulgated by the United States Sentencing Commission under section 994 of title 28 without regard to any statutory minimum sentence, if the court finds at sentencing, after the Government has been afforded the opportunity to make a recommendation, that –

(1) the defendant does not have more than 1 criminal history point, as determined under the sentencing guidelines;
(2) the defendant did not use violence or credible threats of violence or possess a firearm or other dangerous weapon (or induce another participant to do so) in connection with the offense;
(3) the offense did not result in death or serious bodily injury to any person;
(4) the defendant was not an organizer, leader, manager, or supervisor of others in the offense, as determined under the sentencing guidelines and was not engaged in a continuing criminal enterprise, as defined in section 408 of the Controlled Substances Act; and
(5) not later than the time of the sentencing hearing, the defendant has truthfully provided to the Government all information and evidence the defendant has concerning the offense or offenses that were part of the same course of conduct or of a common scheme or plan, but the fact that the defendant has no relevant or useful other information to provide or that the Government is already aware of the information shall not preclude a determination by the court that the defendant has complied with this requirement. 18 U.S.C. 3553(f).

The defendant has the burden of convincing the trial court by a preponderance of the evidence that he satisfies each of the criteria.[24] The appellate courts will afford a sentencing court considerable deference before concluding that the lower court has come to a clearly erroneous conclusion of fact.[25]

Offenses Covered

Section 3553(f) covers the mandatory minimum sentences ordinarily imposed for five offenses:

(1) trafficking in various controlled substances (21 U.S.C. 841);
(2) possession of certain controlled substances (21 U.S.C. 844);
(3) attempt or conspiracy to violate controlled substance provisions carrying mandatory minimum sentences (21 U.S.C. 846);
(4) smuggling controlled substances in violation of 21 U.S.C. 952, 953, 955, 957, or 959); and
(5) attempt or conspiracy to violate the controlled substance import/export provisions (21 U.S.C. 963).

The safety valve is not available to avoid the mandatory minimum sentences that attend other offenses, even those closely related to the listed offenses. For instance, section 860 (21 U.S.C. 860) outlaws violations of section 841 near schools, playgrounds or public housing facilities and sets the penalties for violation at twice what they would be under section 841. Those charged with a violation of section 860 are not eligible for relief under the safety valve provisions.[26] In addition, safety valve relief is not available to those convicted under the

Maritime Drug Law Enforcement Act, even though the Act proscribes conduct closely related to the smuggling and trafficking activities punished under sections 960 and 963.[27]

More than two-thirds of the judges responding to the Sentencing Commission's survey agreed that the safety valve should be expanded to cover any offense with a mandatory minimum.[28] An even higher percentage agreed that it should extended to all drug trafficking offenses[29] and to receipt of child pornography. [30] A number of witnesses at the Commission's hearing also spoke in favor of expanding the number of mandatory minimum statutes covered.[31]

One Point

> [T]he defendant does not have more than 1 criminal history point, as determined under the sentencing guidelines, 18 U.S.C. 3553(f)(1).[32]

The first safety valve criterion demands that a defendant have no more than one criminal history point. The Sentencing Guidelines assign criminal history points based on a defendant's past criminal record. Two or more points are assigned for every prior sentence of imprisonment or juvenile confinement of sixty days or more or for offenses committed while the defendant was in prison, was an escaped prisoner, or was on probation, parole, or supervised release.[33] A single point is assigned for every other federal or state prior sentence of conviction, with certain exceptions.[34]

Foreign sentences of imprisonment are not counted;[35] nor sentences imposed by tribal courts;[36] nor summary court martial sentences;[37] nor sentences imposed for expunged, reversed, vacated, or invalidated convictions;[38] nor sentences for certain petty offenses or minor misdemeanors.[39]

The Sentencing Guidelines list two classes of these minor misdemeanor or petty offenses that are not counted for criminal history purposes and thus for safety valve purposes. One class consists of eight types of minor offenses that are not counted regardless of the sentence imposed, i.e.,

- Fish and game violations,
- Hitchhiking,
- Juvenile status offenses and truancy,
- Local ordinance violations (except those violations that are also violations under state criminal law),
- Loitering,
- Minor traffic infractions (e.g., speeding),
- Public intoxication, [and]
- Vagrancy.[40]

The other class consists of arguable more serious offenses that only counted if the offender was sentenced to imprisonment for thirty days or more and to probation for more than a year, i.e.

- Careless or reckless driving,
- Contempt of court,
- Disorderly conduct or disturbing the peace,
- Driving without a license or with a revoked or suspended license,
- False information to a police officer,
- Gambling,
- Hindering or failure to obey a police officer,
- Insufficient funds check,
- Leaving the scene of an accident,
- Non-support,
- Prostitution,
- Resisting arrest, and
- Trespassing.[41]

Both classes also include similar offenses to those listed "by whatever name they are known."[42]

The Sentencing Guidelines suggest a number of factors to assist in the determination of whether an unlisted offense may be consider "similar" for purposes of section 4A1.2(c):

(i) a comparison of punishments imposed for the listed and unlisted offenses;
(ii) the perceived seriousness of the offense as indicated by the level of punishment;
(iii) the elements of the offense;
(iv) the level of culpability involved; and
(v) the degree to which the commission of the offense indicates a likelihood of recurring criminal conduct.[43]

A sentencing court is bound by the Sentencing Guidelines in its determination of criminal history points for purposes of section 3553(f).[44]

Two-thirds of the judges who responded to the Commission's survey favored expanding the safety valve criminal history criterion to encompass those with 2 or 3 criminal history points,[45] although fewer than one quarter favored expansion of the criterion further.[46] Some of the Commission's hearing witnesses concurred.[47]

Not Violent or Deadly

> [T]he defendant did not use violence or credible threats of violence or possess a firearm or other dangerous weapon (or induce another participant to do so) in connection with the offense, 18 U.SC. 3553(f)(2).48
>
> [T]he offense did not result in death or serious bodily injury to any person, 18 U.S.C. 3553(f)(3).[49]

The disqualification in section 3553(f)(2) turns upon the defendant's conduct or the conduct of those he "aided or abetted, counseled, commanded, induced, procured, or willfully caused."[50] It is not triggered by the conduct of a co-conspirator, unless the defendant aided, abetted, counsel . . . the co-conspirator's violence or possession.[51] Disqualifying firearm possession may be either actual or constructive.[52] Constructive possession is the dominion or control over a firearm or the place where one is located.[53] Disqualification requires the threat of violence or possession of a firearm "in connection with the offense." In many instances, possession of a firearm in a location where drugs are stored or transported, or where transactions occur, will be enough to support an inference of possession in connection with the drug offense of conviction.[54]

The Sentencing Guidelines define 'serious bodily injury" for purposes of section 3553(f)(3) as an "injury involving extreme physical pain or the protracted impairment of a function of a bodily member, organ, or mental faculty; or requiring medical intervention such as surgery, hospitalization, or physical rehabilitation."[55] On its face, the definition would include serious bodily injuries, such as hospitalization, suffered by the defendant as a result of the offense.[56] Unlike the gun and violence disqualification in section 3553(f)(2), the serious injury disqualification in section 3553(f)(3) may be triggered by the conduct of a co-conspirator.[57]

Single or Low Level Offender

> [T]he defendant was not an organizer, leader, manager, or supervisor of others in the offense, as determined under the sentencing guidelines *and was not engaged in a continuing criminal enterprise, as defined in section 408 of the Controlled Substances A*ct, 18 U.S.C. 3553(f)(4)(emphasis added).[58]

The Sentence Guidelines limit disqualification to those who receive a guideline level increase for their aggravated role in the offense.[59] Thus, by implication, it does not require a defendant to have received a guideline increase based on his minimal or minor participation in a group offense nor does it disqualify a defendant who acted alone. [60]

The appellate case law construing section 3553(f)(4) and its Sentencing Guideline counterpart is largely devote to (1) the impact of *Booker*,[61] and (2) the observation that a finding that an defendant merits a sentencing level increase for his aggravating role in the offense under U.S.S.G. §3B1.1 triggers a safety valve disqualification under section 3553(f)(4).[62]

Tell All

> [N]ot later than the time of the sentencing hearing, the defendant has truthfully provided to the Government all information and evidence the defendant has concerning the offense or offenses that were part of the same course of conduct or of a common scheme or plan, but the fact that the defendant has no relevant or useful other information to provide or that the Government is already aware of the information shall not preclude a determination by the court that the defendant has complied with this requirement, 18 U.S.C. 3553(f)(5).[63]

The fifth and most heavily litigated safety valve criterion requires full disclosure on the part of the defendant. The requirement extends not only to information concerning the crimes of conviction, but also to information concerning other crimes that "were part of the same course of conduct or of a common scheme or plan," including uncharged related conduct.[64]

Neither section 3553(f) nor the Sentencing Guidelines explain what form the defendants' full disclosure must take. At least one court has held that under rare circumstances disclosure through the defendant's testimony at trial may suffice. [65] Most often the defendant provides the information during an interview with prosecutors or by a proffer. The defendant must disclose the information to the prosecutor, however. Disclosure to the probation officer during preparation of the presentence report is not sufficient.[66] Moreover, a defendant does not necessarily qualify for relief merely because he has proffered a statement and invited the prosecution to identify any addition information it seeks; for "the government is under no obligation to solicit information from a defendant."[67] On the other hand, past lies do not render a defendant ineligible for relief under the truthful disclosure criterion of the safety value, although they may undermine his creditability. [68]

Author Contact Information

Charles Doyle
Senior Specialist in American Public Law
cdoyle@crs.loc.gov, 7-6968

End Notes

[1] See generally, CRS Report RL32040, *Federal Mandatory Minimum Sentencing Statutes, by Charles Doyle; United States Sentencing Commission, Special Report to the Congress: Mandatory Minimum Penalties in the Federal Criminal Justice System* (1991), available on July 5, 2010 at http://www.ussg.gov/manmin/manmin51.htm; Greenblatt, *How Mandatory Are Mandatory Minimums? How Judges Can Avoid Imposing Mandatory Minimum Sentences*, 36 AMERICAN JOURNAL OF CRIMINAL LAW 1, 27-28 (2008)("[P]rosecutors have power to offer plea deals, reduce charges, limit introduction of evidence, and decide whether to appeal judges' trial management decisions and other orders. Each of these powers gives prosecutors the opportunity to allow a defendant to avoid a mandatory minimum sentence").

[2] Section 4713 of the National Defense Authorization Act for Fiscal Year 2010, found in the Matthew Shepard and James Byrd, Jr., Hate Crimes Prevention Act, P.L. 111-84, 123 Stat. 2843 (2009).

[3] See United States Sentencing Commission, *Results of Survey of United States District Judges January 2010 through March 2010: Question 2. Safety Valve* (June 2010)(*Survey*) available on July 5, 2010 at http://www.ussc.gov/Judge_Survey/2010/JudgeSurvey_20106.pdf.

[4] United States Sentencing Commission, *Public Hearing Agenda Thursday, May 28, 2010* (*Hearing*) available on July 5, 2010 at http://www.ussc.gov/AGENDA/20100527/Agenda.htm.

[5] Section 1007(a) of P.L. 99-570, 100 Stat. 32-07-7 (1986).

[6] In the only amendment to section 3 553(e), section 4002(a)(8) of P.L. 107-273 (2002) changed the phrase "as minimum sentence" to "as a minimum sentence."

[7] "5K1. 1. Substantial Assistance to Authorities (Policy Statement). Upon motion of the government stating that the defendant has provided substantial assistance in the investigation or prosecution of another person who has committed an offense, the court may depart from the guidelines.

(a) The appropriate reduction shall be determined by the court for reasons stated that may include, but are not limited to, consideration of the following:

(1) the court's evaluation of the significance and usefulness of the defendant's assistance, taking into consideration the government's evaluation of the assistance rendered;

(2) the truthfulness, completeness, and reliability of any information or testimony provided by the defendant;

(3) the nature and extent of the defendant's assistance;

(4) any injury suffered, or any danger or risk of injury to the defendant or his family resulting from his assistance;

(5) the timeliness of the defendant's assistance."

[8] *Melendez v. United States*, 518 U.S. 120, 125-26 (1996)("We believe that §3553(e) requires a government motion requesting or authorizing the district court to impose a sentence below a level established by statute as a[a] minimum sentence before the court may impose such a sentence").

[9] *Wade v. United States*, 504 U.S. 181, 186 (1992).

[10] *United States v. Motley*, 587 F.3d 1153, 1159 (D.C. Cir. 2009); *United States v. Smith*, 574 F.3d 521, 525 (8th Cir. 2009); *United States v. Doe*, 445 F.3d 202, 207 (2d Cir. 2006).

[11] *Wade v. United States*, 504 at 186.

[12] *United States v. Freemont*, 513 F.3d 884, 889 (8th Cir. 2008)("The district court may review the government's refusal to make a motion in limited circumstances. First, the district court may review the government's decision for an unconstitutional motive. . . . Second, a district court can compel a §3553(e) motion if the government acknowledges the defendant provided substantial assistance, but refuses to make a motion expressly because the defendant engaged in unrelated misconduct – a reason unrelated to the quality of the defendant's assistance. . . . Third, the district court may be able to compel a motion if the government acted in bad faith by refusing to make a motion"); but see *United States v. Perez*, 526 F.3d 1135, 1138 (8th Cir. 2008)(citing cases evidencing a split within the circuit over whether bad faith provides a sufficient based to compel a government motion).

[13] *Survey, Question 15. Substantial Assistance*. Only 35% of the respondents disagreed with the statement that "Congress should amend 18 USC §3553(e) to authorize judges to sentence a defendant below the applicable statutory mandatory minimum to reflect a defendant's substantial assistance, even if the government does not make a motion," *Id.*

[14] *Melendez v. United States*, 518 U.S. 120, 126 (1996).

[15] *United States v. Burns*, 577 F.3d 887, 894 (8th Cir. 2009)(en banc)("Where a court has authority to sentence below a statutory minimum only by virtue of a government motion under §3553(e), the reduction below the statutory minimum must be based exclusively on assistance-related considerations"); *United States v. Jackson,* 577 F.3d 1032, 1036 (9th Cir. 2009); *United States v. Hood*, 556 F.3d 226, 234 n.2 (4th Cir. 2009), citing *inter alia United States v. Richardson,* 521 F.3d 149, 159 (2d Cir. 2008) and *United States v. Desselle,* 450F.3d 179, 182 (5th Cir. 2006).

[16] *United States v. Gabbard*, 586 F.3d 1046, 1051 (6th Cir. 2009), citing *United States v. Richardson*, 521 F.3d at 159.

[17] Hearing, Testimony of Jeffrey B. Steinback on behalf of the Practitioner's Advisory Group at 8, quoting United States v. Brigham, 977 F.2d 317, 318 (7th Cir. 1992); see also Hearing, Written Statement of Cynthia Hujar Orr, President of the National Ass 'n of Criminal Defense Lawyers at 3 (defendants "who have little or no information to provide the government, end up with far more severe sentences than leaders of conspiracies who run the operations and know the other participants").

[18] *Survey, Question 15. Substantial Assistance*. Only 24% of the respondents disagreed with the statement that "In determining the extent of a reduction below the statutory mandatory minimum under 18 USC §3553(e). . . the court's consideration should not be limited to the nature of the defendant's substantial assistance but also should include consideration of the factors at 18 USC §3553(a)," *Id.*

[19] *United States v. Booker*, 543 U.S. 220, 244 (2005), citing *Apprendi v. New Jersey*, 530 U.S. 466, 490 (2000).

[20] *United States v. Booker*, 543 U.S. at 245.

[21] *Gall v. United States*, 552 U.S. 38, 49-50 (2007).

[22] *United States v. Montes*, 602 F.3d 381, 390 (5th Cir. 2010); see also, *United States v. Christensen*, 582 F.3d 860, 862 (8th Cir. 2009)("Nothing in the reasoning of *United States v. Booker*. . . expands the authority of a district court to sentence below a statutory minimum"); *United States v. Johnson*, 580 F.3d 666, 673 (7th Cir. 2009).

[23] H.Rept. 103-460, at 4 (1994).

[24] *United States v. Gales*, 603 F.3d 49, 52-3 (D.C.Cir. 2010); *United States v. Pena*, 598 F.3d 289, 292 (6th Cir. 2010); *United States v. Larios*, 593 F.3d 82, 89 (1st Cir. 2010); *United States v. Jackson*, 552 F.3d 908, 909 (8th Cir. 2009); *United States v. Altamirano-Quintero*, 511 F.3d 1087, 1098 (10th Cir. 2007); *United States v. Olivas-Ramirez*, 487 F.3d 512, 516-17(7th Cir. 2007); *United States v. Mejia-Pimental*, 477 F.3d 1100, 1104 (9th Cir. 2007).

[25] *United States v. Padilla-Colon*, 578 F.3d 23, 29-3 0 (1st Cir. 2009)("We review de novo safety valve determinations to the extent they rest on conclusions of law. We review for clear error safety-valve determinations to the extent they depend on findings of fact. The clear error standard is extremely deferential. Under it, an appellate court ought not to disturb either findings of fact or conclusions drawn from the record unless the whole of the record compels a strong, unyielding belief that a mistake has been made"); *United States v. Crumley*, 528 F.3d 1053, 1068 (8th Cir. 2008)("We give great weight to a district court's credibility determinations"); see also *United States v. Gales*, 603 F.3d 49, 54 (D.C.Cir. 2010)("The district court did not clearly err in thinking it highly unlikely that Gales did not have any further information on the identity of his steady, supplier, whom he claimed to have known for ten years, beyond the vague description given to the government").

[26] *United States v. Phillips*, 382 F.3d 489, 499-500 (5th Cir. 2004); *United States v. Koons*, 300 F.3d 985, 993 (8th Cir. 2002); *United States v. Kakatin*, 214 F.3d 1049, 1050-51 (9th Cir. 2000); *United States v. Anderson*, 200 F.3d 1344, 1346-348 (1 1th Cir. 2000); *United States v. McQuilkin*, 78 F.3d 105, 108 (3d Cir. 1996). One Commission witness indicated that "in districts where substantial portions of towns and cities fall within protected zones, prosecutors can, and some do, charge violations of 21 U.S.C. §860 for the purpose of preventing safety valve relief for offenders who would otherwise qualify," *Hearings, Statement of Michael Nachmanoff, Federal Public Defender for E.D. Va.* at 31.

[27] *United States v. Gamboa-Cardenas*, 508 F.3d 491, 496-503 (9th Cir. 2007).

[28] *Survey, Section 2. Safety Valve*. Only 18% disagreed; another 12% were neutral, *Id.*

[29] *Id.* Only 12% disagreed; another 12% were neutral, *Id.*

[30] *Id.* Only 15% disagreed; another 13% were neutral, *Id.*

[31] *Hearings, Statement of Michael Nachmanoff, Federal Public Defender for E.D. Va.* at 31 ("We also urge the Commission to recommend to Congress that it expand the safety valve to apply to all mandatory minimums. . . . The problems caused by mandatory minimums are present for all offenses subject to them. Worse, prosecutors in some districts exercise their charging discretion to require mandatory minimum sentences for defendants who would otherwise qualify fort the safety valve"); *Comments of Cory L. Andrews, Washington Legal Foundation* at 5 ("Expanding such mechanisms to other non-violent offenses would allow Congress to maintain the current mandatory minimum sentencing structure while providing district judges with meaningful opportunities to avoid harsh and unintended sentencing results"); *Statement of Jay Rorty, American Civil Liberties Union* at 4.

[32] See also U.S.S.G. §5C1.2(a)(1).

[33] U.S.S.G. §§4A1.1(a), (b), (d); 4A1.2(d).

[34] U.S.C.G. §§4A1.1(c); 4A1.2.

[35] U.S.S.G. §4A1.2(h).

[36] U.S.S.G. §4A1.2(i).

[37] U.S.S.G. §4A1 .2(g). Sentences imposed by general and special courts martial are counted, *id.*

[38] U.S.S.G. §§4A1.2(j); 4A1.2, cmt. n.6.

[39] U.S.S.G. §4A1.2(c).

[40] U.S.S.G. §4A1.2(c)(2).

[41] U.S.S.G. §4A1.2(c)(1).

[42] U.S.S.G. §4A1.2(c)(1), (c)(2).

[43] U.S.S.G. §4A1 .2, cmt. n. 12(A). See e.g., *United States v. DeJesus-Concepcion*, 607 F.3d 303, 305-306 (2d Cir. 2010) (third degree unauthorized use of a vehicle is not a similar offense to careless or reckless driving); *United States v. Calderon Espinosa*, 569 F.3d 1005, 1008 (9th Cir. 2009)(offense of loitering for drug activities is loitering "by whatever name it is known"); *United States v. Russell*, 564 F.3d 200, 206 (3d Cir. 2009)(misdemeanor marijuana possession is not similar to public intoxication); *United States v. Pando*, 545 F.3d 682, 684 (8th Cir. 2008)(driving while intoxicated is not similar to careless or reckless driving, citing U.S.S.G. §4A1.2, cmt. n.5); *United States v. McKenzie*, 539 F.3d 15, 17-18 (1st Cir. 2008)(shoplifting is not similar to "insufficient funds check"); *United States v. Garrett*, 528 F.3d 525, 527-29 (7th Cir. 2008)(bail jumping is similar to contempt of court); *United States v. Sanchez- Cortez*, 530 F.3d 357, 359-60 (5th Cir. 2008)(military AWOL offense was not similar to truancy); *United States v. Cole*, 418 F.3d 592, 599-600 (6th Cir. 2005)(underage (over 18 but under 21) possession of alcohol was similar to a juvenile status offense).

[44] *United States v. Leon-Alvarez*, 532 F.3d 815, 8 18-19 (8th Cir. 2008)("several of our sister circuits have determined that the calculation of criminal history points is not advisory"), citing *United States v. Hernandez*, 473 F.3d 1004, 1007 (9th Cir. 2007); *United States v. McKoy*, 452 F.3d 234, 239-40 (3d Cir. 2006); *United States v. Brehm*, 442 F.3d 1291, 1300 (1 1th Cir. 2006); *United States v. Barrero*, 425 F.3d 154, 1567-58 (2d Cir. 2005); *United States v. Carpenter*, 406 F.3d 915, 917 (7th Cir. 2005).

[45] *Survey, Question 2. Safety Valve*. Only 22% disagreed and another 12% were neutral, *Id.*

[46] *Id.* Asked whether the criterion should be expanded to include offenders with 4, 5 or 6 criminal history points, only 22% agreed; 60% disagreed; and 18% were neutral, *Id.*

[47] *Hearing, Statement of Michael Nachmanoff, Federal Public Defender for E.D. Va.* at 30-31 ("In fiscal year 2009, only 5,447 (35%) of defendants subject to a mandatory minimum qualified for the safety valve, while 10,085 (65%) did not. Yet, 83.2% of all drug trafficking offenses involved no weapon, 94.1% of drug trafficking defendants played no aggravated role or a mitigated role, 51.4% had zero to one criminal history points, and another 11.7% had two to three criminal history points. By requiring no more than one criminal history point, the safety valve excludes many offenders who were not involved in any violence and whose role in the offense was not serious. The safety valve does not distinguish between high- and low-level offenders based on role in the offense, but instead distinguishes among low- level offenders who differ little from each other, i.e., by one criminal history point"); *Statement of Jay Rorty, American Civil Liberties Union* at 4.

[48] See also U.S.S.G. §5C1.2(a)(2).

[49] See also U.S.S.G. §5C1.2(3).

[50] U.S.S.G. §5C1.2, cmt., n.4.

[51] *United States v. Denis*, 560 F.3d 872, 873 (8th Cir. 2009); *United States v. Figueroa-Encarnacion*, 343 F.3d 23, 34 (1st Cir. 2003); *United States v. Sarabia*, 297 F.3d 983, 989 (10th Cir. 2002).

[52] *United States v. Jackson*, 552 F.3d 908, 909-10 (8th Cir. 2009), citing in accord *United States v. Matias*, 465 F.3d 169, 173-74 (5th Cir. 2006); *United States v. Herrera,* 446 F.3d 283, 287 (2d Cir. 2006); *United States v. McLean*, 409 F.3d 492, 501 (1st Cir. 2005); *United States v. Gomez,* 431 F.3d 818, 820-22 (D.C.Cir. 2005); *United States v. Stewart,* 306 F.3d 295, 327 n. 19 (6th Cir. 2002), but noting in apparent disagreement *United States v. Zavalza-Rodriguez*, 379 F.3d 1182, 1186-187 (10th Cir. 2004).

[53] *United States v. Stewart*, 306 F.3d 295, 326 (6th Cir. 2002).

[54] *United States v. Jackson*, 552 F.3d 908, 910 (8th Cir. 2009); *United States v. Stark,* 499 F.3d 72, 80 (1st Cir. 2007); *United States v. Stewart*, 306 F.3d 295, 327 (6th Cir. 2002).

[55] U.S.S.G. §5c1.2, cmt. n.2; §1B1.1, cmt. n.1(L).

[56] The Eleventh Circuit in a nonbinding opinion seems to have come to same conclusion, *United States v. Valencia-Vergara*, 264 Fed.Appx. 832, 836 (11th Cir. 2008)("The district court did not clearly err in denying Valencia-Vergara a reduction under the safety valve provisions. The evidence shows that both he and one of his codefendants sustained second and third degree burns on their bodies, for which they had to be treated at a hospital").

[57] Cf., *United States v. Grimmett*, 150 F.3d 958, 960-61(8th Cir. 1998).

[58] See also U.S.S.G. §5C1.2(a)(4), which notes that the refer to the criminal enterprise section is redundant because "[a]s a practical matter, it should not be necessary to apply this prong of subsection (a)(4) because (i) this [safety valve] section does not apply to a conviction under 21 U.S.C. §848, and (ii) any defendant who 'engaged in a continuing criminal enterprise' but is convicted of an offense to which this section applies will be an 'organizer, leader, manage, or supervisor of others in the offense,'" U.S.S.G. 5C1.2 cmt. n.6.

[59] U.S.S.G. §5C1.2, cmt. n.5 ("'Organizer . . . supervisor of others in the offense, as determined under the sentencing guidelines' as used in subsection (a)(4), means a defendant who receives an adjustment for an aggravating role under §3B1.1 (Aggravating Role)").

[60] See U.S.S.G. §3B1.2 (Mitigating Role).

[61] In *United States v. Booker*, 543 U.S. 220, 244-45 (2005), the Supreme Court held that the Sixth Amendment entitles a criminal defendant to a jury determination, beyond a reasonable doubt, of any fact (other than a prior conviction) which is necessary to increase the maximum penalty for the offense of conviction and that consequently the Sentencing Guidelines may not be afforded binding effect. The First and Second Circuits have distinguished *Booker* and refused to hold that a trial court commits error when it requires a defendant to establish by a preponderance of the evidence his eligibility for safety valve relief (including satisfying the want of leadership requirements of section 3553(f)(4)), *United States v. Zayas*, 568 F.3d 43, 45-46 (1st Cir. 2009); *United States v. Holguin*, 436 F.3d 111, 1 19(2d Cir. 2006).

[62] E.g., *United States v. Gonzalez-Mendoza*, 584 F.3d 726, 729 (7th Cir. 2009); *United States v. Bonilla-Filomeno,* 579 F.3d 852, 858 (8th Cir. 2009); *United States v. Nobari*, 574 F.3d 1065, 1083-84 (9th Cir. 2009); *United States v. Rendon*, 354 F.3d 1320, 1333 (1 1th Cir. 2003).

[63] See also U.S.S.G. §5C1.2(a)(5).

[64] *United States v. Ceballos*, 605 F.3d 468, 472 (8th Cir. 2010); *United States v. Altamirano-Quintero*, 511 F.3d 1087, 1096 (10th Cir. 2007), citing *United States v. Montes*, 381 F.3d 631, 635-36 (7th Cir. 2004); *United States v. Johnson*, 375 F.3d 1300, 1302-303 (1 1th Cir. 2004); *United States v. Salgado*, 250 F.3d 438, 459 (6th Cir. 2001); *United States v. Cruz*, 156 F.3d 366, 371 (2d Cir. 1998); *United States v. Miller*, 151 F.3d 957, 958 (9th Cir. 1998); *United States v. Sabir*, 117 F.3d 750, 753 (3d Cir. 1997).

[65] *United States v. DeLaTorre*, 599 F.3d 1198, 1206 (10th Cir. 2010).

[66] *United States v. Cervantes*, 519 F.3d 1254, 1257 (10h Cir. 2008)(" In making this determination, we join the First, Second, Fourth, Fifth, Seventh, and Ninth Circuits in ruling that a probation officer is not the government for the purposes of the safety valve,"), citing *United States v. Wood*, 378 F.3d 342, 351 (4th Cir. 2004); *Emezuo v. United States*, 357 F.3d 703, 706 n.2(7th Cir. 2004); *United States v. Contreras*, 136 F.3d 1245, 1246 (9th Cir. 1998); *United States v. Jimenez Martinez*, 83 F.3d 488, 495-66 (1st Cir. 1996); *United States v. Rodriguez*, 60 F.3d 193, 195-96 (5th Cir. 1995); and *United States v. Smith*, 174 F.3d 52, 56 (2d Cir. 1999).

[67] *United States v. Milkintas,* 470 F.3d. 1339, 1345 (1 1th Cir. 2006), citing *United States v. O'Dell*, 247 F.3d 655, 675 (6th Cir. 2001); *United States v. Ortiz*, 136 F.3d 882, 884 (2d Cir. 1997); *United States v. Flanagan,* 80 F.3d 143, 146- 47 (5th Cir. 1996); and *United States v. Ivester*, 75 F.3d 182, 185-86 (4th Cir. 1996).

[68] *United States v. Padilla-Colon*, 578 F.3d 23, 31-2 (1st Cir. 2009)(Inconsistencies between statements made during the proffer and statements made to the authorities on other occasions are not necessarily disqualifying. But the court may legitimately consider such inconsistencies in deciding on the truthfulness of the proffer"); *United States v. MejiaPimental*, 477 F.3d 1100, 1108 (9th Cir. 2007)("The district court therefore erred, as a matter of law, in finding MejiaPimental ineligible for safety valve relief on the basis of the lies and delays that preceded his final proffer"); *United States v. Jeffers*, 329 F.3d 94, 99-100 (2d Cir. 2003)("[A] sentencing court may not disqualify a defendant at the threshold from eligibility for safety valve relief based solely on his commission of perjury at trial, where the defendant otherwise fulfills the statutory criteria under 18 U.S.C. §3553(f)(1)-(5). To do so would contradict the plain language of the statute and contravene the statutory deadline for full

compliance with its criteria at the time of the commencement of the sentencing hearing. A court may, of course, consider the relevance of the prior perjury or other obstructive behavior in making a factual finding as to whether the defendant has made a complete and truthful proffer in compliance with 18 U.S.C. §3553(f)(5)").

In: An Examination of Sentencing Levels and Mandatory… ISBN: 978-1-61209-563-9
Editor: Catherine N. Bates

Chapter 4

THREE STRIKE MANDATORY SENTENCING (18 U.S.C. 3559(C)): AN OVERVIEW

Charles Doyle

SUMMARY

The federal three strikes provision calls for a mandatory term of life imprisonment for defendants convicted of a serious violent felony who have two or more federal or state serious violent felony convictions or one or more of such felony conviction plus one or more federal or state serious drug conviction, 18 U.S.C. 3559(c). The qualifying violent felonies are those specifically enumerated within the section—murder, rape, violent robberies, extortion, among others—as well as unenumerated felonies, that is, any state and federal 10-year felony that involves the fact or risk of physical violence. The qualifying serious drug offenses are those punishable by imprisonment for 10 years or more under state or federal law. The section creates an exemption where defendants can prove that an otherwise qualifying conviction involved neither the fact nor risk of injury.

Defendants have regularly challenged the constitutionality of the section and whether their felony convictions constitute convictions for qualified offenses. The question of when a felony should be considered an unenumerated serious violent felony has proven perplexing, but recent Supreme Court construction of the term in another context may be illuminating. The Court has said in *Johnson*, *Chambers*, and *Begay* that for purposes of the Armed Career Criminal Act (ACCA) a violent felony is one that involves the purposeful, aggressive use of force, capable of inflicting physical pain or injury upon another.

Constitutional challenges have been to no avail, at least thus far. Defendants have argued without success (1) that requiring the defendant to prove to a judge by clear and convincing evidence, the inapplicability of an injury free conviction offends the due process and jury trial principles identified in *Apprendi* and its progeny; (2) that the section results in the imposition of cruel and unusual punishment in violation of the Eighth Amendment; (3) that the mandatory sentencing provision impermissibly intrudes upon the constitutional prerogatives of the federal courts in violation of the separation of powers doctrine; (4) that application of the section results in punishment for prior convictions in violation of the double jeopardy clause of the Fifth Amendment, and in some instances of the constitutional prohibition on ex post facto laws; and (5) that, under some circumstances, application of the section constitutes a violation of the equal protection component of the due process clause of the Fifth Amendment.

The text of section 3559(c) is appended.

Introduction

A defendant convicted of a federal "serious violent felony" must be sentenced to life imprisonment under the so-called three strikes law, 18 U.S.C. 3559(c), if he has two prior state or federal violent felony convictions or one such conviction and a serious drug offense conviction.[1]

In the recently enacted hate crime provisions, Congress instructed the United States Sentencing Commission to report to it on the operation of such mandatory minimum sentencing statutes.[2] Over 60% of the federal district court judges responding to a subsequent commission survey indicated they considered federal mandatory minimum sentences too high.[3] Although the survey asked specifically about sentences under other mandatory minimum statutes, it provided no opportunity for a response focused on section 3559(c).[4]

Notice and Objections

Section 3559(c) requires prosecutors to follow the notice provisions of 21 U.S.C. 851(a), if they elect to ask the court to sentence a defendant under the three strikes provision.[5] Section 851(a), in turn, requires prosecutors to notify the court and the defendant of the government's intention to seek the application of section 3559(c) and the description of the prior convictions upon which the government will rely.[6] Without such notice, the court may not impose an enhanced sentence.[7] The purpose of the requirement "is to ensure the defendant is aware before trial that he faces possible sentence enhancement as he assesses his legal options and to afford him a chance to contest allegations of prior convictions."[8] As long as that dual purpose is served, however, a want of meticulous compliance or complete accuracy will not preclude enhanced sentencing.[9] The objections most often raised are constitutional challenges and those that question the qualifications of prior convictions as predicate offenses.

Predicate Offenses

Serious Drug Offenses

Serious drug offenses for purposes of section 3559(c) consist of (a) federal drug kingpin offenses;[10] (b) the most severely punished of the federal drug trafficking offenses;[11] (c) the smuggling counterpart of the such trafficking offenses;[12] and (d) state equivalents of any of these three.[13] When the prosecution relies upon a state drug trafficking conviction, for example, it must show that the amount of drugs involved warranted treating it as an equivalent. [14]

Serious Violent Felonies

The federal three strikes provision recognizes convictions for two categories of serious violent felonies—one enumerated, the other general. The inventory of enumerated serious violent felonies consists of the federal or state crimes of

- murder (as described in section 1111);
- manslaughter other than involuntary manslaughter (as described in section 1112);
- assault with intent to commit murder (as described in section 113(a));
- assault with intent to commit rape; aggravated sexual abuse and sexual abuse (as described in sections 2241 and 2242);
- abusive sexual contact (as described in sections 2244(a)(1) and (a)(2);
- kidnapping;[15]
- aircraft piracy (as described in section 46502 of Title 49);
- robbery (as described in section 2111, 2113, or 2118);
- carjacking (as described in 2119);
- extortion;[16]
- arson;[17]
- firearms use;[18]
- firearms possession (as described in section 924(c)); or
- attempt, conspiracy, or solicitation to commit any of the above offenses.[19]

The more general, unenumerated category consists of "any other [state or federal] offense punishable by a maximum term of imprisonment of 10 years or more that has as an element the use, attempted use, or threatened use of physical force against the person of another or that, by its nature, involves a substantial risk that physical force against the person of another may be used in the course of committing the offense."[20]

There are statutory exceptions for both categories. Among the enumerated offenses, arson offenses do not qualify as predicate offenses, if the defendant can establish by clear and convincing evidence that he reasonably believed the offense posed no threat to human life and that it in fact did not.[21] Moreover, neither robbery, attempted robbery, conspiracy to commit robbery, nor solicitation to commit robbery qualify, if the defendant can establish by clear and convincing evidence that the offense involved neither the use nor threatened use of a dangerous weapon and that no one suffered serious bodily injury as a consequence of the crime.[22]

Among the unenumerated offenses, this same no-weapon, no-injury standard applies—those otherwise qualifying 10-year felonies, marked by the use or threatened use of physical force against another, do not qualify as predicate offenses, if the defendant can establish by clear and convincing evidence that no weapon was used, and no injury sustained, in the course of the offense.[23]

The question of what constitutes a conviction for an unenumerated "serious violent felony" under section 3559(c) seems to have proven as perplexing as what constitutes a "violent felony" conviction under the Armed Career Criminal Act (ACCA).[24] Recent Supreme Court construction of the term "violent felony" in the ACCA may provide clarification for future cases arising under section 3559(c).[25] In *Johnson*, *Chambers*, and *Begay*, the Court has made it clear that the ACCA's reference to violent felonies refers to purposeful, aggressive use of force capable of inflicting physical pain or injury upon another.[26] One circuit, however, has noted that conviction for a "serious violent felony" includes a state escape conviction, notwithstanding the holding in *Chambers* that held in another context that a failure-to-report offense lacked the intentional, aggressive use of force necessary to qualify as a violent felony.[27]

CONSTITUTIONAL CONSIDERATIONS

Defendants have challenged the constitutionality of section 3559(c) on a number of grounds. They have argued (1) that requiring the defendant to prove to a judge by clear and convincing evidence the inapplicability of an injury free conviction offends the principles identified in *Apprendi* and its progeny; (2) that the section results in the imposition of cruel and unusual punishment in violation of the proscription of the Eighth Amendment; (3) that the mandatory sentencing provision impermissibly intrudes upon the constitutional prerogatives of the federal courts in violation of the separation of powers doctrine; (4) that section 3559(c) results in punishment for prior convictions in violation of the double jeopardy clause of the Fifth Amendment and in some instances of the constitutional prohibition on ex post facto laws; and (5) that, under some circumstances, application of section 3559(c) constitutes a violation of the equal protection component of the due process clause of the Fifth Amendment.

Apprendi and Related Matters

Defendants sentenced under section 3559(c) have argued variously (1) that allowing the court, rather than the jury, to determine whether a defendant has sufficient, qualifying predicate offense convictions to warrant imposition of a mandatory minimum sentence violates the defendant's constitutional right to a jury trial; (2) that for the same reason allowing the court, rather than the jury, to determine whether a defendant's predicate offense conviction involved an injury free offense violates the defendant's constitutional right to a jury trial; (3) that requiring the defendant to prove that a predicate offense conviction involved an injury free offense in order to avoid the mandatory minimum sentence shifts the burden of proof from the government in violation of the defendant's constitutional right to due process; and (4) that the use of a clear and convincing standard rather than a proof beyond a reasonable doubt standard to judge whether a conviction involved an injury free offense also violates the defendant's constitutional right to due process.

Jury Trial—Prior Conviction

In *Apprendi* and the cases that followed, the Supreme Court has said that any fact relied upon to enhance a defendant's sentence beyond the maximum otherwise set by statute must be proven to the jury beyond a reasonable doubt unless the defendant waives that right. Those declarations, however, have always included a caveat—except for the fact of a prior conviction.[28] The caveat reflects a pre-*Apprendi* decision, *Almendarez-Torres*, in which Court held that the fact of a prior conviction might be treated as a sentencing factor to be determined by the sentencing court without offending the defendant's right to grand jury indictment, or by implication his right to a jury trial and conviction only on proof beyond a reasonable doubt.[29]

Pointing to the *Apprendi* caveat or *Almendarez-Torres* or both, the lower federal appellate courts have rejected the contention that section 3559(c) offends constitutional norms when it authorizes a sentencing court to determine whether a defendant has prior predicate offense convictions sufficient to trigger the section's mandatory minimum provisions.[30]

No Injury Exception

Almendarez-Torres does not speak to the validity of assigning sentencing courts the task of determining whether a defendant has shown by clear and convincing evidence that his robbery or arson convictions involved offenses free of physical injury or free of the involvement of dangerous weapons. Instead, the courts have rejected constitutional challenges on such grounds by pointing to other pre-*Apprendi* cases, *Patterson* and *Parke*, which held that once the elements of an offense have been constitutionally established a statute may assign the task of determining the existence of mitigating sentencing considerations to the sentencing court under any burden or standard.[31]

Cruel and Unusual Punishment

The Eighth Amendment prohibits infliction of cruel and unusual punishments.[32] Defendants sentenced under section 3559(c) have occasionally contended that a sentence of life imprisonment without the possibility of parole—since there is no parole in the federal criminal justice system for any crime committed after 1987—violates this prohibition. The Supreme Court precedents provide some limited support, but are not as helpful as they might be. In *Solem*, the Court held that the imposition of a sentence of life imprisonment without the possibility of parole under a state recidivist statute constituted a cruel and unusual punishment when based on three relatively minor property offenses.[33] In *Graham*, it held that imposition of a sentence of life imprisonment without the possibility of parole constituted a cruel and unusual punishment when imposed upon a child for a nonhomicide offense.[34] Yet in between the two, in *Harmelin* and *Ewing* a divided Court found no Eighth Amendment impediment to imposition of a sentence of life imprisonment without the possibility of parole for a serious drug offense or to imposition of a lengthy prison term under a state three strike statute following serious property offense convictions.[35]

The Court has yet to address the issue in a case arising under section 3559(c), but each of the lower federal appellate courts to consider the question has rejected the Eighth Amendment argument.[36]

Separation of Powers

The Constitution vests the judicial power of the United States in the Supreme Court "and in such inferior Courts as the Congress may from time to time ordain and establish."[37] Defendants sentenced under section 3559(c) have sometimes argued that by denying judges sentencing discretion, the section impermissibly intrudes upon the judicial power of the courts. The argument has been undermined by Supreme Court pronouncements in other contexts that "Congress has the power to define criminal punishments without giving the courts any sentencing discretion."[38] The lower federal appellate courts have yet to find the argument compelling.[39]

Double Jeopardy and Ex Post Facto

The Fifth Amendment ensures that no "person be subject for the same offence to be twice put in jeopardy of life or limb."[40] The double jeopardy clause protects against both successive prosecutions and successive punishments for the same offense.[41] Defendants sentenced under section 3559(c) have occasionally argued that to do so is to punish them twice for their underlying predicate offenses. The courts have met the argument with the observation that "the Supreme Court has long since determined that recidivist statutes do not violate double jeopardy because 'the enhanced punishment imposed for the later offense is not to be viewed as either a new jeopardy or additional penalty for the earlier crimes, but instead as a stiffened penalty for the latest crime, which is considered to be an aggravated offense because a repetitive one.'"[42]

Ex post facto contentions have failed for much the same reason. The Constitution forbids the passage of ex post facto laws by either the United States or the states.[43] The proscription covers

> 1st. Every law that makes an action done before the passing of the law, and which was innocent when done, criminal; and punishes such action. 2d. Every law that aggravates a crime, or makes it greater than it was, when committed. 3d. Every law that changes the punishment, and inflicts a greater punishment, than the law annexed to the crime, when committed. 4th. Every law that alters the legal rules of evidence, and receives less, or different, testimony, than the law required at the time of the commission of the offense, in order to convict the offender.[44]

In the case of section 3559(c), "the use of predicate felonies to enhance a defendant's sentence does not violate the Ex Post Facto Clause because such enhancements do not represent additional penalties for earlier crimes, but rather stiffen the penalty for the latest crime committed by the defendant."[45]

Equal Protection

The equal protection component of the due process clause of the Fifth Amendment prohibits prosecution "based on an unjustifiable standard such as race, religion, or other arbitrary classification."[46] To prevail on an equal protection claim, a defendant must show an intentionally motivated discriminatory effect.[47] Defendants who claimed that section 3559(c) has a disparate racial impact have been unable to show that it was crafted for that purpose.[48]

APPENDIX. 18 U.S.C. 3559(C)(TEXT)

(c) **Imprisonment of certain violent felons.—**

(1) **Mandatory life imprisonment.—**Notwithstanding any other provision of law, a person who is convicted in a court of the United States of a serious violent felony shall be sentenced to life imprisonment if—

(A) the person has been convicted (and those convictions have become final) on separate prior occasions in a court of the United States or of a State of—

(i) 2 or more serious violent felonies; or

(ii) one or more serious violent felonies and one or more serious drug offenses; and

(B) each serious violent felony or serious drug offense used as a basis for sentencing under this subsection, other than the first, was committed after the defendant's conviction of the preceding serious violent felony or serious drug offense.

(2) **Definitions.—**For purposes of this subsection—

(A) the term "assault with intent to commit rape" means an offense that has as its elements engaging in physical contact with another person or using or brandishing a weapon against another person with intent to commit aggravated sexual abuse or sexual abuse (as described in sections 2241 and 2242);

(B) the term "arson" means an offense that has as its elements maliciously damaging or destroying any building, inhabited structure, vehicle, vessel, or real property by means of fire or an explosive;

(C) the term "extortion" means an offense that has as its elements the extraction of anything of value from another person by threatening or placing that person in fear of injury to any person or kidnapping of any person;

(D) the term "firearms use" means an offense that has as its elements those described in section 924(c) or 929(a), if the firearm was brandished, discharged, or otherwise used as a weapon and the crime of violence or drug trafficking crime during and relation to which the firearm was used was subject to prosecution in a court of the United States or a court of a State, or both;

(E) the term "kidnapping" means an offense that has as its elements the abduction, restraining, confining, or carrying away of another person by force or threat of force;

(F) the term "serious violent felony" means—
   (i) a Federal or State offense, by whatever designation and wherever committed, consisting of murder (as described in section 1111); manslaughter other than involuntary manslaughter (as described in section 1112); assault with intent to commit murder (as described in section 113(a)); assault with intent to commit rape; aggravated sexual abuse and sexual abuse (as described in sections 2241 and 2242); abusive sexual contact (as described in sections 2244(a)(1) and (a)(2); kidnapping; aircraft piracy (as described in section 46502 of Title 49); robbery (as described in section 2111, 2113, or 2118); carjacking (as described in 2119); extortion; arson; firearms use; firearms possession (as described in section 924(c)); or attempt, conspiracy, or solicitation to commit any of the above offenses; and
   (ii) any other offense punishable by a maximum term of imprisonment of 10 years or more that has as an element the use, attempted use, or threatened use of physical force against the person of another or that, by its nature, involves a substantial risk that physical force against the person of another may be used in the course of committing the offense;

(G) the term "State" means a State of the United States, the District of Columbia, and a commonwealth, territory, or possession of the United States; and

(H) the term "serious drug offense" means—
   (i) an offense that is punishable under section 401(b)(1)(A) or 408 of the Controlled Substances Act (21 U.S.C. 841(b)(1)(A), 848) or section 1010(b)(1)(A) of the Controlled Substances Import and Export Act (21 U.S.C. 960(b)(1)(A); or
   (ii) an offense under State law that, had the offense been prosecuted in a court of the United States, would have been punishable under section 401(b)(1)(A) or 408 of the Controlled Substances Act (21 U.S.C. 841(b)(1)(A), 848), or section 1010(b)(1)(A) of the Controlled Substances Import and Export Act (21 U.S.C. 960(b)(1)(A)).

(3) **Nonqualifying felonies.**—

(A) **Robbery in certain cases.**—Robbery, an attempt, conspiracy, or solicitation to commit robbery; or an offense described in paragraph (2)(F)(ii) shall not serve as a basis for sentencing under this subsection if the defendant establishes by clear and convincing evidence that—
   (i) no firearm or other dangerous weapon was used in the offense and no threat of use of a firearm or other dangerous weapon was involved in the offense; and
   (ii) the offense did not result in death or serious bodily injury (as defined in section 1365) to any person.

(B) **Arson in certain cases.**—Arson shall not serve as a basis for sentencing under this subsection if the defendant establishes by clear and convincing evidence that—
   (i) the offense posed no threat to human life; and
   (ii) the defendant reasonably believed the offense posed no threat to human life.

(4) **Information filed by United States Attorney.**—The provisions of section 411(a) of the Controlled Substances Act (21 U.S.C. 851(a)) shall apply to the imposition of sentence under this subsection.
(5) **Rule of construction.**—This subsection shall not be construed to preclude imposition of the death penalty.
(6) **Special provision for Indian country.**—No person subject to the criminal jurisdiction of an Indian tribal government shall be subject to this subsection for any offense for which Federal jurisdiction is solely predicated on Indian country (as defined in section 1151) and which occurs within the boundaries of such Indian country unless the governing body of the tribe has elected that this subsection have effect over land and persons subject to the criminal jurisdiction of the tribe.
(7) **Resentencing upon overturning of prior conviction.**—If the conviction for a serious violent felony or serious drug offense that was a basis for sentencing under this subsection is found, pursuant to any appropriate State or Federal procedure, to be unconstitutional or is vitiated on the explicit basis of innocence, or if the convicted person is pardoned on the explicit basis of innocence, the person serving a sentence imposed under this subsection shall be resentenced to any sentence that was available at the time of the original sentencing.

End Notes

[1] 18 U.S.C. 3559(c).

[2] P.L. 111-84, sec. 4713, 123 Stat. 2843 (2009).

[3] United States Sentencing Commission, *Results of Survey of United States District Judges: January 2010 through March 2010, Question 1. Mandatory Minimums* (June 2010), available at http://www.ussc.gov/Judge_ Survey/2010/ JudgeSurvey_201006.pdf.

[4] *Id.* A majority found the statutory mandatory minimums appropriate for trafficking in heroin, powder cocaine and methamphetamine; for firearms offenses; for aggravated identity theft; for production and distribution of child pornography; and for other child exploitation offenses. On the other hand, a majority found them too high for trafficking in crack cocaine (76%) or marijuana (54%); or receipt of child pornography (7 1%). *Id.*

[5] 18 U.S.C. 3559(c)(4).

[6] 21 U.S.C. 851(a)(1)("No person who stands convicted of an offense under this part shall be sentenced to increased punishment by reason of one or more prior convictions, unless before trial, or before entry of a plea of guilty, the United States attorney files an information with the court (and serves a copy of such information on the person or counsel for the person) stating in writing the previous convictions to be relied upon...."). See e.g., *United States v. Sanchez*, 586 F.3d 918, 929-30 (1 1th Cir. 2009)("Prior to trial, the Government notified the district court and Camejo, pursuant to 18 U.S.C. §851, that if Camejo was found guilty of Counts 3, 4, or 5, it would ask the court to impose a life sentence, pursuant to 18 U.S.C. §3559(c), because he previously had been convicted in Florida circuit court of what §3559(c)(1)(A) deemed a 'serious violent felony' and two 'serious drug offenses'").

[7] *United States v. Hood*, 615 F.3d 1293, 1302 (10th Cir. 2010); *United States v. Baugham*, 613 F.3d 291, 294 (D.C. Cir. 2010); *United States v. Morales*, 560 F.3d 112, 113 (2d Cir. 2009).

[8] *United States v. Baugham*, 613 F.3d at 294-95; *United States v. Lane*, 591 F.3d 921, 927 (7th Cir. 2010).

[9] *United States v. Hood*, 615 F.3d at 1302 (noting the appropriateness of "harmless error analysis" rather than "hypertechnical approach"); *United States v. Baugham*, 613 F.3d at 295 ("Our caselaw also makes clear, however, that to comply with §851(a) the information need not be perfect with respect to every jot and tittle"); *United States v. Boudreau*, 564 F.3d 431, 437 (6th Cir. 2009)("Indeed, we have regularly held that actual notice satisfies the requirements of Section 851(a)").

[10] 21 U.S.C. 848.

[11] 21 U.S.C. 841(b)(1)(A).

[12] 21 U.S.C. 960(b)(1)(A).

[13] 18 U.S.C. 3559(c)(2)(H).

[14] *United States v. Sanchez*, 586 F.3d 918, 930 (1 1th Cir. 2009)(parenthetical citations in the original)("A state drug offense qualifies as a 'serious drug offense' under §3559(c) only if the offense, if prosecuted in federal court, would have been punishable under [21 U.S.C. §841(b)(1)(A)] or [21 U.S.C. §960(b)(1)(A)].... [For example,] to qualify as a 'serious drug offense' under §3559(c)(2)(H)(ii), the drug offenses must have been punishable under 21 U.S.C. §841(b)(1)(A). Section 841(b)(1)(A), however, is limited only to offenses involving '5 kilograms or more' of cocaine or '50 grams or more' of cocaine base").

[15] 18 U.S.C. 3559(c)(2)(E)("the term 'kidnapping' means an offense that has as its elements the abduction, restraining, confining, or carrying away of another person by force or threat of force").

[16] 18 U.S.C. 3559(c)(2)(C)("the term 'extortion' means an offense that has as its elements the extraction of anything of value from another person by threatening or placing that person in fear of injury to any person or kidnapping of any person").

[17] 18 U.S.C. 3559(c)(2)(B)("the term 'arson' means an offense that has as its elements maliciously damaging or destroying any building, inhabited structure, vehicle, vessel, or real property by means of fire or an explosive").

[18] 18 U.S.C. 3559(c)(2)(D)("the term 'firearms use' means an offense that has as its elements those described in section 924(c) or 929(a), if the firearm was brandished, discharged, or otherwise used as a weapon and the crime of violence or drug trafficking crime during and relation to which the firearm was used was subject to prosecution in a court of the United States or a court of a State, or both").

[19] 18 U.S.C. 3559(c)(2)(F)(i).

[20] 18 U.S.C. 3559(c)(2)(F)(ii).

[21] 18 U.S.C. 3559(c)(3)(B).

[22] 18 U.S.C. 3559(c)(3)(A).

[23] *Id.*

[24] E.g., *United States v. Abraham*, 386 F.3d 1033, 1038 (1 1th Cir. 2004)(escape constitutes a serious violent felony for purposes of section 3559(c)); *United States v. Dobbs*, 449 F.3d 904, 913-14 (8th Cir. 2006)(burglary is not a serious violent felony for purposes of section 3559(c)); *United States v. Evans*, 478 F.3d 1332, 1342 (1 1th Cir. 2007) (conviction for an anthrax threat against a federal building is not a serious violent felony for purposes of section 3559(c)).

[25] See *United States v. Rose*, 587 F.3d 695, 703-704 (5th Cir. 2009)(noting that circuit precedent construing the term "violent felony" in ACCA may be instructive when construing the term "serious violent felony" in section 3559(c)). The ACCA defines the term "violent felony" to mean "any crime punishable by imprisonment for a term exceeding one year ... that—(i) has as an element the use, attempted use, or threatened use of physical force against the person of another; or (ii) is burglary, arson, or extortion, involves use of explosives, or otherwise involves conduct that presents a serious potential risk of physical injury to another," 18 U.S.C. 924(e)(2)(B).

[26] See *Johnson v. United States*, 130 S.Ct. 1265, 1271 (2010)(emphasis in the original)("We think it clear that in the context of a statutory definition of '*violent* felony,' the phrase 'physical force' means *violent* force—that is force capable of causing physical pain or injury to another person"); *Chambers v. United States*, 129 S.Ct. 687, 692 (2009)("Conceptually speaking, the crime [of failing to report] amounts to a form of inaction, a far cry from the 'purposeful, violent, and aggressive conduct' potentially at issue when an offender [commits an enumerated offense, e.g.,] uses explosives against property, commits arson, burgles a dwelling or residence, or engages in certain forms of extortion"); *Begay v. United States*, 553 U.S. 137, (2008)("DUI differs from the [enumerated] crimes—burglary, arson, extortion, and crimes involving the use explosives—in at lease one pertinent, and import, respect. the [enumerated crimes all typically involve purposeful, 'violent,' and 'aggressive' conduct").

[27] *United States v. Sanchez*, 586 F.3d 918, 932 n.33 (11th Cir. 2009)("[W]e are mindful of the Supreme Court's recent decision in *Chambers v. United States*, 555 U.S. ___, 129 S.Ct. 687, 172 L.Ed. 2d 484 (2009) (holding that the Illinois crime of failure to report for imprisonment is not a violent felony for purposes of the Armed Career Criminal Act). We nonetheless find that decision inapposite. There, the Court held that a criminal defendant sentenced to 11 weekends of imprisonment could not have been found to have had the '"purposeful, 'violent,' and 'aggressive' conduct"' required to meet the statutory definition of a 'violent felony' by failing to report to the prison for four of those weekends. *Id.* at ___, 129 S.Ct. at 692 (quoting *Begay v. United States*, 553 U.S. 137, 128 S.Ct. 1581, 1586 (2008). This case is distinct. Here, Antonio Sanchez pled guilty to escape, not a failure to report. Moreover, the record suggests that he had the specific intent to escape from prison-he used the scheduled release as a ruse to leave the institution of his confinement for more than a month"). The prosecution indicated that Sanchez might have prevailed had he been able to establish that "his escape conviction was indeed for a nonviolent 'walkaway,'" *Id.* at 933 n. 35.

[28] *Apprendi v. New Jersey*, 530 U.S. 466, 490 (2000)("Other than the fact of a prior conviction, any fact that increases the penalty for a crime beyond the prescribed statutory maximum must be submitted to a jury, and proved beyond a reasonable doubt"); *Blakely v. Washington*, 542 U.S. 296, 301 (2004)(quoting *Apprendi* language); *United States v. Booker*, 543 U.S. 220, 244 (2005)("Any fact (other than a prior conviction) which

is necessary to support a sentence exceeding the maximum authorized by the facts established by a plea of guilty or a jury verdict must be admitted by the defendant or proved to a jury beyond a reasonable doubt").

29 *Almendarez-Torres v. United States*, 523 U.S. 224, 226-27, 247 (1998).

30 *United States v. Snype*, 441 F.3d 119, 148 (2d Cir. 2006)("Thus, *Almendarez-Torres* continues to bind this court in its application of *Apprendi*.... With this understanding of the law, we identify no Sixth Amendment error in the district court's findings as to the fact of Snype's prior state robbery convictions. Four of our sister circuits have considered this question and reached the same conclusion"), citing *United States v. Cooper*, 375 F.3d 1041, 1053 n.3 (10th Cir. 2004); *United States v. Bradshaw*, 281 F.3d 278, 294 (1st Cir. 2002); *United States v. Weaver*, 267 F.3d 231, 251 (3d Cir. 2001); *United States v. Davis*, 260 F.3d 965, 969 (8th Cir. 2001).

31 *United States v. Matthews*, 545 F.3d 223, (2d Cir. 2008), citing *Patterson v. New York*, 432 U.S. 197, 207-208 (1977) and *Parke v. Raley*, 506 U.S. 20, 26-7 (1992), and citing in accord *United States v. Contreras*, 536 F.3d 1167, 1173-174 (10th Cir. 2008); *United States v. Bradshaw*, 281 F.3d at 296-97; *United States v. Davis*, 260 F.3d at 970; *United States v. Gray*, 260 F.3d 1267, 1279 (1 1th Cir. 2001); *United States v. Ferguson*, 211 F.3d 878, 886-86 (5th Cir. 2000); *United States v. Gatewood*, 230 F.3d 186, 190 (6th Cir. 2000); *United States v. Kaluna*, 192 F.3d 1188, 1196 (9th Cir. 1999); *United States v. Wicks*, 132 F.3d 383, 388-89 (7th Cir. 1997).

32 U.S. Const. Amend. VIII.

33 *Solem v. Helm*, 463 U.S. 277, 303 (1983).

34 *Graham v. Florida*, 130 S.Ct. 2011, 2034 (2010).

35 *Harmelin v. Michigan*, 501 U.S. 957, 904, 1004 (1991); *Ewing v. California*, 538 U.S. 11, 30-1 (2003).

36 *United Stats v. Rose*, 587 F.3d 695, 704-705 (5th Cir. 2009); *United States v. Gurule*, 461 F.3d 1238, 1247 (10th Cir. 2006); *United States v. Snype*, 441 F.3d 119, 152 (2d Cir. 2006); *United States v. Kaluna*, 192 F.3d 1188, 1199-200 (9th Cir. 1999); *United States v. DeLuca*, 137 F.3d 24, 40 n. 19 (1st Cir. 1998); *United States v. Washington*, 109 F.3d 335, 337-38 (7th Cir. 1997); *United States v. Farmer*, 73 F.3d 836, 840 (8th Cir. 1996).

37 U.S. Const. Art. III, §1.

38 *Chapman v. United States*, 500 U.S. 453, 467 (199); see also *Mistretta v. United States*, 488 U.S. 361, 364 (1989)("the scope of judicial discretion with respect to a sentence is subject to congressional control").

39 *United States v. Gurule*, 461 F.3d 1238, 1246 (10th Cir. 2006)("As for the Three Strikes statute in particular, the few reported decisions of which we are aware from other circuits are unanimous in rejecting this [separation of powers] argument.... We agree with these precedents"), citing *United States v. Kaluna*, 192 F.3d 1188, 1199 (9th Cir. 1999); *United States v. Rasco*, 123 F.3d 222, 226-27 (5th Cir. 1997); *United States v. Washington*, 109 F.3d 335, 338 (7th Cir. 1997).

40 U.S. Const. Amend. V.

41 *United States v. Dixon*, 509 U.S. 688, 696 (1993); *North Carolina v. Pearce*, 395 U.S. 711, 717 (1969).

42 *United States v. Kaluna*, 192 F.3d at 1198-199, quoting *Witte v. Untied States*, 515 U.S. 389, 400 (1995) and *Gryger v. Burke*, 334 U.S. 728, 732 (1948); see also *United States v. Washington*, 109 F.3d at 338; *United States v. Farmer,* 73 F.3d 836, 840 (8th Cir. 1996).

43 U.S. Const. Art. I, §§9, 10.

44 *Stogner v. California*, 539 U.S. 607, 612 (2003), quoting *Calder v. Bull*, 3 Dall. (3 U.S.) 386, 390 (1798); see also *Johnson v. United States*, 529 U.S. 694, 699 (2000).

45 *United States v. Abraham*, 386 F.3d 1033, 1038 (11th Cir. 2004); *United States v. Kaluna*, 192 F.3d at 1199; *United States v. Rasco*, 123 F.3d 222, 227 (5th Cir. 1997); *United States v. Washington*, 109 F.3d at 338; *United States v. Farmer*, 73 F.3d at 840-41.

46 *United States v. Armstrong*, 517 U.S. 456, 464 (1996).

47 *Id.* at 465.

48 *United States v. Washington*, 109 F.3d 335, 338 (7th Cir. 1997); *United States v. Farmer*, 73 F.3d 836, 841 (8th Cir. 1996). Equally unsuccessful was a defendant who claimed an equal protection violation based on disparate sentencing patterns from one state to another, *United States v. Wicks*, 132 F.3d 383, 389 (7th Cir. 1997)("Certain felonies—those described in (F)(i)—it [(Congress)] considered serious enough to include no matter how Draconian or lenient their treatment may be under state law, while others—those described in (F)(ii)—are subject to a congressional leveler through the requirement of the ten-year term of imprisonment. There is no federalism or equal protection issue at all in (F)(i), and none that survives rational basis analysis in (F)(ii)").

In: An Examination of Sentencing Levels and Mandatory… ISBN: 978-1-61209-563-9
Editor: Catherine N. Bates

Chapter 5

ARMED CAREER CRIMINAL ACT (18 U.S.C. 924(E)): AN OVERVIEW

Charles Doyle

SUMMARY

The Armed Career Criminal Act (ACCA), 18 U.S.C. 924(e), requires imposition of a minimum 15-year term of imprisonment for recidivists convicted of unlawful possession of a firearm under 18 U.S.C. 922(g). Section 924(e) applies only to those defendants who have three prior state or federal convictions for violent felonies or serious drug offenses.

Violent felonies for purposes of section 924(e) are those that either (1) have an element of threat, attempt, or use of physical force against another or (2) that involve burglary, arson, or extortion, or some similar offense. Serious drug offenses are those punishable by imprisonment for 10 years or more.

Constitutional challenges to the application of section 924(e) have been generally unsuccessful, regardless of whether they were based on arguments of cruel and unusual punishment, double jeopardy, due process, grand jury indictment or jury trial rights, the right to bear arms, or limits on Congress's legislative authority.

INTRODUCTION

The Armed Career Criminal Act (ACCA), 18 U.S.C. 924(e), establishes a 15-year mandatory minimum term of imprisonment for defendants convicted of unlawful possession of a firearm under section 18 U.S.C. 922(g) who have three prior convictions for violent felonies or serious drug offenses.[1] Although section 922(g) bans firearm possession for nine categories of individuals, section 924(e) applies most often to defendants with prior felony convictions for obvious reasons.[2] More often than not, the prior convictions are for violations of state law.

Congress directed the United States Sentencing Commission to report by October 28, 2010, on the impact on the federal criminal justice system of mandatory minimum sentencing provisions like section 924(e).[3] As part of its study, the Commission solicited the views of federal trial judges. Almost sixty percent of those responding to a Sentencing Commission survey indicated that they considered the section 924(e) mandatory minimum sentences appropriate.[4]

PREDICATE OFFENSES

Section 924(e) requires conviction for three predicate offenses. The offenses must constitute either violent felonies or serious drug offenses and must have been committed on different occasions.[5] "[T]o trigger a sentence enhancement under the ACCA, a defendant's prior felony convictions must involve separate criminal episodes. However, offenses are considered distinct criminal episodes if they occurred on occasions different from one another. Two offenses are committed on occasions different from one another if it is possible to discern the point at which the first offense is completed and the second offense beings."[6] Thus, separate drug deals on separate days will constitute offenses committed on different occasions though they involve the same parties and location.[7] The fact that two crimes occurred on a different occasion, however, must be clear on the judicial record; recourse to police records will not do.[8]

Application of section 924(e) provides no opportunity to challenge the validity of the underlying predicate offenses.[9]

Serious Drug Offenses

The section defines serious drug offenses as those violations of state or federal drug law punishable by imprisonment for 10 years or more. [10] Conviction under a statute which carries a 10-year maximum for repeat offenders qualifies, even though the maximum term for first-time offenders is five years.[11] It is the maximum permissible term which determines qualification, even when discretionary sentencing guidelines called for a term of less than 10 years,[12] or when the defendant was in fact sentenced to a lesser term of imprisonment.[13] The appellate courts are divided over the question of whether the offense must be at least a 10-year felony at the time of conviction for predicate offenses or at the time of sentencing under section 924(e).[14]

As long as the attempt is punishable by imprisonment for 10 years or more, the term "serious drug offense" includes attempts to commit a serious drug offense. [15]

Violent Felonies

The assessment of whether a past crime constitutes a violent felony for purposes of section 924(e) is more complicated than whether a drug offense is a serious drug offense for such purposes. The task involves an examination of "how the law defines the offense and not how an individual offender might have committed on a particular occasion."[16] Violent felony predicates come in two varieties: offenses involving the use of physical force and offenses of the burglary/arson/ extortion class.[17]

Physical force. The physical force category consists of those offenses that have "as an element the use, attempted use, or threatened use of physical force against the person of another."[18] "Physical force" here means "violent force—that is, force capable of causing physical pain or injury to another person."[19] Thus, it does not include state convictions for intentional touching of another, such as the Florida statute in Johnson.[20]

Burglary et al. The second variety of violent felony predicates consists of the crimes of burglary, arson, extortion, use of explosives, and any other offense that "otherwise involves conduct that presents a serious potential risk of physical injury to another."[21] The crimes found in the residual clause (crimes that "otherwise involve ...") are only those similar to the enumerated crimes of burglary, arson, extortion and the use of explosives, those marked by "purposeful, violent and aggressive conduct."[22] Thus, they do not include convictions for driving under the influence of alcohol or failing to report to begin serving a term of imprisonment.[23]

SUBSTANTIAL ASSISTANCE

Federal mandatory minimum sentencing statutes, including section 924(e), are subject to a general exception under 18 U.S.C. 3553(e) in cases where the defendant has provided the government with substantial assistance.[24] A defendant is entitled to a sentence below an otherwise applicable statutory minimum under the provisions of section 3553(e) only if the government agrees.[25] The courts have acknowledged that due process or equal protection or other constitutional guarantees may provide a narrow exemption. "Thus, a defendant would be entitled to relief if a prosecutor refused to file a substantial-assistance motion, say, because of the defendant's race or religion."[26] A defendant is entitled to relief if the government's refusal constitutes a breach of its plea agreement.[27] A defendant is also "entitled to relief if the prosecutor's refusal to move was not rationally related to any legitimate Government end."[28] Some courts have suggested that a defendant is entitled to relief if the prosecution refuses to move under circumstances that "shock the conscience of the court," or that demonstrate bad faith, or for reasons unrelated to substantial assistance.[29] A majority of the judges who answered the Sentencing Commission's survey agreed that relief under section 3553(e) should be available even in the absence of motion from the prosecutor. [30]

A motion under section 3553(e) for a sentence beneath the mandatory minimum and a motion under U.S.S.G. §5K1.1 for a sentence beneath the applicable Sentencing Guideline range are not the same. Thus, a motion under section 5K1.1 will ordinarily not be construed as a motion under section 3553(e).[31]

Any sentence imposed below the statutory minimum by virtue of section 3553(e) must be based on the extent of the defendant's assistance; it may not reflect considerations unrelated to such assistance. [32] It has been suggested that a court may use the section 5K1 .1 factors for that determination, i.e., "(1) the court's evaluation of the significance and usefulness of the defendant's assistance, taking into consideration the government's evaluation of the assistance rendered; (2) the truthfulness, completeness, and reliability of any information or testimony provided by the defendant; (3) the nature and extent of the defendant's assistance; (4) any injury suffered, or any danger or risk of injury to the defendant or his family resulting from his assistance; [and] (5) the timeliness of the defendant's assistance," U.S.S.G. §5K1.1(a).[33]

The substantial assistance exception makes possible convictions that might otherwise be unattainable. Yet, it may also lead to "inverted sentencing," i.e., a situation in which "the more serious the defendant's crimes, the lower the sentence—because the greater his wrongs, the more information and assistance he had to offer to a prosecutor;" while in contrast the exception is of no avail to the peripheral offender who can provide no substantial assistance.[34] Perhaps for this reason, most of the judges who responded to the Sentencing Commission survey agreed that a sentencing court should not be limited to assistance-related factors and should be allowed use the generally permissible sentencing factors when calculating a sentence under section 3553(e).[35]

Constitutional Considerations

Defendants have raised a number of constitutional challenges to the application of section 924(e). They have argued that Congress lacked the constitutional authority to enact the section, that application in their case violates the Second Amendment, the Fifth Amendment, the Sixth Amendment, and/or the Eighth Amendment. Their arguments have yet to succeed.

Legislative Authority

The Constitution vests Congress with authority to enact legislation "necessary and proper" to carry into execution the powers which the Constitution grants the Congress or any other officer, department, or agency of the United States.[36] Those powers which cannot be traced to an enumeration within the Constitution are reserved to the states and the people.[37] Congress's constitutional authority to regulate interstate and foreign commerce is among its most sweeping prerogatives, but the power is not boundless. It permits regulation of the use of the channels of commerce, of the instrumentalities of commerce, of the things that move there, and of those activities which substantially impact commerce.[38] Absent such a nexus, it does not permit Congress to enact legislation proscribing possession of a firearm on school grounds, as the Supreme Court observed in *Lopez*.[39] Section 922(g)[40] outlaws receipt by a felon of a firearm "which has been shipped or transported in interstate or foreign commerce." This, in the view of the circuit courts to address the issue, is sufficient to bring within Congress's commerce clause power the prohibitions of section 922(g), that section 924(e) makes punishable.[41]

Second Amendment

The Second Amendment provides that "A well regulated Militia, being necessary to the security of a free State, the right of the people to keep and bear Arms, shall not be infringed."[42] The Supreme Court in *Heller* declared that "the Second Amendment confer[s] an individual right to keep and bear arms ... [but] the right in not unlimited... ."[43] It explained, however, that "nothing in our opinion should be taken to cast doubt on longstanding prohibitions on possession of firearms by felons...."[44]

The lower appellate courts have taken this to mean that 18 U.S.C. 922(g)(1) which prohibits firearm possession by a felon does not offend the Second Amendment.[45] From which it seems to follow that section 924(e), which imposes a mandatory minimum sanction upon felons who violate section 922(g)(1), is similarly inoffensive.[46]

Apprendi and its Progeny

The Supreme Court in *Almendarez-Torres* identified the fact of a prior conviction as a sentencing factor. It rejected the argument that the Fifth and Sixth Amendments required that the fact of a defendant's prior conviction be charged in the indictment and found by the jury beyond a reasonable doubt.[47] Yet almost immediately thereafter, it seemed to repudiate the broad implications of *Almendarez-Torres*, while clinging to its narrow holding, "under the Due Process Clause of the Fifth Amendment and the notice and jury trial guarantees of the Sixth Amendment, any fact (*other than prior conviction*) that increases the maximum penalty for a crime must be charged in an indictment, submitted to a jury, and proven beyond a reasonable doubt."[48]

And so the Court continued in *Blakely* and *Booker*—unless the defendant waived, a jury must decide any sentence enhancing fact, other than the fact of a prior conviction.[49] The Court waivered slightly in *Shepard* where a plurality held that a sentencing court may look no further than the judicial record of a prior conviction when faced with a dispute over whether a section 924(e) defendant was convicted earlier of a qualifying predicate offense. [50] Justice Thomas, upon whose concurrence the result rested, however, opined that "*Almendarez-Torres* ... has been eroded by this Court's subsequent Sixth Amendment jurisprudence, and a majority of the Court now recognizes that *Almendarez-Torres* was wrongly decided."[51]

Nevertheless, the lower federal courts continued to adhere to *Almendarez-Torres* in section 924(c) cases—the fact of a prior qualifying conviction need not be charged in the indictment nor proved to the jury beyond a reasonable doubt.[52]

Eighth Amendment

Defendants sentenced under section 924(e) have suggested two Eighth Amendment issues. First, they argue that their sentences are disproportionate to their offenses. Second, they contend that crimes committed when they were juveniles may not be used as predicates.

The Eighth Amendment prohibits the infliction of cruel and unusual punishments.[53] It has been said to prohibit sentences that are "grossly disproportionate" to the crime.[54] Under varying theories, the Supreme Court has held that it permits the imposition of life imprisonment without the possibility of parole of a first-time offender convicted of large scale drug trafficking;[55] and permits the imposition of a sentence of imprisonment for 25 years to life following a "three strikes" conviction resting on three nonviolent grand theft convictions.[56] On the other hand, the Court held in *Ewing* that the Eighth Amendment precludes execution for a capital offense committed by a juvenile,[57] and most recently in *Graham* that it precludes imprisonment for life without parole for a non-homicide offense committed by a juvenile. [58]

The lower federal courts have consistently rejected general claims that sentences under 924(e) were grossly disproportionate to the crimes involved.[59] In cases decided before *Graham*, the lower federal courts had also rejected claims that the Eighth Amendment precluded use of a juvenile predicate offense to trigger sentencing of an adult under section 924(e).[60] To date, there have been no subsequent federal appellate court decision directly on point. Two circuits, however, have found no Eighth Amendment impediment to mandatory life imprisonment sentences imposed under provisions other than section 924(e) upon adults convicted of drug trafficking and based in part on predicate juvenile offenses.[61]

Double Jeopardy

The Fifth Amendment ensures that no "person be subject for the same offence to be twice put in jeopardy of life or limb."[62] The double jeopardy clause protects against both successive prosecutions and successive punishments for the same offense.[63] The test for whether a defendant has been twice tried or punished for the same offense or tried or punished for two different offenses is whether each of the two purported offenses requires proof that the other does not.[64] Defendants have argued to no avail that the double jeopardy clause bars reliance on the predicate offenses or on section 922(g) to trigger section 924(e).[65]

APPENDIX. 18 U.S.C. 924(E)(TEXT)

(e)(1) In the case of a person who violates section 922(g) of this title and has three previous convictions by any court referred to in section 922(g)(1) of this title for a violent felony or a serious drug offense, or both, committed on occasions different from one another, such person shall be fined under this title and imprisoned not less than fifteen years, and, notwithstanding any other provision of law, the court shall not suspend the sentence of, or grant a probationary sentence to, such person with respect to the conviction under section 922(g).

(2) As used in this subsection—

(A) the term "serious drug offense" means—

(i) an offense under the Controlled Substances Act (21 U.S.C. 801 et seq.), the Controlled Substances Import and Export Act (21 U.S.C. 951 et seq.), or chapter 705 of title 46, for which a maximum term of imprisonment of ten years or more is prescribed by law; or

(ii) an offense under State law, involving manufacturing, distributing, or possessing with intent to manufacture or distribute, a controlled substance (as defined in section 102 of the Controlled Substances Act (21 U.S.C. 802)), for which a maximum term of imprisonment of ten years or more is prescribed by law;

(B) the term "violent felony" means any crime punishable by imprisonment for a term exceeding one year, or any act of juvenile delinquency involving the use or carrying of a firearm, knife, or destructive device that would be punishable by imprisonment for such term if committed by an adult, that—

(i) has as an element the use, attempted use, or threatened use of physical force against the person of another; or

(ii) is burglary, arson, or extortion, involves use of explosives, or otherwise involves conduct that presents a serious potential risk of physical injury to another; and

(C) the term "conviction" includes a finding that a person has committed an act of juvenile delinquency involving a violent felony.

End Notes

[1] 18 U.S.C. 924(e)(1)("In the case of a person who violates section 922(g) of this title and has three previous convictions by any court referred to in section 922(g)(1) of this title for a violent felony or a serious drug offense, or both, committed on occasions different from one another, such person shall be fined under this title and imprisoned not less than fifteen years, and, notwithstanding any other provision of law, the court shall not suspend the sentence of, or grant a probationary sentence to, such person with respect to the conviction under section 922(g)"). The ACCA is not to be confused with the federal three strikes statute, 18 U.S.C. 3559(c), which establishes a mandatory term of life imprisonment upon a third serious violent felony conviction, or with its two strike counterpart in 18 U.S.C. 3 559(e), relating to mandatory life imprisonment for repeated child sex offenders.

[2] The other disqualified categories cover fugitives, drug addicts, mental defectives, unlawful aliens, dishonorably discharged members of the armed forces, individuals who have renounced their U.S. citizenship, those under a domestic violence restraining order, and those convicted of misdemeanor domestic violence, 18 U.S.C. 922(g)(2)-(9).

[3] Section 4713, P.L. 111-84, 123 Stat. 2843 (2009).

[4] United States Sentencing Commission, *Results of Survey of United States District Judges: January 2010 through March 2010, Question 1. Mandatory Minimums* (June 2010), available at http://www.ussc.gov/Judge_Survey/2010/ JudgeSurvey_201006.pdf.

[5] 18 U.S.C. 924(e)(1).

[6] *United States v. Martin*, 526 F.3d 926, 938-39 (6th Cir. 2008)(internal citations omitted).

[7] *United States v. Ross*, 569 F.3d 821, 823 (8th Cir. 2009).

[8] *United States v. Tucker*, 603 F.3d, 260, 266 (4th Cir. 2010)("Here, the district court relied on the PSR's [Probation Service's Presentence Report] recitation of the facts about the burglaries, but the PSR relied on the police incident report, which is not allowed ..."); *United States v. Sneed*, 600 F.3d 1326, 1332-333(1 1th Cir. 2010), each citing *Shepard v. United States*, 544 U.S. 13 (2005).

[9] *Custis v. United States*, 511 U.S. 485, 487 (1994)("a defendant has no such right (with the sole exception of convictions obtained in violation of the right to counsel) to collaterally attack prior convictions"); *United States v. Greer*, 607 F.3d 559, 565 (8th Cir. 2010); *United States v. Dean*, 604 F.3d 169, 174-75 (4th Cir. 2010); *United States v. Covington*, 565 F.3d 1336, 1345 (1 1th Cir. 2009); *United States v. Buie*, 547 F.3d 401, 403-404 (2d Cir. 2008); *United States v. Goodman*, 519 F.3d 310, 318 (6th Cir. 2008); *United States v. Krejcarek*, 453 F.3d 1290, 1297 10th Cir. 2006).

[10] 18 U.S.C. 924(e)(2)(A)("the term 'serious drug offense' means—(i) an offense under the Controlled Substances Act (21 U.S.C. 801 et seq.), the Controlled Substances Import and Export Act (21 U.S.C. 951 et seq.), or chapter 705 of title 46, for which a maximum term of imprisonment of ten years or more is prescribed by law; or (ii) an offense under State law, involving manufacturing, distributing, or possessing with intent to manufacture or distribute, a controlled substance (as defined in section 102 of the Controlled Substances Act (21 U.S.C. 802), for which a maximum term of imprisonment of ten years or more is prescribed by law").

[11] *United States v. Rodriquez*, 533 U.S. 377, 380 (2008).

[12] *United States v. Rodriquez*, 533 U.S. at 390; *United States v. Mayer*, 560 F.3d 948, 963(9th Cir. 2009).

[13] *United States v. Buie*, 547 F.3d 401, 404 (2d Cir. 2008); *United States v. Williams*, 508 F.3d 724, 728 (4th Cir. 2007); *United States v. Henton*, 473 F.3d 467, 470 (7th Cir. 2004).

[14] *United States v. McNeill*, 598 F.3d 161, 164-66 (4th Cir. 2010)("the maximum sentence for a predicate conviction under the ACCA is determined as of the time of the underlying offense"), noting in accord *United States v. Hinojosa*, 349 F.3d 200, 205 (5th Cir. 2003), and to the contrary *United States v. Darden*, 539 F.3d 116, 122 (2d Cir. 2008) ("judges should examine the state law in place at the time of federal sentencing"); *United States v. Morton*, 17 F.3d 911, 915 (6th Cir. 1994).

[15] *United States v. Williams*, 499 F.3d 1004, 1009 (D.C. Cir. 2007).

[16] *Begay v. United States*, 553 U.S. 137, 141 (2008).

[17] 18 U.S.C. 924(e)(2)(B)("the term 'violent felony' means any crime punishable by imprisonment for a term exceeding one year, or any act of juvenile delinquency involving the use or carrying of a firearm, knife, or destructive device that would be punishable by imprisonment for such term if committed by an adult, that—(i) has as an element the use, attempted use, or threatened use of physical force against the person of another; or (ii) is burglary, arson, or extortion, involves use of explosives, or otherwise involves conduct that presents a serious potential risk of physical injury to another").

[18] 18 U.S.C. 924(e)(2)(B)(i).

[19] *Johnson v. United States*, 130 S.Ct. 1265, 1271 (2010); *United States v. Forrest*, 611 F.3d 908, 910 (8th Cir. 2010); *United States v. Ramon Silva*, 608 F.3d 663, 669 (10th Cir. 2010); *United States v. Hughes*, 602 F.3d 669, 673-74 (5th Cir. 2010).

[20] *Johnson v. United States*, 130 S.Ct. at 1272.

[21] 18 U.S.C. 924(e)(2)(B)(ii).

[22] *Begay v. United States*, 553 U.S. 137, 144-45 (2008); *Chambers v. United States*, 129 S.Ct. 687, 692 (2009); *United States v. Alexander*, 609 F.3d 1250, 1254-255 (1 1th Cir. 2010).

[23] *Begay v. United States*, 533 U.S. at 139; *Chambers v. United States*, 129 S.Ct. at 693.

[24] The discussion of section 3553(e) which follows has been borrowed largely from CRS Report R41326, *Federal Mandatory Minimum Sentences: The Safety Valve and Substantial Assistance Exceptions*, by Charles Doyle.

[25] *Melendez v. United States*, 518 U.S. 120, 125-26 (1996)("We believe that §3553(e) requires a government motion requesting or authorizing the district court to impose a sentence below a level established by statute as [a] minimum sentence before the court may impose such a sentence").

[26] *Wade v. United States*, 504 U.S. 181, 186 (1992).

[27] *United States v. Motley*, 587 F.3d 1153, 1159 (D.C. Cir. 2009); *United States v. Smith*, 574 F.3d 521, 525 (8th Cir. 2009); *United States v. Doe*, 445 F.3d 202, 207 (2d Cir. 2006).

[28] *Wade v. United States*, 504 at 186; *United States v. Davis*, 583 F.3d 1081, 1098 (8th Cir. 2009).

[29] *United States v. Freemont*, 513 F.3d 884, 889 (8th Cir. 2008)("The district court may review the government's refusal to make a motion in limited circumstances. First, the district court may review the government's decision for an unconstitutional motive.... Second, a district court can compel a §3553(e) motion if the government acknowledges the defendant provided substantial assistance, but refuses to make a motion expressly because the defendant engaged in unrelated misconduct—a reason unrelated to the quality of the defendant's assistance.... Third, the district court may be able to compel a motion if the government acted in bad faith by refusing to make a motion"); but see *United States v. Perez*, 526 F.3d 1135, 1138 (8th Cir. 2008)(citing cases evidencing a split within the circuit over whether bad faith provides a sufficient basis to compel a government motion).

[30] *Survey, Question 15. Substantial Assistance*. Only 35% of the respondents disagreed with the statement that "Congress should amend 18 USC §3553(e) to authorize judges to sentence a defendant below the applicable statutory mandatory minimum to reflect a defendant's substantial assistance, even if the government does not make a motion," *Id.*

[31] *Melendez v. United States*, 518 U.S. 120, 126 (1996).

[32] *United States v. Burns*, 577 F.3d 887, 894 (8th Cir. 2009)(en banc)("Where a court has authority to sentence below a statutory minimum only by virtue of a government motion under §3553(e), the reduction below the statutory minimum must be based exclusively on assistance-related considerations"); *United States v. Jackson*, 577 F.3d 1032, 1036 (9th Cir. 2009); *United States v. Hood*, 556 F.3d 226, 234 n.2 (4th Cir. 2009), citing *inter alia United States v. Richardson*, 521 F.3d 149, 159 (2d Cir. 2008) and *United States v. Desselle,* 450 F.3d 179, 182 (5th Cir. 2006).

[33] *United States v. Gabbard*, 586 F.3d 1046, 1051 (6th Cir. 2009), citing *United States v. Richardson*, 521 F.3d at 159.

[34] *Hearing, Testimony of Jeffrey B. Steinback on behalf of the Practitioner's Advisory Group* at 8, quoting *United States v. Brigham*, 977 F.2d 317, 318 (7th Cir. 1992); see also *Hearing, Written Statement of Cynthia Hujar Orr, President of the National Ass 'n of Criminal Defense Lawyers* at 3 (defendants "who have little or no information to provide the government, end up with far more severe sentences than leaders of conspiracies who run the operations and know the other participants").

[35] *Survey, Question 15. Substantial Assistance*. Only 24% of the respondents disagreed with the statement that "In determining the extent of a reduction below the statutory mandatory minimum under 18 USC §3553(e) ... the court's consideration should not be limited to the nature of the defendant's substantial assistance but also should include consideration of the factors at 18 USC §3553(a)," *Id.*

[36] U.S. Const. Art. I, §8, cl. 18.

[37] U.S. Const. Amend. X.

[38] *United States v. Lopez*, 516 U.S. 549, 558-59 (1995); *United States v. Morrison*, 529 U.S. 598, 609 (2000).

[39] *United States v. Lopez,* 514 U.S. at 552.

[40] 18 U.S.C. 922(g).

[41] *United States v. Vallejo*, 373 F.3d 855, 860-61 (7th Cir. 2004), *citing in accord, United States v. Thompson*, 361 F.3d 918, 922 (6th Cir. 2004); *United States v. Leathers*, 354 F.3d 955, 599 (8th Cir. 2003); *United States v. Dunn*, 345 F.3d 1285, 1297 (1 1th Cir. 2003); *United States v. Darrington,* 351 F.3d 632, 634 (5th Cir. 2003).

[42] U.S. Const. Amend. II.

[43] *District of Columbia v. Heller*, 128 S.Ct. 2783, 2799 (2008).

[44] *Id.* at 2816-817.

[45] *United States v. Scroggins*, 599 F.3d 433, 451 (5th Cir. 2010); *United States v. Vongxay*, 594 F.3d 1111, 1114-1 15(9th Cir. 2010); *United States v. Mc Cane*, 573 F.3d 1037, 1047 (10th Cir. 2009).

[46] *United States v. Rozier*, 598 F.3d 768, 771-72 (1 1th Cir. 2010)(holding section 922(g)(1) a permissible limitation of the defendant's Second Amendment right and upholding his sentence under section 924(e)).

[47] *Almendarez-Torres v. United States*, 523 U.S. 224, 247 (1998).

[48] *Apprendi v. New Jersey*, 530 U.S. 466, 476 (2000)(emphasis added), quoting dicta in *Jones v. United States*, 526 U.S. 227, 243 n.6 (1999).

[49] *Blakely v. Washington*, 542 U.S. 296, 301 (2004)("Other than the fact of a prior conviction, any fact that increases the penalty for a crime beyond the prescribed statutory maximum must be submitted to a jury, and proved beyond a reasonable doubt"), quoting *Apprendi v. New Jersey*, 530 U.S. at 490; *United States v. Booker*, 543 U.S. 220, 231 (2005), quoting the same passage from *Apprendi*.

[50] *Shepard v. United States*, 544 U.S. 13, 16 (2005)("We hold that ... a later court determining the character of an admitted burglary is generally limited to examining the statutory definition, charging document, written plea agreement, transcript of plea colloquy, and any explicit factual finding by the trial judge to which the defendant assented").

[51] *Id.* at 27 (Thomas, J. concurring in part and concurring in the judgment).

[52] *United States v. Charlton*, 600 U.S. 43, 55 (1st Cir. 2010)("This court normally is bound by a Supreme Court precedent unless and until the Court itself disavows that precedent. For that reason, we recently have rejected a parade of similarly sculpted challenges to the continued vitality of *Almendarez-Torres* in the context of the ACCA. We reiterate those holdings today"); *United States v. Rozier*, 598 F.3d 768, 771-72 (1 1th Cir. 2010)("Rozier argues that because these prior convictions were not included within the indictment, nor proven to a jury, any sentence over the 120-month maximum of §924(a)(2) is unconstitutional. This argument runs contrary to the established law of the Supreme Court and this Circuit. See *Almendarez-Torres v. United States*"); *United States v. Jones*, 574 F.3d 546, 553- 54 (8th Cir. 2009); *United States v. Salahuddin*, 509 F.3d 858, 863 (7th Cir. 2007); *United States v. Coleman*, 451 F.3d 154, 159-60 (3d Cir. 2006).

[53] U.S. Const. Amend. VIII ("Excessive bail shall not be required, nor excessive fines imposed, nor cruel and unusual punishments inflicted").

[54] *Graham v. Florida,* 130 S.Ct. 2011, 2021 (2010); *Harmelin v. Michigan*, 501 U.S. 957, 1001 (1991)(Kennedy, J. concurring in part and concurring in the judgment); *Ewing v. California*, 538 U.S. 11, 21 (2003)(opinion of O'Connor, J.).

[55] *Harmelin v. Michigan*, 501 U.S. at 994.

[56] *Ewing v. California*, 538 U.S. at 30-1.

[57] *Roper v. Simmons,* 543 U.S. 551, 560 (2005).

[58] *Graham v. Florida,* 130 S.Ct. at 2034.

[59] *United States v. Helm*, 502 F.3d 366, (5th Cir. 2007), citing in accord *United States v. Cardoza*, 129 F.3d 6, 18 (1st Cir. 1997); *United States v. Rudolph*, 970 F.2d 467, 469-70 (8th Cir. 1992); *United States v. Crittendon*, 883 F.2d 326, 331 (4th Cir. 1989); *United States v. Pedigo*, 879 F.2d 1315, 1320 (6th Cir. 1989); *United States v. Dombrowski*, 877 F.2d 520, 526 (7th Cir. 1989); *United States v. Baker,* 850 F.2d 1365, 1372 (9th Cir. 1988); see also *United States v. Lyons*, 403 F.3d 1248, 1256-257 (11th Cir. 2005).

[60] *United States v. Jones*, 574 F.3d 546, 552-53 (8th Cir. 2009); *United States v. Salahuddin*, 509 F.3d 858, 863-64 (7th Cir. 2007); *United States v. Wilks*, 464 F.3d 1240, 1243 (1 1th Cir. 2006).

[61] *United States v. Scott*, 610 F.3d 1009, 1017 (8th Cir. 2010)("Scott argues that the Eighth Amendment prohibits enhancing his sentence based on his previous felony drug convictions because he was a juvenile when he committed those crimes.... [W]e have upheld the use of juvenile court adjudications to enhance subsequent sentences for adult convictions.... The U.S. Supreme Court cases that Scott cites, *Roper* and Graham, do not change this result. These decisions established constitutional limits on certain sentences for offenses committed by juveniles. However, Scott was twenty-five years old at the time he committed the conspiracy offense in this case. Neither *Roper* nor *Graham* involved the use of prior offenses committed as a juvenile to enhance an adult conviction, as here.... the Court's analysis in *Graham* was limited to defendants sentenced to life in prison without parole for crimes committed as juveniles. The Court in *Graham* did not call into question the constitutionality of using prior convictions, juvenile or otherwise, to enhance the sentence of a convicted adult. Therefore, we affirm the constitutionality of Scott's life sentence under 21 U.S.C. §841(b)(1)(A)"); *United States v. Graham*, ___ F.3d , ___ (6th Cir. Sept. 21, 2010)(2010 WL 3632 149)(same).

[62] U.S. Const. Amend. V.

[63] *United States v. Dixon*, 509 U.S. 688, 696 (1993); *North Carolina v. Pearce*, 395 U.S. 711, 717 (1969).

[64] *Blockburger v. United States*, 284, U.S. 299, 304 (1932); *United States v. Dixon*, 509 U.S. at 696 (1993); *United States v. Faulds*, 612 F.3d 566, 569 (7th Cir. 2010); *United States v. Ayala*, 601 F.3d 256, 265 (4th Cir. 2010); *United States v. Mahdi*, 598 F.3d 883, 888 (D.C. Cir. 2010).

[65] *United States v. Keesee*, 358 F.3d 1217, 1220 (9th Cir. 2004); *United States v. Studifin*, 240 F.3d 415, 419 (4th Cir. 2001); *United States v. Bates*, 77 F.3d 1101, 1106 (8th Cir. 1996); *United States v. Wallace*, 889 F.2d 580, 584 (5th Cir. 1989).

In: An Examination of Sentencing Levels and Mandatory… ISBN: 978-1-61209-563-9
Editor: Catherine N. Bates

Chapter 6

DRUG OFFENSES: MAXIMUM FINES AND TERMS OF IMPRISONMENT FOR VIOLATION OF THE FEDERAL CONTROLLED SUBSTANCES ACT AND RELATED LAWS

Brian T. Yeh

SUMMARY

This is a chart of the maximum fines and terms of imprisonment that may be imposed as a consequence of conviction for violation of the federal Controlled Substances Act (CSA) and other drug supply and drug demand related laws.

It lists the penalties for: heroin, cocaine, crack, PCP, LSD, marihuana (marijuana), amphetamine, methamphetamine, listed (precursor) chemicals, paraphernalia, date rape drugs, rave drugs, designer drugs, ecstasy, drug kingpins, as well as the other substances including narcotics and opiates assigned to Schedule I, Schedule II, Schedule III, Schedule IV, and Schedule V of the Controlled Substances Act and the Controlled Substances Import and Export Act (Title II and Title III of the Comprehensive Drug Abuse and Control Act).

It maps the penalty structure for violations of 21 U.S.C. 841 (drug trafficking), 21 U.S.C. 841(b)(5) (cultivation on federal property), 21 U.S.C. 841(b)(6) (environmental damage from illegal manufacturing), 21 U.S.C. 841 (b)(7) (crime of violence), 21 U.S.C. 841(c) (offenses involving listed chemicals), 21 U.S.C. 841(d)(booby traps on federal lands), 21 U.S.C. 841(f) (distribution/possession of listed chemicals), 21 U.S.C. 841(g) (Internet sales of date rape drugs), 21 U.S.C. 841(h) (dispensing controlled substances that are prescription drugs by means of the Internet), 21 U.S.C. 842 (regulatory offenses), 21 U.S.C. 843 (communications-related offenses), 21 U.S.C. 844 (simple possession), 21 U.S.C. 846, 963 (attempt and conspiracy), 21 U.S.C. 849 (drug dealing at truck stops), 21 U.S.C. 848 (continuing criminal enterprises (CCE)), 21 U.S.C. 854, 855 (investment of illicit drug profits), 21 U.S.C. 856 (establishing manufacturing operations), 21 U.S.C. 858 (endangering human life), 21 U.S.C. 859 (distribution to infants, minors, children, juveniles, and those under 18 years of age), 21

U.S.C. 860 (distribution in school zones), 21 U.S.C. 861 (distribution to pregnant women), 21 U.S.C. 863 (trafficking in drug paraphernalia), 21 U.S.C. 864 (theft of anhydrous ammonia, or transportation of stolen anhydrous ammonia), 21 U.S.C. 865 (smuggling methamphetamine into the United States), 21 U.S.C. 960 (illicit drug import and export), 21 U.S.C. 960a (narco-terrorism), 21 U.S.C. 962 (recalcitrant drug smugglers), 21 U.S.C. 1906 (financial transactions with designated foreign narcotics traffickers), 18 U.S.C. 545 (smuggling goods into the United States), 18 U.S.C. 546 (smuggling goods into foreign countries), 18 U.S.C. 924(c) (firearms and armor piercing ammunition in connection to drug trafficking crime), 18 U.S.C. 924(e) (armed career criminals), 18 U.S.C. 1952 (Travel Act), 18 U.S.C. 1956 (money laundering), 18 U.S.C. 1957 (monetary transactions in property derived from unlawful activity), 18 U.S.C. 1959 (compensated crime of violence in aid of racketeering), 18 U.S.C. 1963 (racketeering (RICO)), 18 U.S.C. 3559(c)(three strikes), 19 U.S.C. 1590 (aviation smuggling), 26 U.S.C. 7201 (tax evasion), 26 U.S.C. 7203 (failure to file required returns), 26 U.S.C. 7206 (fraud and false statements), 31 U.S.C. 5322 (currency transaction reporting (smurfing)), 31 U.S.C. 5332 (bulk cash smuggling into or out of the United States), 46 U.S.C. 70506 (maritime drug law enforcement).

This report reflects amendments to the Controlled Substances Act made by the Fair Sentencing Act of 2010 (P.L. 111-220) that increased the quantities of crack cocaine necessary to trigger certain penalties and also increased the fine amounts for major drug traffickers.

TRAFFICKING

Unlawful distribution, possession with intent to distribute, manufacture, importation and exportation, etc. (21 U.S.C. 841, 960, 962, and 46 U.S.C. 70506)[1]

1st offense			
Substance	**Amount**	**Fine**	**Imprisonment**
Heroin			
	One kilogram[2] or more	$10/50 million	10 years to life
	100 to 999 grams	$5/25 million	5 to 40 years
	Less than 100 grams	$1/5 million	Up to 20 years
Coca leaf and derivatives			
	5 kilograms or more	$10/50 million	10 years to life
	500 to 4999 grams	$5/25 million	5 to 40 years
	Less than 500 grams	$1/5 million	Up to 20 years
Ecgonine (a cocaine precursor)			
	5 kilograms or more	$10/50 million	10 years to life
	500 to 4999 grams	$5/25 million	5 to 40 years
	Less than 500 grams	$1/5 million	Up to 20 years
Coca leaves, cocaine, or ecgonine containing cocaine base ("Crack," etc.)			
	280 grams or more	$10/50 million	10 years to life
	28 to 279 grams	$5/25 million	5 to 40 years

(Continued)

Substance	Amount	Fine	Imprisonment
	Less than 28 grams	$1/5 million	Up to 20 years
PCP (phencyclidine)			
	100 grams or more	$10/50 million	10 years to life
	10 to 99 grams	$5/25 million	5 to 40 years
	Less than 10 grams	$1/5 million	Up to 20 years
Mixture or substance containing detectable amount of PCP			
	1 kilogram or more	$10/50 million	10 years to life
	100 to 999 grams	$5/25 million	5 to 40 years
	Less than 100 grams	$1/5 million	Up to 20 years
LSD (lysergic acid diethylamide)			
	10 grams or more	$10/50 million	10 years to life
	1 to 9 grams	$5/25 million	5 to 40 years
	Less than 1 gram	$1/5 million	Up to 20 years
	N-phenyl-N-[1-(2-phenylethyl)-4-piperidinyl] propanamide (Fentanyl, i.e., "synthetic heroin") 400 grams or more (or 100 grams or more of a mixture or substance containing a detectable amount of any analogue of it)	$10/50 million	10 years to life
	40 to 399 grams (or 10-99 grams of a mixture containing a detectable amount of any analogue of it)	$5/25 million	5 to 40 years
	Less than 40 grams	$1/5 million	Up to 20 years
Marijuana			
	1000 kilograms or more or 1000 or more plants[3]	$10/50 million	10 years to life
	100 to 999 kilograms or 100 to 999 plants	$5/25 million	5 to 40 years
	50 to 99 kilograms or 50 to 99 plants	$1/5 million	Up to 20 years
	Under 50 kilograms[4], 10 kilograms of hashish, one kilogram of hashish oil, or 1 to 49 plants	$250,000/$1 million	Up to 5 years
Methamphetamine			
	50 grams or more or 500 grams or more of a mixture	$10/50 million	10 years to life

(Continued)

Substance	Amount	Fine	Imprisonment
	5 to 49 grams or 50 to 499 grams of a mixture	$5/25 million	5 to 40 years
	Less than 5 grams or less than 50 grams of a mixture	$1/5 million	Up to 20 years
Gamma hydroxybutyric acid			
	any weight	$1/5 million	Up to 20 years
Flunitrazepam[5]			
	1 gram	$1/5 million	Up to 20 years
	Less than 1 gram	$250,000/$1 million	Up to 5 years
Any other Schedule I or II substance			
	any weight	$1/5 million	Up to 20 years
Any other Schedule III substance			
	any weight	$500,000/$2.5 million	Up to 15 years[6]
Any other Schedule IV substance			
	any weight	$250,000/$1 million	Up to 5 years[7]
Any Schedule V substance			
	any weight	$100,000/$250,000	Up to 1 year
2nd offense[8]			
Heroin			
	One kilogram or more	$20/75 million	20 years to life
	100 to 999 grams	$8/50 million	10 years to life
	Less than 100 grams	$2/10 million	Up to 30 years
Coca leaf and derivatives			
	5 kilograms or more	$20/75 million	20 years to life
	500 to 4999 grams	$8/50 million	10 years to life
	Less than 500 grams	$2/10 million	Up to 30 years
Ecgonine (a cocaine precursor)			
	5 kilograms or more	$20/75 million	20 years to life
	500 to 4999 grams	$8/50 million	10 years to life
	Less than 500 grams	$2/10 million	Up to 30 years
Coca leaves, cocaine, or ecgonine containing cocaine base ("Crack," etc.)			
	280 grams or more	$20/75 million	20 years to life
	28 to 279 grams	$8/50 million	10 years to life
	Less than 28 grams	$2/10 million	Up to 30 years
PCP (phencyclidine)			
	100 grams or more	$20/75 million	20 years to life
	10 to 99 grams	$8/50 million	10 years to life
	Less than 10 grams	$2/10 million	Up to 30 years

(Continued)

Substance	Amount	Fine	Imprisonment
Mixture or substance containing detectable amount of PCP			
	1 kilogram or more	$20/75 million	20 years to life
	100 to 999 grams	$8/50 million	10 years to life
	Less than 100 grams	$2/10 million	Up to 30 years
LSD(lysergic acid diethylamide)			
	10 grams or more	$20/75 million	20 years to life
	1 to 9 grams	$8/50 million	10 years to life
	Less than 1 gram	$2/10 million	Up to 30 years
N-phenyl-N-[1-(2-phenylethyl)-4-piperidinyl] propanamide (Fentanyl, i.e., "synthetic heroin") 400 grams or more (or 100 grams or more of a mixture or substance containing a detectable amount of any analogue of it)		$20/75 million	20 years to life
	40 to 399 grams (or 10-99 grams of a mixture containing a detectable amount of any analogue of it)	$8/50 million	10 years to life
	Less than 40 grams	$2/10 million	Up to 30 years
Marijuana			
	1000 kilograms or more or 1000 or more plants)	$20/75 million	20 years to life
	100 to 999 kilograms or 100 to 999 plants)	$8/50 million	10 years to life
	50 to 99 kilograms or 50 to 99 plants[9]	$2/10 million	Up to 30 years
	Less than 50 kilograms,10 [10] kilograms of hashish, one kilogram of hashish oil, or 1 to 49 plants	$500,000/$2 million	Up to 10 years
Methamphetamine			
	50 grams or more	$20/75 million	20 years to life
	5 to 49 grams	$8/50 million	10 years to life
	Less than 5 grams	$2/10 million	Up to 30 years
Gamma hydroxybutyric acid			
	any weight	$2/10 million	Up to 30 years
Flunitrazepam11			
	1 gram	$2/10 million	Up to 30 years
	Less than 1 gram	$500,000/$2 million	Up to 10 years
Any other Schedule I or II substance			
	any weight	$2/10 million	Up to 30 years
Any other Schedule III substance			

(Continued)

Substance	Amount	Fine	Imprisonment
	any weight	$1 million/$5 million	Up to 30 years
Any other Schedule IV substance			
	any weight	$500,000/$2 million	Up to 10 years
Any Schedule V substance			
	any weight	$200,000/$500,000	Up to 4 years
3rd offense			
A Schedule I or II substance singled out for special penalty treatment (as indicated above) in amounts constituting a top level offense		Same as 2nd offense	Life
Cultivation on Federal property (21 U.S.C. 841(b)(5))			
Any offense			
All substances/all weights		Greater of $500,000/ $1 million or the maximum fine for distribution of the substance involved	Maximum term for distribution of the substance involved
Environmental damage on Federal property resulting from controlled substance manufacturing or distribution (21 U.S.C. 841(b)(6))			
Any offense[12]			
	All substances	Up to $250,000	Up to 5 years
Offenses involving essential (listed) chemicals, generally (21 U.S.C. 841(c))			
Any offense[13]			
	List I chemicals [under 21 U.S.C. 802(34)]	Up to $250,000	Up to 20 years
	List II chemicals [under 21 U.S.C. 802(35)]	Up to $250,000	Up to 10 years
Wrongful distribution or possession of essential (listed) chemicals (21 U.S.C. 841(f))			
Knowing unlawful distribution			
Listed chemicals [under 21 U.S.C. 802 (33)]		Up to $250,000	Up to 5 years
Knowing possession of unreported listed chemicals			
Listed chemicals [under 21 U.S.C. 802 (33)]		Up to $100,000	Up to 1 year
Internet Sales of Date Rape Drugs (21 U.S.C. 841(g))			
Knowingly using the Internet to distribute a date rape drug[14]		Up to $250,000	Up to 20 years
Dispensing Controlled Substances by Means of the Internet (21 U.S.C. 841(h))			
Knowingly or intentionally using the Internet to deliver, distribute, or dispense a controlled substance without a valid prescription[15] (or aiding or abetting such activity)		Sentences determined according to the penalties authorized under 21 U.S.C. 841(b)[16]	
Regulatory offenses & use of communications to facilitate distribution (21 U.S.C. 842, 843)			

(Continued)

Substance	Amount	Fine	Imprisonment
1st offense			
Generally[17]		Up to $100,000	Up to 1 year
Deception offenses, etc.[18]		Up to $250,000	Up to 4 years
Methamphetamine equipment offenses		Up to $250,000	Up to 10 years
Advertisement offenses[19]		Up to $250,000	Up to 4 years
2nd offense			
Generally		Up to $250,000	Up to 2 years
Deception offenses, etc.		Up to $250,000	Up to 8 years
Methamphetamine equipment offenses		Up to $60,000	Up to 20 years
Advertisement offenses		Up to $250,000	Up to 8 years
Manufacturing or Distributing Controlled Substances Within 1000 Feet of a Truck Stop or Highway Rest Area (21 U.S.C. 849)			
1st offense			
All substances		Up to twice the penalties otherwise authorized	
2nd offense			
All substances		Up to three times the penalties otherwise authorized	
Distribution to persons under age 21 by those age 18 or older (21 U.S.C. 859)			
1st offense			
All substances		Up to twice the penalties otherwise authorized[20]	
2nd offense			
All substances		Up to three times the penalties otherwise authorized	
Distribution or manufacturing in or near schools, colleges, or certain youth-centered recreational facilities (21 U.S.C. 860, 860a)[21]			
1st offense			
All substances (except methamphetamine)		Up to twice the penalties otherwise authorized for distribution or manufacture but at least 1 year in prison[22]	
2nd offense			
All substances (except methamphetamine)		Up to three times the penalties otherwise authorized for distribution or manufacture but at least 3 years in prison	
Any offense involving methamphetamine		Other sentence as imposed plus imprisonment for no more than 20 years	
Trafficking in drug paraphernalia (21 U.S.C. 863)			
Interstate or foreign sale and transportation of, or use of the mails to sell, drug paraphernalia		Up to $250,000	Up to 3 years

Possession

Simple possession (21 U.S.C. 844)[23]		
1st offense	Not less than $1,000	Up to 1 year
2nd offense[24]	Not less than $2,500	15 days to 2 years
3rd offense	Not less than $5,000	90 days to 3 years
Flunitrazepam	Up to $250,000	Up to 3 years

Controlled Substance Violations and Other Crimes/Activity

Attempt and conspiracy (21 U.S.C. 846, 963)		
Any offense		
All substances	Same as penalties for the underlying offense	
Use of a controlled substance to commit a crime of violence (21 U.S.C. 841(b)(7))		
Any offense[25]		
All substances	Up to $250,000	Up to 20 years
Boobytraps on Federal property (21 U.S.C. 841(d))[26]		
1st offense	Up to $250,000	Up to 10 years
2nd offense	Up to $250,000	Up to 20 years
Continuing Criminal Enterprise (CCE) ("kingpin") (21 U.S.C. 848)[27]		
1st offense		
All substances	Up to $2 million	20 years to life
2nd offense		
All substances	Up to $4 million	30 years to life
Any offense, if the offender is a major participant, involving an enterprise that grosses $10 million a year or more or involving 300 times[28] the amount of controlled substances required to trigger the most severe distribution penalties of 21 U.S.C. 841		
All substances	Up to $4 million	life
Establishing manufacturing operations (21 U.S.C. 856)		
Opening, maintaining, financing or making available a place for unlawful manufacture, distribution or use of controlled substances		
All substances	Up to $500,000	Up to 20 years
Endangering human life while illegally manufacturing a controlled substance (21 U.S.C. 858)		
Any offense		

(Continued)

All substances	Up to $250,000	Up to 10 years
Employment of persons under 18 years of age (for violation of the CSA) or unauthorized distribution to a pregnant individual (21 U.S.C. 861)		
1st offense		
Generally	Up to twice the penalties otherwise authorized for the underlying offense but at least 1 year in prison[29]	
2nd offense		
Generally	Up to three times the penalties otherwise authorized for the underlying offense but at least 1 year in prison[30]	
Any offense		
Use of person under 14 or distribution to a person under 18	Up to $50,000	Up to 5 years
Narco-Terrorism (21 U.S.C. 960a)		
Engaging in prohibited drug activity knowing or intending to provide anything of pecuniary value to terrorists	Up to $250,000	At least twice the minimum punishment authorized under 21 U.S.C. 841(b)(1).
Theft of anhydrous ammonia, or transportation of stolen anhydrous ammonia with intent or knowledge that such will be used to manufacture a controlled substance (21 U.S.C. 864)		
1st offense	Up to $250,000	Up to 4 years
2nd offense	Up to $250,000	Up to 8 years
Violation of regulations proscribing financial transactions with significant foreign narcotics traffickers (21 U.S.C. 1906)		
Any offense (individual)	Up to $250,000	Up to 10 years
Any offense (organization)	Up to $10,000,000	
Any offense (organization officer or agent)	Up to$5,000,000	Up to 30 years
Travel Act: use of interstate facilities in aid of a racketeering enterprise involving controlled substances (18 U.S.C. 1952)		
Any substance and the intent to commit the following act:		
A crime of violence in furtherance of the racketeering enterprise	Up to $250,000	Up to 20 years, or any term of years or life if death results
Distributing the proceeds from the racketeering enterprise	Up to $250,000	Up to 5 years
Promotion or facilitation of the racketeering enterprise	Up to $250,000	Up to 5 years

(Continued)

18 U.S.C. 924(c) (use or possession of firearms or armor piercing ammunition in connection to a drug trafficking crime)[31]		
1st offense involving a firearm		
Generally		Not less than 5 years
If a firearm is brandished		Not less than 7 years
If a firearm is discharged		Not less than 10 years
If firearm is a short-barreled rifle, short-barreled shotgun, or semiautomatic assault weapon		Not less than 10 years
If firearm is a machinegun or destructive device, or equipped with a silencer/muffler		Not less than 30 years
2nd or subsequent offense involving a firearm		
Generally		Not less than 25 years
If firearm is a machinegun or destructive device, or equipped with a silencer/muffler		life
Any offense involving armor piercing ammunition		
Use or possession		Not less than 15 years
If such ammunition is used for murder		Any term of years or life
If such ammunition is used for manslaughter	Up to $250,000	Up to 10 years
If such ammunition is used for manslaughter	Up to $250,000	Up to 6 years
Armed career criminal: possession of a firearm by a convicted felon or other disqualified person with 3 or more prior serious controlled substance convictions (drug crimes punishable by imprisonment for 10 years or more) or prior violent crime convictions (18 U.S.C. 924(e))		
Any offense		
All substances	Up to $250,000	Not less than 15 years
Three strikes: commission of a serious violent felony by an individual with a prior serious controlled substance conviction (drug kingpin or most seriously punished trafficking offense) and a prior serious violent felony conviction or 2 or more prior serious violent felony convictions (18 U.S.C. 3559(c))		
Any offense		
All substances	Up to $250,000	life

Racketeering

Commission of a pattern of racketeering activity including one or more narcotic or dangerous drug felony to invest in, acquire, operate or participate in the affairs of an interstate enterprise ((RICO)(18 U.S.C. 1963))		
Any offense Narcotic and dangerous drugs	Up to $250,000	Up to 20 years or life if the maximum for the predicate is life
Compensated crime of violence in aid of RICO (18 U.S.C. 1959)		
Any offense involving any substance and the following criminal act: Murder	Up to $250,000	life
Kidnapping	Up to $250,000	Up to life in prison
Maiming	Up to $250,000	Up to 30 years
Serious injury	Up to $250,000	Up to 20 years
Threats	Up to $250,000	Up to 5 years
Attempt or conspiracy to murder or kidnap	Up to $250,000	Up to 10 years

Smuggling

Smuggling Goods into the United States (18 U.S.C. 545)		
Any offense		
All substances	Up to $250,000	Up to 20 years
Smuggling Goods into Foreign Countries (18 U.S.C. 546)		
Any offense		
All substances	Up to $250,000	Up to 2 years
Smuggling methamphetamine or methamphetamine precursor chemicals into the United States while using facilitated entry programs (21 U.S.C. 865)		
Any offense	Imprisonment Sentence for Methamphetamine Offense Enhanced By Up to 15 years	
Aviation smuggling (19 U.S.C. 1590)		
Any offense		
All substances	Up to $250,000 Up to 20 years	

Laundering Money from Controlled Substance Violations

Laundering (18 U.S.C. 1956)		
Any offense		
All substances	Up to greater of $500,000 or 2X the amount of $ laundered	Up to 20 years
Monetary traffic in property derived from unlawful activity (18 U.S.C. 1957)		
Any offense		
All substances	Up to greater of $250,000 or 2X the amount of $ laundered	Up to 10 years
Currency transaction and transportation reporting (31 U.S.C. 5322)		
1st offense		
All substances	Up to $250,000	Up to 5 years
2nd offense		
All substances	Up to $500,000	Up to 10 years
Bulk cash smuggling into or out of the United States (31 U.S.C. 5332)		
Knowingly concealing more than $ 10,000 across a U.S. border		Up to 5 years
Investment of illicit drug profits (21 U.S.C. 854, 855)		
Any offense		
All substances	Up to the greater of 2X profit/proceeds or $50,000	Up to 10 years

Tax Offenses

Attempted evasion [concerning income from controlled substance violations] (26 U.S.C. 7201)		
Any offense		
All substances	Up to $250,000	Up to 5 years
Willful failure to file return [concerning income for such violations] (26 U.S.C. 7203)		
Any offense		
All substances	Up to $250,000	Up to 5 years
Fraud and false statements [concerning income from such violations] (26 U.S.C. 7206)		
Any offense		
All substances	Up to $250,000	Up to 3 years

End Notes

[1] All trafficking offenses involving Schedule I and II substances (and gamma hydrobutyric acid and flunitrazepam) are subject to the same imprisonment penalty—20 years to life—if death or serious bodily injury results from

the use of the substance involved. Unless otherwise indicated, weights apply to any mixture containing a detectable amount of the substance regardless of the weight of the substance in the mixture.
A reference to a fine of "$5/25 million" means a fine of no more than $5 million for an individual and no more than $25 million for a defendant other than an individual. A reference to "10 years to life" means a term of imprisonment of not less than 10 years nor more than life.

[2] 1 kilogram is equal to 35.27 ounces; 1 gram is equal to 0.04 ounces.

[3] Unlike the penalties for manufacturing, distribution, dispensing, or possession, those for importation or exportation do not distinguish between quantities of marihuana plants in excess of 100. Importation or exportation of any marihuana plants in excess of 100 is subject to higher penalties than those for less than 50 kilograms of marihuana, etc.

[4] Except in the case of 50 or more marihuana plants regardless of weight, and except that under section 841(b)(4) distribution of a small amount of marihuana for no remuneration is treated as a simple possession offense and punished under section 844, *infra*.

[5] Importation or exportation of any quantity of flunitrazepam is subject to a fine of $ 1/5 million and up to 20 years imprisonment.

[6] *Id.*

[7] *Id.*

[8] A second offense is one committed after a prior conviction for a felony drug offense has become final.

[9] *See supra* note 3.

[10] Except in the case of 50 or more marihuana plants regardless of weight and except that distribution of a small amount of marihuana is punishable as simple possession under section 844, *infra*.

[11] *See supra* note 5.

[12] Creating a serious hazard to human or animal life, or harming the environment, or causing water pollution as a result of using poisons, chemicals or other hazardous substances on Federal property while in the course of unlawfully manufacturing or otherwise distributing a controlled substance

[13] Possession with intent to use for unauthorized manufacture of a controlled substance; possession or distribution knowing that the chemical will be used for unauthorized manufacture of a controlled substance; or, with intent of causing evasion of the record-keeping or reporting requirements of 21 U.S.C. 830 (or regulations pursuant thereto), receipt or distribution of a reportable amount in units small enough so that the making of records or filing of reports is not required.

[14] "Date rape drug" means gamma hydroxybutyric acid (GHB) or any controlled substance analogue of GHB, including gamma butyrolactone (GBL) or 1,4-butanediol; ketamine; flunitrazepam; or any substance which the Attorney General designates, through a rulemaking proceeding, to be used in committing rape or sexual assault. 21 U.S.C. 841(g)(2)(A).

[15] Examples of prohibited activities include knowingly or intentionally: (1) delivering, distributing, or dispensing a controlled substance by means of the Internet by an online pharmacy that is not validly registered with the Drug Enforcement Administration (DEA); (2) writing a prescription for a controlled substance for the purpose of delivery, distribution, or dispensation by means of the Internet; (3) serving as an agent, intermediary, or other entity that causes the Internet to be used to bring together a buyer and seller to engage in such distribution; (4) offering to fill a prescription for a controlled substance based solely on a consumer's completion of an online medical questionnaire; and (5) making a material false, fictitious, or fraudulent statement or representation on the homepage of Internet sites operated by an online pharmacy regarding the pharmacy's compliance with federal and state controlled substance laws. 21 U.S.C. 841(h)(2).

[16] See pages 1-5 of this report for these penalties, which vary by type of substance, weight or other factual circumstances, and repeat offender status. 21 U.S.C. 841(h)(4).

[17] Knowingly distributing a controlled substance to an unauthorized person by a registrant, removing required labels, unlawful use of information acquired during a controlled substance inspection, failing to keep required records, etc. For more information about these federal requirements pertaining to the lawful handling of controlled substances, see CRS Report RL34635, *The Controlled Substances Act: Regulatory Requirements*, by James E. Nichols and Brian T. Yeh,

[18] To knowingly: use fictitious, revoked, suspended or expired registration number; obtain a controlled substance by fraud, forgery, or other form of deceit; provide false information; use labels and other markings to render a drug a counterfeit substance; unlawfully possess certain controlled substance manufacturing equipment; being a registrant, unlawfully distribute a controlled substance in the course of legitimate business; create or receive a mixture containing listed chemicals to evade regulatory requirements.

[19] Knowingly placing in any newspaper, magazine, handbill, or other publications, any written advertisement that has the purpose of seeking or offering illegally to receive, buy, or distribute a schedule I controlled substance. 21 U.S.C. 843(c). However, this offense does not include any advertisement that merely advocates the use of a schedule I controlled substance and does not attempt to propose or facilitate an actual transaction in a schedule I controlled substance. Id. The Ryan Haight Online Pharmacy Consumer Protection Act of 2008, P.L. 110-425, creates an additional advertisement offense, new subsection 21 U.S.C. 843(c)(2): knowingly or intentionally using the Internet to advertise the sale of, or to offer to sell, distribute, or dispense a controlled substance in a

manner that is not authorized by federal controlled substances law, including directing prospective buyers to online pharmacies that are not registered with the DEA. The penalties for the offense are the same as those for advertising in printed publications.

[20] Except that violation carries a mandatory minimum of no less than one year unless the offense involves marihuana in an amount of 5 grams or less.

[21] The offense includes distribution or manufacturing in or on, or within 1,000 feet of the real property comprising a public or private elementary, vocational, or secondary school or a public or private college, junior college, or university, or a playground, or housing facility owned by a public housing authority, or within 100 feet of a public or private youth center, public swimming pool, or video arcade facility.

[22] Also, at least twice any term of supervised released otherwise authorized for a first offense. An exception to the mandatory 1-year minimum is provided with respect to an offense involving 5 grams or less of marihuana. Where the statute provides for a different mandatory penalty, the higher prevails.

[23] If convicted of a simple possession offense, the defendant is required, if able, to pay the "reasonable costs" of the investigation and prosecution of the offense. Penalties for simple possession are also applicable to distribution of a "small amount" of marihuana for no remuneration.

[24] For purposes of the section under which the possession penalties are imposed, a prior conviction includes conviction of *any* offense under the Controlled Substances Act or the Controlled Substances Import and Export Act and any drug or narcotic offense chargeable under state law.

[25] Distributing a controlled substance to another with the intent to commit a crime of violence upon the victim.

[26] Assembly, maintenance, or placement—in connection with the manufacture, distribution, or dispensing of a controlled substance.

[27] Under the statute, a person is considered to be engaged in a continuing criminal enterprise if (1) he commits any felony violation of the Controlled Substances Act or the Controlled Substances Import and Export Act, (2) the violation is a part of a continuing series of violations of those statutes (A) which are undertaken by the person in concert with five or more other persons with respect to whom such person occupies a position of organizer, a supervisory position, or any other position of management, and (B) from which such person obtains substantial income or resources. Note that some violations carry the death penalty as discussed *supra*.

[28] Except in the case of methamphetamine, where these provisions apply to any enterprise that grosses $5 million or more a year, or involves 200 times of the amount of controlled substances required under 21 U.S.C. 841.

[29] Also, at least twice any term of supervised release otherwise authorized for a first offense. Any higher mandatory penalty otherwise authorized for the offense would prevail.

[30] Also, at least three times any term of supervised release otherwise authorized for a first offense. Penalties for third and subsequent offenses are governed by 21 U.S.C. 841(b)(1)(A).

[31] The penalties listed for this offense apply *in addition* to the punishment provided for the drug trafficking crime.

In: An Examination of Sentencing Levels and Mandatory... ISBN: 978-1-61209-563-9
Editor: Catherine N. Bates

Chapter 7

TESTIMONY OF THE HONORABLE JUDGE JULIE E. CARNES, CHAIR OF THE CRIMINAL LAW COMMITTEE ON BEHALF OF THE JUDICIAL CONFERENCE, BEFORE THE SUBCOMMITTEE ON CRIME, TERRORISM AND HOMELAND SECURITY, HEARING ON "MANDATORY MINIMUM SENTENCES"

Mr. Chairman and Distinguished Members of the Committee,

I am pleased to testify on behalf of the Judicial Conference of the United States and its Criminal Law Committee and to offer you a judicial perspective on mandatory minimum sentencing statutes and the harms that we judges, first-hand, have seen them visit on our federal sentencing system.

I start by attributing no ill will or bad purpose to any Congressional member who has promoted or supported particular mandatory minimums sentences. To the contrary, many of these statutes were enacted out of a sincere belief that certain types of criminal activity were undermining the order and safety that any civilized society must maintain and out of a desire to create an effective weapon that could be wielded against those who refuse to comply with these laws. For example, 18 U.S.C. § 924(c), which provides a mandatory minimum sentence for the use of a gun in a crime of violence, was enacted following the assassinations of Martin Luther King, Jr. and Robert F. Kennedy.[1] Likewise, the mandatory minimum sentencing statute for crack cocaine was enacted in response to the death of basketball star Len Bias, and grew out of a concern that crack cocaine was a dangerous substance that could devastate the poorest and most vulnerable communities in our society.[2]

Yet, as well-intentioned as the proponents of mandatory minimum legislation may have been, these kinds of sentencing statutes have created what the late Chief Justice Rehnquist aptly identified as "unintended consequences."[3] Indeed, appropriately echoing the Chief Justice's phrase, this hearing is focused on "Mandatory Minimums and Unintended Consequences."

What are some of those consequences? First, because these statutes typically focus on one factor only, such as drug weight, to the exclusion of all other potentially relevant factors, they sweep quite broadly. Therefore, a severe penalty that might be appropriate for the most egregious of offenders will likewise be required for the least culpable violator, as long as the one factor identified in the statute is present. The ramification for this less culpable offender can be quite stark, as such an offender will often be serving a sentence that is greatly disproportionate to his or her conduct.

Unjust mandatory minimum statutes also have a corrosive effect on our broader society. To function successfully, our judicial system must enjoy the respect of the public. The robotic imposition of sentences that are viewed as unfair or irrational greatly undermines that respect. Further, as I will explain later in my testimony, some of these statutes do not produce merely questionable results; instead, a few produce truly bizarre outcomes.

Excessive mandatory sentences also squander scarce resources. It costs $25,895 a year to incarcerate a federal prisoner.[4] While this is money well-spent when the punishment fits the crime, these funds are wasted when they are used to incarcerate an individual whose sentence greatly exceeds what would be deemed a reasonable sentence.

In my testimony today on behalf of the Judicial Conference, I will touch on three points. In Part I, I will explain why mandatory minimum statutes are systemically flawed and will rarely avoid undesirable outcomes. In Part II, I will set out the history of the Judicial Conference's consistent and vigorous opposition to mandatory minimum sentences. In Part III, I will describe two recent cases in which use of mandatory minimum sentencing provisions produced sentences that greatly exceeded what even the toughest sentencer would consider an appropriate punishment. In Part IV, I will conclude by providing the Committee with some preliminary thoughts about approaches that Congress may begin to take to ameliorate the current situation and about a specific recommendation on one statute that the Conference has made.

Part I. The Systemic Flaw in Mandatory Minimum Sentences, and Why it Will Always be Problematic to Draft a Mandatory Minimum Statute that Will Work

As I note in Part II, the Judicial Conference has, for decades, opposed mandatory minimum sentences. While this opposition has been clearly communicated, the reasons for the opposition may sometimes have been misinterpreted by Congress and others. My sense is that some believe that judicial opposition to mandatory minimums arises strictly out of a sense of wounded autonomy: that is, district judges believe that they should have the absolute right to impose whatever sentence they consider appropriate, unfettered by outside constraints. In other words, according to this theory, district judges do not believe that they should be dictated to in this manner.

In reality, however, district judges are continually dictated to in a variety of ways, in both civil and criminal cases. In fact, much of a judge's daily activity is consumed with executing "mandatory" tasks, using a decision-making process that is "mandated" by some other entity.

Thus, a judge must adjudicate a civil case, according to the prescribed standards, whether or not the judge agrees with the policy judgment made by Congress that gave rise to the cause of action or to the recognized defenses. A judge must instruct a jury as to what the applicable statute and precedent require, regardless of the judge's possible disagreement with some of these instructions. Myriad other examples abound.

Judges understand and accept these constraints because judges know that they do not create the law; this is Congress's role. Rather, judges interpret that law and apply it to the facts of the case, within whatever ambit of discretion is deemed permissible for the particular issue. Likewise, as to mandatory minimum statutes, the Judicial Conference's opposition derives not from a narrow defense of a district judge's prerogatives but from a recognition, gained through years of experience, that mandatory minimum sentencing provisions have created untenable results and that they simply do not hang together in any coherent or rational way. As Chief Justice Rehnquist noted, they almost invariably create unintended, as well as undesirable, consequences.

The reason for this phenomenon lies in the way that mandatory minimum statutes must be constructed. A contrast with the federal sentencing guidelines system is instructive. The guidelines were premised on a "heartland" theory.[5] That is, the United States Sentencing Commission identified the typical core conduct that comprised a particular offense—the "heartland"—and assigned a numerical base offense level to that conduct. Then, the Sentencing Commission identified potential aggravating and mitigating conduct that could occur in connection with that offense and assigned a numerical value to that conduct, which number would either be added to or subtracted from the base offense level. A very calibrated criminal history formula was devised and included in the guidelines' calculation. Finally, a judge was given some limited departure authority to adjust a sentence up or down if "an aggravating or mitigating circumstance of a kind, or to a degree, not adequately taken into consideration by the Sentencing Commission in formulating the guidelines[6] was found to exist.

It is true that some judges and others have criticized the severity of some of the sentences prescribed by the guidelines. Some also believe that the sentencing ranges are too narrow and that departure authority is too cramped.[7] Whatever criticisms can be made as to the substance of the Guidelines, however, it is clear that the Guidelines' system looks at multiple factors that relate to culpability and consequences of the commission of criminal conduct and dangerousness of the offender. In short, the federal guidelines allow for some flex in the joints.[8]

In contrast, mandatory minimum statutes typically identify just one aggravating factor, and then pin the prescribed enhanced sentence totally on that one factor, without regard to the possibility of mitigating factors surrounding the commission of the offense. For such a sentence to be reasonable in every case, then, the particular conduct triggering the mandatory minimum must necessarily *always* warrant the mandated sentence, regardless of any of the circumstances of the offense or the offender. There are perhaps a few types of criminal conduct that are so unambiguous or heinous in nature that no examination of any fact other than the commission of the crime itself is necessary to persuade a reasonable person that the prescribed mandatory penalty is appropriate. Most criminal conduct, however, does not lend itself to such narrow scrutiny.

In short, mandatory minimum statutes are a blunt and inflexible tool. There is an inherent structural challenge in drafting a mandatory minimum statute that can truly apply to every case. Such a statute, to be just in every case, must not over-punish the most benign conduct that could be prosecuted under the particular criminal statute. Thus, the drafter of a proportional and fair mandatory minimum sentencing provision must consider the "minimum" *conduct, circumstances* and *offender type* that could be punished under the statute. In this sense, the word "minimum" should not refer only to the minimum penalty for a typical offense, but instead to the "minimum"—or most extenuated—conduct that could satisfy the statutory elements of the offense. Having envisioned the most sympathetic hypothetical offender possible, the drafter should only then determine what would be an appropriate minimum penalty for that offender.

Yet, when one examines the approximately 170 mandatory minimum statutory provisions in the federal code, it appears that the above approach has infrequently been taken by Congress. Instead the approach has frequently resembled a search for severity, whereby the particular statute appears to envision the most culpable offender and offense conduct possible, and the minimum penalty is then pegged to that hypothetical person. Such an approach will necessarily mean that any offender who is convicted of the particular statute, but whose conduct has been extenuated in ways not taken into account in fixing the penalty, will necessarily be given a sentence that is excessive.

Let me give you an example. Title 21 U.S.C. § 841(b)(1)(A) provides that, when a defendant has been convicted of a drug distribution offense involving a quantity of drugs that would trigger a mandatory minimum sentence of 10 years imprisonment—e.g., 5 kilograms of cocaine—the defendant's 10-year mandatory sentence shall be doubled to a 20-year sentence if he has been previously convicted of a drug distribution-type offense.

Now, if our defendant is a drug kingpin running a long-standing, well-organized, and extensive drug operation who has been previously convicted of another serious drug offense, a 20-year sentence may sound just fine. But, kingpins are, by definition, few in number, and they are not the most typical drug defendant that we see in federal court.

Instead, envision a low-level defendant who is one of several individuals hired to provide the manual labor used to offload a large drug shipment arriving in a boat. The quantity of drugs in the boat will easily qualify for a 10-year mandatory sentence. Further, assume that this off- loader has one prior conviction for distributing a small-quantity of marijuana, for which he served no time in prison. Further, assume that since his one marijuana conviction, he has led a law-abiding life until he lost his job and made the poor decision to offload this drug shipment in order to help support his wife and children. This defendant will now be subject to a 20-year sentence. Many persons would question the proportionality of this sentence.

I do not want to leave you with the impression that mandatory minimum sentencing provisions necessarily result in an unfair and excessive sentence in all cases. They do not. In some cases, the mandatory penalty will seem appropriate and reasonable. When that happens, judges do not typically fret that the sentence was also called for by a mandatory sentencing provision, because the judge believes the sentence to be fair. In other words, the "minimum" made sense in that particular case.

Unfortunately, however, given the severity of many of the mandatory sentences that are most frequently utilized in our system, judges are often required to impose a mandatory sentence in which the minimum term seems greatly disproportionate to the crime and terribly cruel to the human being standing before the judge for sentencing. It is this unintended consequence of a mandatory minimum statute that has created such concern and dismay.

PART II. THE JUDICIAL CONFERENCE'S HISTORY OF OPPOSITION TO MANDATORY MINIMUM SENTENCES

For more than fifty years, the Judicial Conference has consistently opposed mandatory minimum sentences. At its September 1953 meeting, the Conference endorsed a resolution from the Judicial Conference of the District of Columbia Circuit, opposing enactment of laws that compelled judges to impose minimum sentences and that denied judges the ability to place certain defendants on probation.[9]

Since then, the Judicial Conference of the United States has condemned mandatory minimum sentences with considerable regularity. In September 1961, the Conference considered several criminal bills pending before Congress.[10] The Conference took no position on the substantive merits of the bills, but "disapproved in principle those provisions requiring the imposition of mandatory minimum sentences.[11] By the next year, opposition to mandatory minimum sentences was considered to be the well-established position of the Judicial Conference. In March 1962, the Conference supported a bill easing parole restrictions, "consistent with the *established policy* of the Conference concerning mandatory minimum sentences."[12] Legislation containing mandatory minimum sentencing provisions was opposed on these grounds in 1965,[13] 1967,[14] and 1971.[15]

In 1976, the Conference affirmed its opposition, noting that there was no demonstrated need for legislation imposing mandatory minimum terms for certain offenses, and concluding that such legislation would "unnecessarily prolong the sentencing process and engender additional appellate review and would increase the expenditure of public funds without increase in additional benefits."[16]

In 1981, the Conference disapproved of a bill that would have imposed extended and strengthened mandatory penalties for the use of firearms in federal felonies.[17] The Conference noted that proposed legislation typically required the imposition of a minimum term while prohibiting probation and parole eligibility.[18] The Conference noted, "Statutes of this type limit judicial discretion in the sentencing function and tend to increase the number of criminal trials and the number of appeals in criminal cases. Upon the recommendation of the Committee the Conference reaffirmed its opposition to legislation requiring the imposition of mandatory minimum sentences."[19]

In March 1990, the Conference noted that the Third, Eighth, Ninth, and Tenth Circuits had all passed resolutions against mandatory minimum sentences, and voted to "urge the Congress to reconsider the wisdom of mandatory minimum sentence statutes and to restructure such statutes so that the U.S. Sentencing Commission may unifomily establish guidelines for all criminal statutes to avoid unwarranted disparities."[20] In May 1990, the Executive Committee of the Judicial Conference, acting on the Conference's behalf, reaffirmed this position in the form of approving a recommendation of the Federal Courts Study Committee that mandatory minimum sentencing provisions should be repealed, whereupon the Sentencing Commission should reconsider the guidelines applicable to the affected offenses.[21]The Conference's longstanding opposition to mandatory minimum terms was reaffirmed in July and August of 1991 by the Executive Committee, acting on behalf of the Judicial Conference, when it opposed amendments to the Violent Crime Control Act of 1991.[22]

In September 1991, the Conference approved a proposed statutory amendment that would provide district judges with authority to impose a sentence below a mandatory minimum when a defendant has limited involvement in an offense.[23] The Conference noted that "[w]hile the judiciary's overriding goal is to persuade Congress to repeal mandatory minimum sentences, for the short term, a safety valve of some sort is needed to ameliorate some of the harshest results of mandatory minimums.[24]

In March 1993, in the context of a long-range planning initiative, the Conference again agreed to renew efforts to reverse the trend of enacting mandatory minimum prison sentences.[25] Later, in September 1993, the Conference considered the Controlled Substances Minimum Penalty — Sentencing Guideline Reconciliation Act of 1993, legislation presented by the Chairman of the Sentencing Commission that attempted to reconcile mandatory minimum sentences with the sentencing guidelines.[26] "The Committee on Criminal Law believed that, although the proposed legislation would not solve all of the problems associated with mandatory minimum sentences, it addresses the essential incompatibility of mandatory minimums and sentencing guidelines and represents a promising approach."[27] On recommendation of the Committee on Criminal Law, the Conference endorsed the concept.[28]

On May 17, 1994, the Executive Committee, acting on behalf of the Judicial Conference, agreed not to oppose retroactivity of "safety valves" included in pending crime legislation to ameliorate some of the harshest results of mandatory minimum sentences despite the burden that retroactivity may impose upon the judiciary.[29]

The Long Range Plan for the Federal Courts, adopted in 1995, reiterated the Conference position that Congress should be discouraged from prescribing mandatory minimum sentences.[30] More recently, when considering the appropriate responses to the Supreme Court's decision in *Booker v. U.S.,* 543 U.S. 220 (2005), the Conference resolved to "oppose legislation that would respond to the Supreme Court's decision by (1) raising directly the upper limit of each guideline range or (2) expanding the use of mandatory minimum sentences."[31] In 2006, the Conference also considered the consequences of mandatory minimum terms in opposing the existing differences between crack and powder cocaine sentences.[32]

Most recently, upon the recommendation of the Criminal Law Committee, the Judicial Conference has endorsed seeking legislation that would "unstack" penalties under 18 U.S.C. § 924(c) and permit the statute to operate as a true recidivist statute.[33]

In short, for more than fifty years, the Judicial Conference has consistently and vigorously opposed mandatory minimum sentencing.

PART III. TWO EXAMPLES OF INJUSTICE WROUGHT BY MANDATORY MINIMUM SENTENCES

The description of an actual case can often convey more effectively than any abstract analysis the very real injustice that some specific mandatory minimum statutes have caused.

A. The Case of Weldon Angelos

Just over two years ago, my predecessor as Chair of the Criminal Law Committee, then-Judge, now-Professor Paul G. Cassell, testified before the Subcommittee on Crime, Terrorism, and Homeland Security,[34] and described in considerable detail the case of *United States v. Angelos.*[35] The sentencing of Weldon Angelos was a source of considerable distress for Judge Cassell,[36] and his description of that event stands as a powerful example of the unintended consequences that can result from well-intended legislation. I will not explore the intricacies of the case as deeply as did Judge Cassell, but I will review some of the key facts, as they may prove instructive.

When Mr. Angelos was sentenced in November of 2004, he was a twenty-four-year-old, first-time offender, arrested for trafficking marijuana. For his offense of dealing marijuana and related offenses, both the Government and the defense agreed that he should serve between six and eight years in prison. Under the U.S. Sentencing Guidelines, his crimes resulted in a total offense level of 28,[37] and, because Mr. Angelos had no significant prior criminal history, he was treated as a first-time offender (criminal history category I) under the Guidelines, resulting in a prescribed Guidelines sentence between 78 to 97 months.

But in imposing his sentence, Judge Cassell was also required to consider three additional firearms counts, pursuant to 18 U.S.C. § 924(c), a mandatory minimum statute that requires a court to impose a consecutive sentence of five years in prison the first time a drug dealer carries a gun and a twenty-five-year consecutive sentence for each subsequent time.[38]

Two of the § 924(c) counts arose because Mr. Angelos carried a handgun to two separate $350 marijuana deals. The third count arose out of the discovery by police, during the execution of a search warrant, of several additional handguns at Angelos' home. As a result of his conviction on these three counts, the Government insisted that Mr. Angelos must serve the statutory minimum, which was a *de facto* life sentence. Specifically, the Government contended that the court had to sentence Mr. Angelos to a prison term of no less than 61[1]/2 years: 61/2 years for drug dealing, followed by *55 additional years* for the three counts of possessing a firearm in connection with a drug offense.

It is also worth noting that the original indictment issued against Mr. Angelos contained only three counts of distribution of marijuana,[39] one § 924(c) count, and two other lesser charges.[40]The Government had told Mr. Angelos, through counsel, that if he pled guilty to the drug distribution count and the § 924(c) count, the Government would agree to drop all other charges, not supersede the indictment with additional counts, and recommend a prison sentence of 15 years. However, the Government also warned that if he rejected the offer, prosecutors would obtain a new superseding indictment adding several § 924(c) counts that could lead to Mr. Angelos facing more than 100 years of mandatory prison time. In short, Mr. Angelos faced the choice of accepting 15 years in prison or insisting on a trial by jury at the risk of a life sentence. He elected to go to trial. As promised, the Government obtained two superseding indictments, charging a total of twenty counts, including five § 924(c) counts that alone carried a minimum mandatory sentence of 105 years (5 + 25 + 25 + 25 + 25).

At trial, the jury found Mr. Angelos guilty on sixteen of the twenty counts, including three § 924(c) counts. Those counts, alone, produced a mandatory 55 year term (5 + 25 + 25). Judge Cassell was troubled by the sentence, viewing it as unjust, cruel, and irrational,'[41] but his role in evaluating § 924(c) was limited. A judge may ignore a statutorily-mandated sentence typically only on constitutional grounds under the Fifth or Eighth Amendment, i.e., if it produces irrational punishment without any conceivable justification or is so excessive as to constitute cruel and unusual punishment.

Judge Cassell considered these arguments carefully, noting that adding 55 years on top of a 61/2 year sentence for drug dealing is *far* beyond the roughly two-year-increase in sentence that the United States Sentencing Guidelines indicated to be appropriate for possessing firearms under the same circumstances,[42] and also noting that the sentence exceeded what the jury recommended to the court.[43] Judge Cassell also contrasted the sentence of Mr. Angelos with the sentences that would be imposed for various serious crimes under the Sentencing Guidelines.[44] He noted that the sentence exceeded the sentences prescribed for these much more serious crimes. In fact, the punishment imposed in Mr. Angelos' case so exceeded the penalties associated with these other, serious crimes that it is impossible to credibly contend that the sentence was proportional to the penalties for those offenses at the time.[45] See Table I, below.

Table I. Comparison of Mr. Angelos' Sentence with Federal Sentences for Other Crimes

Offense and Offense Guideline	Offense Calculation	Maximum Sentence
Mr. Angelos with Guidelines sentence plus § 924(c) counts	Base Offense Level 28 + 3 § 924(c) counts (55 years)	738 Months
Kingpin of major drug trafficking ring in which death resulted U.S.S.G. §2D1.1(a)(2)	Base Offense Level 38	293 Months
Aircraft hijacker U.S.S.G. §2A5.1	Base Offense Level 38	293 Months
Terrorist who detonates a bomb in a public place intending to kill a bystander U.S.S.G. § 2K1.4(a)(1)	Total Level 36 (by cross reference to § 2A2.1(a)(2) and terrorist enhancement in § 3A1.4(a))	235 Months
Racist who attacks a minority with the intent to kill U.S.S.G. § 2A2.1(a)(1) & (b)(1)	Base Level 28 + 4 for life threatening + 3 for racial selection under § 3A1.1	210 Months
Spy who gathers top secret information U.S.S.G. § 2M3.2(a)(1)	Base Offense Level 35	210 Months
Second-degree murderer U.S.S.G. § 2A1.2	Base Offense Level 33	168 Months
Criminal who assaults with the intent to kill U.S.S.G. § 2A2.1(a)(1) & (b)	Base Offense Level 28 + 4 for intent to kill = 32	151 Months
Kidnapper U.S.S.G. § 2A4.1(a)	Base Offense Level 32	151 Months
Saboteur who destroys military materials U.S.S.G. § 2M2.1(a)	Base Offense Level 32	151 Months

Table I. (Continued)

Offense and Offense Guideline	Offense Calculation	Maximum Sentence
Marijuana dealer who shoots an innocent person during drug transaction U.S.S.G. § 2D1.1(c)(13) & (b)(2)	Base Offense Level 16 + 1 § 924(c) count	146 Months
Rapist of a 10-year-old child U.S.S.G. § 2A3.1(a) & (B)(4)(2)(A)	Base Offense Level 27 + 4 for young child = 31	135 Months
Child pornographer who photographs a 12-year-old. in sexual positions U.S.S.G. § 2G2.1(a) &(b)	Base Offense Level 27 + 2 for young child = 29	108 Months
Criminal who provides weapons to support a foreign terrorist organization U.S.S.G. § 2M5.3(a) & (b)	Base Offense Level 26 +2 for weapons = 28	97 Months
Criminal who detonates a bomb in an aircraft U.S.S.G. § 2K1.4(a)(1)	By cross reference to § 2A2.1(a)(1)	97 Months
Rapist U.S.S.G. § 2A3.1	Base Offense Level 27	87 Months

It would be myopic to suggest that drug trafficking is a non-violent offense,[46] but the *potential for* violence associated with Mr. Angelos' carrying a firearm to his drug deals certainly did not cause the kind of *actual violence* associated with aircraft hijacking, murder, and rape. Yet, as indicated in Table I, Mr. Angelos faced a prison term more than double the sentence of, for example, an aircraft hijacker (293 months), a terrorist who detonates a bomb in a public place (235 months), a racially-motivated defendant who attacks a minority victim with the intent to kill and inflicts permanent or life-threatening injuries (210 months), or a second-degree murderer (168 months). Indeed, Mr. Angelos faced a prison term more than *five times as long* as the Guidelines sentence of someone who rapes a ten-year-old child (135 months) and more than eight times as long as that of a rapist (87 months).

In fact, on the very same day that Judge Cassell sentenced Weldon Angelos, he imposed sentence in another case, *United States v. Visinaiz:*[47] In the Visinaiz case, the defendant had beaten a 68-year-old woman to death by striking her in the head with a log, before hiding her body and then dumping it in a river, weighed down with cement blocks. The Sentencing Guidelines required a sentence for this brutal second-degree murder of between 210 to 262 months.[48] Upon the Government's recommendation, Judge Cassell imposed a sentence of 262 months, which was less than half the sentence he was compelled to impose on Mr. Angelos.

But despite that contrasting experience and notwithstanding all the above considerations, controlling precedent required Judge Cassell to reject Mr. Angelos' constitutional challenges and Judge Cassell imposed the mandatory 55-years sentence. Troubled by an unjust but unavoidable sentence, Judge Cassell wrote to the Office of the Pardon Attorney, asking the President to commute Mr. Angelos' sentence to no more than 18 years in prison (the average recommended by jurors in the case).[49] He also recommended that Congress modify § 924(c) so that its harsh provisions for 25-year multiple sentences apply only to "true" recidivist drug offenders: those who have been sent to prison for a particular crime, but who have failed to learn their lesson and repeat the same crime after release.[50] Judge Cassell also testified about the *Angelos* case, twice, when appearing before the House Subcommittee on Crime, Terrorism and Homeland Security in 2006 and 2007.[51]

B. The Case of Marion Hungerford

Another case illustrating the cruelly harsh results that can emanate from the "stacking effect" of § 924(c) is *United States v. Hungerford,*[52] a case from the Ninth Circuit Court of Appeals. Although Marion Hungerford never held a weapon during the robberies that her boyfriend carried out, she was involved in the planning of the crimes and she enjoyed the spoils of the offense. She would not agree to a plea bargain, and in accordance with the law she was convicted of conspiracy and seven counts of robbery and using a firearm in relation to a crime of violence.[53] Because of the seven stacked § 924(c) counts, Hungerford was sentenced to slightly more than 159 years in prison.[54] Although the evidence indicated that Marion Hungerford suffered from a severe case of borderline personality disorder,[55] the Ninth Circuit followed established precedent, rejected her claims, and affirmed her sentence.[56]

In short, as the above two cases illustrate, mandatory minimum sentencing laws can be grenades: powerful, but crude, and lacking in the ability to distinguish meaningfully between serious offenders and those who are substantially less culpable. With mandatory minimum sentences, there is no discretion afforded to judges at either the trial or appellate level to correct sentences that are obviously greatly disproportionate to the offense.

PART IV. SUPPORT OF THE JUDICIAL CONFERENCE AND OTHERS FOR EFFORTS TO RESCIND MANDATORY MINIMUM STATUTES OR TO AMELIORATE THEIR DELETERIOUS EFFECTS

As the Conference has consistently opposed mandatory minimum sentencing provisions over the last five decades, we are pleased that Congress is taking steps to address the problems created by these statutes. Indeed, three bills have already been introduced, and additional approaches will likely be suggested by Congressional members.

A. Previous Suggested Approaches

Approximately 170 mandatory minimum sentencing provisions are found throughout the federal criminal code. Any thorough reform should ultimately address all of them. In considering what approach to take, Congress can draw on the views of many knowledgeable observers who have considered the question over the years. The Judicial Conference has offered several ideas in the past, which might usefully serve as a basis for reform now. For example, the Conference has long sought the repeal of mandatory minimum sentences.[57] As interim or partial solutions, the Judicial Conference has supported other measures. In September 1991, the Judicial Conference approved a proposed statutory amendment that would provide district judges with authority to impose a sentence below a mandatory minimum when a defendant has limited involvement in an offense.[58] In 1993, the Conference endorsed a proposal offered by Judge William W. Wilkins, Jr., in his capacity as chair of the Sentencing Commission, in which the guidelines would trump the statutory mandatory minimum.[59]

Over the years, at the same time that the Conference has been maintaining its opposition to mandatory minimum sentences, several Members of Congress have proposed alternatives to them. In February 1993, Representative Don Edwards introduced the Sentencing Uniformity Act of 1993. The Act sought to amend the federal criminal code and other federal laws to abolish mandatory minimums.[60] Although the bill had 36 co-sponsors, it never left the subcommittee. Later that year, Senator Orrin G. Hatch, citing the Sentencing Commission's special report on mandatory minimums, suggested that Congress should begin using methods other than mandatory minimums to shape sentencing policy. Among the recommendations cited were: (1) specific statutory directives to the Sentencing Commission (e.g., instructing the Commission to adjust the guidelines by a specific number of levels), (2) general directives (e.g., highlighting Congress' concerns for the Commission's consideration when amending the guidelines), (3) increased statutory maximums, and (4) diligent oversight of federal sentencing policy (e.g., relying on data and research, conducting oversight hearings).[61]

Simultaneously with the Judicial Conference, groups such as the American Bar Association[62] and the Sentencing Project[63] have called for the outright repeal of all mandatory minimums. The Constitution Project has called for the enactment of mandatory minimum sentences "only in the most extraordinary circumstances."[64]The members of Families Against Mandatory Minimums (FAMM) have been active over the years in the debate concerning mandatory minimums and, true to the name of their organization, they have repeatedly challenged "inflexible and excessive penalties required by mandatory sentencing laws."' They have traditionally supported three primary strategies to be used in lieu of mandatory minimums.

First, they have recommended restoring sentencing discretion to judges. To insure a judge's decision will meet standards for appropriate punishment, the prosecutor or the defendant would be able to appeal the judge's sentence.[66] Second, FAMM supports the use of sentencing guidelines. Finally, FAMM recommends that Congress consider sentencing alternatives--such as substance abuse treatment, drug court supervision, probation, and community correctional programs--as well as incarceration.[67]

Congress could use the Sentencing Commission as a starting point for reform. Congress created the Commission in 1984 as part of its efforts to reduce sentencing disparities and improve the transparency of federal sentencing. The irony, however, is that Congress. has created two conflicting federal sentencing systems: the Guidelines system and mandatory minimum statutes.

While guidelines and mandatory minimums can occasionally be reconciled,[68] far more often they seem to cut in opposite directions. As the Sentencing Commission has cogently explained, the two systems are "structurally and functionally at odds."[69] In the *Angelos* case, for example, the guidelines called for a sentence for Mr. Angelos that was more than forty years lower than what he ultimately received as a result of mandatory minimum penalties. Moreover, because of the transparency of the Guidelines system, it was possible to calculate precisely how far Angelos' sentence exceeded what he would have received for committing other more serious crimes such as aircraft hijacking, second degree murder, espionage, kidnapping, aggravated assault, and rape.

In reforming the system today, Congress should, at a minimum, examine offenses in which mandatory minimum provisions have produced sentences significantly different from those produced by the Guidelines. As noted, the Judicial Conference has previously endorsed a proposal that would allow the court to "depart" from the mandatory minimum sentence to impose any sentence that would be proper under the Sentencing Guidelines.[70]

In short, there are a variety of ways to address and ameliorate the unintended and deleterious effects of mandatory minimum sentencing provisions: from outright repeal to other more incremental steps. The Judicial Conference is supportive of Congress' efforts to make a thoughtful and thorough assessment of this continuing problem.

B. The Need to Unstack § 924(c) Penalties

The Conference recognizes the significance and scope of any undertaking to revise the current mandatory minimum regime. At the same time, we hope that the Congress will attempt to identify expeditiously and address those most egregious mandatory minimum provisions that produce the unfairest, harshest, and most irrational results in the cases sentenced under their provisions. The Conference, at the recommendation of the Criminal Law Committee, has identified one such provision—the stacking aspect of § 924(c) penalties—and has explicitly endorsed seeking legislation that would unstack § 924(c) penalties and permit the statute to operate as a true recidivist statute.[71]

To understand the basis for this recommendation, a familiarity with the history of this section is instructive. Title 18 U.S.C. § 924(c) was proposed and enacted in a single day as an amendment to the Gun Control Act of 1968, which had been prompted by the assassinations of Martin Luther King, Jr. and Robert F. Kennedy. Congress intended the Act to address the "increasing rate of crime and lawlessness and the growing use of firearms in violent crime."[72]Because § 924(c) was offered as a floor amendment, there are no congressional hearings or committee reports regarding its original purpose,[73] and only a few statements made during floor debate are available.[74]

As originally enacted, § 924(c) gave judges considerable discretion in sentencing and was not nearly as harsh as it has become. When passed in 1968, § 924(c) imposed an enhancement of "not less than one year nor more than ten years" for the person who "uses a firearm to commit any felony for which he may be prosecuted in a court of the United States" or "carries a firearm unlawfully during the commission of any felony for which he may be prosecuted in a court of the United States."[75] If the person was convicted of a "second or subsequent" violation of § 924(c), the additional penalty was "not less than 2 nor more than 25 years," which could not run "concurrently with any term of imprisonment imposed for the commission of such felony."[76]

One of the first questions involving the statute concerned whether a defendant could be sentenced under § 924(c) when the underlying felony statute already included an enhancement for use of a firearm. In 1972, in *Simpson v. United States*,[77] the Supreme Court, relying on floor statements from Representative Poff, held that "the purpose of § 924(c) is already served whenever the substantive federal offense provides enhanced punishment for the use of a dangerous weapon" and that "to construe the statute to allow the additional sentence authorized by § 924(c) to be pyramided upon a sentence already enhanced under § 2113(c) would violate the established rule that 'ambiguity concerning the ambit of criminal statutes should be resolved in favor of lenity."[78]

In 1980, in *Busic v. United States,*[79] the Court reaffiiuied its decision in *Simpson* and went one step further, holding that prosecutors could not file a § 924(c) count instead of the enhancement provided for in the underlying federal statute. In support of this decision, the Court noted that, in 1971, the Department of Justice had advised prosecutors not to proceed under § 924(c) if the predicate felony statute provided for "increased penalties where a firearm was used in the commission of the offense."[80]

In response to *Simpson* and *Busic,* Congress amended § 924(c) in 1984 "so that its sentencing enhancement would apply regardless of whether the underlying felony statute `provides for an enhanced punishment if committed by the use of a deadly or dangerous weapon or device."[81] The 1984 amendment also established a five-year mandatory minimum for use of a firearm during commission of a crime of violence.[82]

In 1986, as part of the Firearms Owner's Protection Act, Congress amended § 924(c) so that it also applied to drug-trafficking crimes, and increased the mandatory minimum to ten years for certain types of firearms.[83] In later amendments, Congress increased the penalty for a "second or subsequent" § 924(c) conviction to a mandatory minimum of twenty years, which twenty years later became twenty-five years.[84]

The increased penalties for "second or subsequent" § 924(c) convictions gave rise to litigation over whether multiple convictions in the same proceeding constituted "second or subsequent" convictions subject to the enhanced penalty. In essence, the issue was whether Congress intended § 924(c) to be a "true" recidivist statute or one that applies enhanced penalties to successive counts of carrying a firearm during a crime of violence within a single proceeding. Most courts, including the Tenth Circuit, did not apply the twenty-year penalty when the "second" conviction was just the second § 924(c) count in an indictment.[85]

In *Deal v. United States,*[86] however, the Supreme Court, in a six-to-three decision, construed the statute more broadly. Deal had been convicted of committing six different bank robberies on six different dates, each time using a gun. He was sentenced to five years for the first § 924(c) charge, and twenty years consecutive for each of the other five § 924(c) charges, for a total of 105 years. In affirming his sentence, the Court held that a "second or subsequent" conviction could arise from a single prosecution.[87] The Court stated, "We choose to follow the language of the statute, which give no indication that punishment of those who fail to learn the `lesson' of prior conviction or of prior punishment is the sole purpose of § 924(e)(1), to the exclusion of other penal goals such as taking repeat offenders off the streets for especially long periods or simply visiting society's retribution upon repeat offenders more severely.[88]

Less than two weeks after *Deal,* the Court again interpreted the statute in *Smith v. United States.*[89] In *Smith,* the Court held that exchanging a gun for drugs constitutes "use" of a firearm "during and in relation to . . . [a] drug trafficking crime." The Court rejected the defendant's argument that "use" of a firearm required use as a *weapon.*[90] The majority noted than when Congress enacted the relevant version of § 924(c), it was no doubt responding to concerns that drugs and guns were a "dangerous combination."[91] Justice Scalia argued in dissent that it was "significant" that the portion of § 924(c) relating to drug trafficking was affiliated with the preexisting provision pertaining to use of a fireaun in relation to a crime of violence.[92] He therefore construed the word "use" in relation to a crime of violence to mean use as a weapon, and concluded that this definition of use should carry over to the addition of drug trafficking to the statute.[93]

Additional rulings further broadened the applicability and effect of § 924(c). The Court again interpreted § 924(c) in *United States v. Gonzales,*[94] where it held that a sentence under § 924(c) could not be served concurrently with an unrelated sentence from a state conviction.[95] Finally, in *Muscarello v. United States,*[96] the Court held that, as used in § 924(c), "carries" is not limited to a firearm that is carried by the felon on his person, but also includes a gun found in the glove compartment of a vehicle that was present at the drug transaction.

The Conference recommends that, at the least, Congress should establish § 924(c) as a "true" recidivist statute. This would be particularly important in cases like *Angelos* that do not involve direct violence, but instead only the possession of a gun. A "true" recidivist statute would mean that the "second and subsequent" enhancement would apply only to defendants who have been previously convicted of a § 924(c) offense prior to the firearm possession that led to the § 924(c) charge being sentenced. It is an approach that we believe makes good sense.

CONCLUSION

The Conference supports Congress's efforts to review and ameliorate the deleterious and unwanted consequences spawned by mandatory minimum sentencing provisions. A predecessor chair of the Criminal Law Committee of the Judicial Conference, the late and wise Senior Judge Vincent L. Broderick, summarized the conclusion that many reach concerning mandatory minimum sentences when he testified about the mandatory minimum sentences before the House Judiciary Subcommittee on Crime and Criminal Justice of the House Committee in 1993. What he said then still makes a great deal of sense today.

> I firmly believe that any reasonable person who exposes himself or herself to this [mandatory minimum] system of sentencing, whether judge or politician, would come to the conclusion that such sentencing must be abandoned in favor of a system based on principles of fairness and proportionality. In our view, the Sentencing Commission is the appropriate institution to carry out this important task.[97]

I hope that Congress will act swiftly to reform mandatory minimums to eliminate the great injustices that they are creating.

End Notes

[1] See H.R. REP. NO. 90-1577 at 1698, 90th Cong., 2d Sess., 7 (1968), 1968 U.S.C.C.A.N. 4410, 4412.

[2] See, e.g., *Restoring Fairness to Federal Sentencing: Addressing the Crack-Powder Disparity Before the Senate Subcomm. on Crime and Drugs*, 111th Cong. (Statement of Lanny A. Breuer, Assistant Attorney General, Criminal Division, Department of Justice) (attributing high profile overdose death of Len Bias as a source of congressional interest in cocaine sentencing policy).

[3] *See* William H Rehnquist, *Luncheon Address* (June 18, 1993), *in* United States Sentencing Commission, *Proceedings of the Inaugural Symposium on Crime and Punishment in the United States* 286 (1993) (suggesting that federal mandatory minimum sentencing statutes are "perhaps a good example of the law of unintended consequences").

[4] *See* Matthew Rowland, Deputy Assistant Director, Administrative Office of the United States Courts Memorandum (May 6, 2009), Cost of Incarceration and Supervision (on file) (reporting the annual cost of Bureau of Prisons confinement as $25,894.50 as opposed to $3743.23 per year for supervision outside of confinement.)

[5] *See* United States Sentencing Commission, Guidelines Manual Ch. 1, Pt. A.(4)(b) (2008) ("The Commission intends the sentencing courts to treat each guideline as carving out a "heartland," a set of typical cases embodying the conduct that each guideline describes.").

[6] 18 U.S.C. § 3553(b).

[7] *In Koon v. United States*, 518 U.S. 81 (1996), the Supreme Court expanded departure authority, holding that whether a given sentencing factor was a legitimate ground for departure was a factual matter to be determined by the sentencing judge, subject to an abuse of discretion standard. With the 2003 passage of the PROTECT Act (Pub. L. No. 108-21, § 401(d)), however, *Koon* was overturned and departure authority was substantially restricted.

[8] *See* United States Sentencing Commission, Report to Congress, Downward Departures From the Federal Sentencing Guidelines (October 2003).

The Committee does not intend that the Guidelines be imposed in a mechanistic fashion. *It believes that the sentencing judge has an obligation to consider all the factors in a case and to impose sentences outside the Guidelines in an appropriate case.* The purpose of the sentencing Guidelines is to provide a structure for evaluating the fairness and appropriateness of the sentence for an individual offender as compared to similarly situated offenders, not to eliminate the imposition of thoughtful individualized sentences.

Id. at B-9 (quoting S. Rep. No. 97-307 at 969) (emphasis added).

[9] JCUS-SEP 53, pp. 28-29.

[10] JCUS-SEP 61, pp. 98-99.

[11] *Id.* at 99.

[12] JCUS-MAR 62, p. 22 (emphasis added).

[13] JCUS-MAR 65, p. 20.

[14] JCUS-SEP 67, pp. 79-80 ("The Conference approved a recommendation of its Committee confirming the general opposition of the Conference to mandatory minimum sentences.").

[15] JCUS-OCT 71, p. 40 ("The Conference reaffirmed its disapproval of mandatory minimum sentences.").

[16] ICUS-APR 76, p. 10.

[17] JCUS-SEP 81, p. 90.

[18] JCUS-SEP 81, p. 93.

[19] *Id.*

[20] ICUS-MAR 90, p. 16.

[21] JCUS-SEP 90, p. 62.

[22] JCUS-SEP 91, p. 45 (opposing mandatory minimum sentencing amendments to S. 1241, 102nd Congress).

[23] JCUS-SEP 91, p. 56.

[24] *Id.*

[25] JCUS-MAR 93, p. 13.

[26] JCUS-SEP 93, p. 46.

[27] *Id.*

[28] *Id.*

[29] JCUS-SEP 94, p. 42.

[30] JCUS-SEP 95, p. 47.

[31] JCUS-MAR 05, pp. 15-16.

[32] JCUS SEP 06,, p 18 ("Under the anti-drug abuse act of 1986 (Pub. L. no. 99-570), 100 times as much powder cocaine as crack cocaine is needed to trigger the same mandatory minimum sentences.")

[33] JCUS-MAR 09, pp. 16-17.

[34] *Mandatory Minimum Sentencing Laws — The Issues Before the House Subcomm. on Crimes, Terrorism and Homeland Security*, 110th Cong. (Statement of Paul G. Cassell, Chair, Criminal Law Committee of the Judicial Conference).

[35] 345 F. Supp. 2d 1227 (D. Utah 2004).

[36] *See* J.C. Oleson, *The Antigone Dilemma: When the Paths of Law and Morality Diverge,* 29 CARDOZO L. REV. 669, 682 (2007) ("Judge Cassell appears to have agonized over the decision, aching to strike down the fifty-five year sentence on Equal Protection and Eighth Amendment grounds...."). *Id.* at 683 (describing Judge Cassell's feeling of being "ethically obligated to bring this injustice to the attention of those who are in a position to do something about it.") (citing U.S. v. Angelos, at 1261).

[37] U.S. v. Angelos. Tr. 9/14/04 at 27 (based on U.S.S.G. § 2D1.1(c)(7) & § 2S1.1(b)(2)(B)).

[38] 18 U.S.C. § 924(c)(1)(A)(I), (C)(i), and (D)(ii).
[39] 18 U.S.C. § 841(b)(1).
[40] *See supra* note 34 (describing Judge Cassell's account of plea negotiations).
[41] *Angelos,* 345 F. Supp 2nd at 1251.
[42] *See* U.S.S.G. § 2D1.1(b)(1) (describing gun enhancement for drug offenses). If Angelos' sentence had been calculated under the Sentencing Guidelines rather than stacked 924 (c) counts, it would have increased his offense level from 28 to 30, resulting in 24 additional months of imprisonment.
[43] Following the trial — over the government's objection — Judge Cassell sent each of the *Angelos* jurors the relevant information about Mr. Angelos' limited criminal history, described the abolition of parole in the federal system, and asked the jurors what they believed was the appropriate penalty for Mr. Angelos. Nine jurors responded and provided the following recommendations: (1) 5 years; (2) 5-7 years; (3) 10 years; (4) 10 years; (5) 15 years; (6) 15 years; (7) 15-20 years; (8) 32 years; and (9) 50 years. Averaging these answers, the jurors recommended a mean sentence of about 18 years and a median sentence of 15 years.
[44] The 2003 Guidelines were used in all calculations. All calculations assume a first offender, like Mr. Angelos, in Criminal History Category I.
[45] *See* Harmelin v. Michigan, 501 U.S. 957, 1004 (1991) (Kennedy J., concurring) (noting that "[c]omparisons can be made in light of the harm caused or threatened to the victim or society, and the culpability of the offender").
[46] Hamelin, at 1002 (Kennedy J., concurring).
[47] 344 F. Supp. 2d 1310 (2004).
[48] U.S.S.G. *2A1.1 (offense level of 33) + &3A1.1(b) (two-level increase for vunlnerable victim) + *3C1.1 (two level increase for onstruction of justice)
[49] *See* United States v. Angelos, 345 F. Supp. 2d at 1261-62.
[50] *See id.* at 1262-63.
[51] *See Oversight Hearing on* United States v. Booker: *One Year Later—Chaos or Status Quo? Before the House Subcomm. on Crime, Terrorism, and Homeland Security,* 109th Cong. (2006) (statement of Paul Cassell, Chair, Criminal Law Committee of the Judicial Conference); *Mandatory Minimum Sentencing Laws — The Issues, supra* note 4.
[52] 465 F.3d 1113 (2006).
[53] *M.* at 1114.
[54] *Id.* at 1119.
[55] *Id.*
[56] *Id.* at 1118.
[57] *See supra* notes 24 and 25.
[58] *Supra* note 23.
[59] *Supra* note 26. *See also* Paul J. Hofer, *The Possibilities for Limited Legislative Reform of Mandatory Minimum Penalties,* 6 FED. SENTENCING REP. 2, at 63 (September 1993) (explaining that Judge Wilkins' proposal was seen as "too sweeping" by Congress).
[60] H.R. 957, 103rd Congress (February 7, 1993).
[61] *See* Orrin G. Hatch, *The Role of Congress in Sentencing: The United States Sentencing Commission, Mandatory Minimum Sentences, and the Search for a Certain and Effective Sentencing System,* 28 WAKE FOREST L. REV. 185 (1993).
[62] *See* American Bar Association, Justice Kennedy Commission, *Reports with Recommendations to the House of Delegates* 9 (Aug. 2004).
[63] Ryan S. King, The Sentencing Project, *Changing Direction? State Sentencing Reforms 2004-2006* (2007), available at http://sentencingproiect.org/Admin/Documents/publications/sentencingrefonnforweb.pdf.
[64] Constitution Project, *Principles for the Design and Reform of Sentencing Systems: A Background Report* (March 15, 2006), available at http://www.constitutionproject.org/pdf/Sentencing_Principles_Background_Report.pdf.
[65] Families Against Mandatory Minimums, FAMMGRAM, *The Case Against Mandatory Minimums* (Winter 2005), available at http://www.famm.org/Repository/Files/PritnerFinal.pdf.
[66] *Id.* See also, Christina N. Davilas, *Prosecutorial Sentence Appeals: Reviving the Forgotten Doctrine in State Law as an Alternative to Mandatory Sentencing Laws,* 87 CORNELL L. REV. 1259 (July 2002) (suggesting that prosecutorial sentence appeals maintain judicial discretion while at the same time providing a mechanism for correcting judicial mistakes, including "unreasonable" sentences).
[67] *Id.*
[68] *See, e.g.,* 18 U.S.C. §§ 3553(e) and (f).
[69] See United States Sentencing Commission, Special Report to Congress, Mandatory Minimum Penalties in the Federal Criminal Justice System 25 (August 1991).
[70] *Supra* notes 23 and 26.
[71] JCUS-MAR 09, pp. 16-17.
[72] H.R. REP. No. 90-1577 at 1698, 90th Cong., 2d Sess., 7 (1968), 1968 U.S.C.C.A.N. 4410, 4412.
[73] *Cf. Jung v. Association of American Medical Colleges,* 339 F.Supp.2d 26,40, 2004 WL 1803198 at * 11 (D.D.C. 2004) (noting interpretive difficulties created when legislation is passed without legislative hearings).

[74] *Busic v. United States,* 446 U.S. 398, 405 (1980).
[75] *Simpson v. United States,* 435 U.S. 6, 7-8 (1978) (citing 18 U.S.C. § 924(c) (1968)).
[76] Id.
[77] Id.
[78] Id. at 13, 14.
[79] 446 U.S. 398 (1980).
[80] *Id.* at 406 (quoting 19 U.S. Atty's Bull. No. 3, p.63 (U.S. Dept. of Justice, 1981)).
[81] *United States v. Gonzales,* 520 U.S. 1, 10 (1997)(citing Comprehensive Crime Control Act of 1984, Pub. L. 9847. § 1005(a), 98 Stat. 2128-39).
[82] *Id.*
[83] Pub. L. No. 99-308, § 104(a)(2)(A)-(F).
[84] Pub. L. No. 100-690, § 6212, 102 Stat. 4181, 4360 (1988).
[85] *See, e.g., United States v. Chalan,* 812 F.2d 1302, 1315 (10th Cir. 1987), *cert. denied,* 488 U.S. 983 (1988).
[86] 508 U.S. 129 (1993).
[87] *Id.* at 133-34.
[B8] *Id.* at 136.
[89] 508 U.S. 223 (1993).
[90] *Id.* at 228.
[91] *Id.* at 239.
[92] *Id.* at 244 (Scalia J., dissenting).
[93] *Id.*
[94] 520 U.S. 1 (1997).
[95] *Id.* at 9-10.
[96] 524 U.S. 125 (1998).
[97] Senior Judge Vincent L. Broderick, Southern District of New York, speaking for the Judicial Conference Committee on Criminal Law in testimony before the Subcommittee on Crime and Criminal Justice of the House Committee on the Judiciary, July 28, 1993.

In: An Examination of Sentencing Levels and Mandatory… ISBN: 978-1-61209-563-9
Editor: Catherine N. Bates

Chapter 8

STATEMENT OF JULIE STEWART, PRESIDENT, FAMILIES AGAINST MANDATORY MINIMUMS, BEFORE THE SUBCOMMITTEE ON CRIME, TERRORISM, AND HOMELAND SECURITY, HEARING ON "MANDATORY MINIMUMS AND UNINTENDED CONSEQUENCES"

I am Julie Stewart, President of Families Against Mandatory Minimums. FAMM is a national nonprofit, nonpartisan organization whose mission is to promote fair and proportionate sentencing policies. FAMM does not oppose prison; we simply want the punishment to fit the crime.

I want to thank Chairman Scott, ranking member Gohmert and distinguished members of the Committee, for the opportunity to testify before the Subcommittee on Crime, Terrorism and Homeland Security and for your commitment to sentencing reform.

As some of you know, I started FAMM 18 years ago after watching my brother get sentenced to five years for growing marijuana in a garage. My brother, Jeff, deserved to be punished because he broke the law. And some time in prison might have even been appropriate. But five years seemed excessive then and still seems that way to me now. A lot can happen in five years – a lot of missed birthdays, holidays and family gatherings, and in Jeff's case, the death of our Dad. That's a blow that's hard to bear from a prison cell.

But what motivated me to start an organization to repeal mandatory minimum sentences was not really the length of my brother's sentence – it was witnessing the judge's inability to give my brother the sentence he wanted to. At sentencing, the judge stated that his "hands were tied" by mandatory sentencing laws. It seemed counterintuitive to me that the person who knew all the facts of Jeff's case could not deliver the sentence that was appropriate for Jeff and his role in the offense. I thought in this country we sentenced individuals - not crimes. I thought courts imposed sentence, not lawmakers miles away in Washington.

It seemed utterly un-American. It still does.

Sixteen years ago I made that same argument before this same subcommittee on this same subject: mandatory minimum sentencing. Sitting beside me at the witness table that day in 1993 was a young woman named Nicole Richardson. She was dressed in a prison jumpsuit and brought into the hearing room in shackles. Nicole had been convicted of drug trafficking for giving her boyfriend's phone number to an informant who wanted to pay him for some LSD. Even though she cooperated with the DEA, she was charged with conspiracy to distribute LSD. Her boyfriend, the drug dealer, had incriminating information about others to give the prosecutors. He received a five-year sentence as a reward for his cooperation. Nicole had no one to finger, so she bore the brunt of the government's case and at the age of 18 was sentenced to ten years in federal prison without parole. Nicole's judge did not want to sentence her to such a long prison term, and when the jury foreman later found out the sentence Nicole received, he said, "If I had known she would receive a mandatory 10-year prison sentence, we would still be sitting in that jury room today."

At that same 1993 subcommittee hearing, Judge Vincent Broderick, then chair of the Criminal Law Committee of the Judicial Conference of the United States, testified that Nicole's case was not an isolated horror story. Rather, Judge Broderick said, "I respectfully submit that the mandatory minimum system in place is itself the 'horror story'. ... [and] ...that mandatory minimums are the major obstacle to the development of a fair, rational, honest, and proportional federal criminal justice sentencing system."

The upshot of that hearing was the passage the following year of the "safety-valve," which allows the courts to sentence below the mandatory minimum for a narrow band of drug defendants. The safety valve was a great first step, but it did not go far enough. Since 1995, over 200,000 people have received mandatory prison sentences of five or ten years. That's an enormous number of families devastated by one-size-fits-all sentences.

Now is the time to take the next step. This hearing sets us on that path.

We are here today in part, because of the mandatory minimum sentences imposed on border agents Ignacio Ramos and Jose Alonso Compean. Their sentences angered many Americans who saw the agents as heroes and who feared their convictions and long sentences might have a chilling effect on those who work on the border or other front lines of law enforcement.

Whatever your thoughts about the border agents' case, those of us who have been fighting against mandatory sentencing for years would caution Members of this Committee and Congress against seeing it as an anomaly. In reality, it is just one more of the all-too-common failures of one-size-fits-all sentencing.

Consider the following facts: First, you had a prosecutor following the instructions of his superiors – in this case, Attorney General Ashcroft's memo of 2003, ordering all federal prosecutors to bring "the most serious readily provable chargeable offense" and to oppose downward departures at sentencing. Second, a jury of peers delivered guilty verdicts. Finally, you had a sentencing judge whose discretion was extinguished by a mandatory sentencing law passed by Congress.

Mr. Chairman, this happens every day in federal court rooms all across this country.

Consider the case of Michael Mahoney. In 1979, when he was 24 years old, Michael was living in Texas, using methamphetamine and selling small amounts to support his habit. Within a one-month period, he made three sales totaling less than $300 dollars to an undercover officer and was arrested. He pled guilty and was convicted of three felonies and served almost two years in jail in Texas. When he got out, he moved home to Tennessee and turned his life around. He opened a successful local restaurant and pool hall, paid taxes, employed people, and was a productive member of society for more than a decade. One day, Michael decided to purchase a gun from a pawn shop to protect himself when he made deposits after closing. The pawn shop owner, who said he was also an attorney, told Michael it was okay to own a gun because his convictions were more than ten years old. Michael thought this made sense because he had been allowed to get a liquor license after a ten-year waiting period.

Sometime later, Michael's gun was stolen. Concerned that it might be used to commit a crime, he reported the theft to authorities. He returned to the pawn shop and bought another gun. In a routine check of the pawnshop's records, the Bureau of Alcohol, Tobacco, and Firearms, discovered the sale and arrested Michael as a felon in possession of a firearm. Michael was found guilty of the "crime" and federal prosecutors decided to count the three 14 year-old drug sales as separate convictions at Michael's sentencing in 1994. This decision meant the difference between a five-year and 15-year mandatory minimum. Rather than receiving a sentence designed for a simple felon in possession of a firearm, he received a sentence intended for hardened career criminals.

Michael's judge was a Reagan appointee with a reputation for being extremely tough on crime. But, at sentencing, he said, "...it seems to me this sentence is just completely out of proportion to the defendant's conduct in this case. ... [I]t just seems to me this is not what Congress had in mind." At the end of the day, however, he had no choice. He handed down the 15-year sentence required by law. Seven years into his 15-year sentence, Michael died in prison.

The judge who sentenced Jesus Esparza, expressed similar frustration when sentencing Jesus to 10 years in prison. Jesus, who had served his country honorably in the armed forces, accompanied a friend from Michigan to Seattle, where his friend picked up one kilogram of cocaine. On the return trip, they were stopped in Wyoming by state troopers. The troopers found the cocaine and a loaded handgun under the friend's seat. Jesus pled guilty and accepted responsibility for his role in the offense. The sentencing guidelines called for a sentence of 46-5 7 months. But the mandatory minimum statutes required the judge to sentence Jesus to five years for the cocaine and another five years for the gun.

The judge said, "When it comes to mandatory minimums, the powers of the Court.. .and the consideration of underlying facts ... pretty much flies out the window. [The Court] could have considered... your role in that offense as a person who essentially went along to help drive [your codefendant] as a favor to him... and measure the seriousness of your conduct as compared to that of [your codefendant], who brought the gun."

I believe as fervently as I did 15 years ago when I testified from this table that you should use your power to repeal mandatory minimum sentences. I do not want to be sitting at this same table 15 or 16 years from now asking for the same sentencing reforms I urged back then and again, today. After two decades of experimenting with mandatory minimum sentencing policies, the verdict is in: mandatory minimums are a failure. They are a failure today, just as they were in 1970 when a bipartisan Congress voted to repeal the Bogg's Act, which required mandatory minimum sentences for drug offenses. That repeal is the focus of a FAMM report, *Correcting Course,* which urges that we learn from history and repeal mandatory minimums once more.[1]

The reasons that led Congress to repeal mandatory minimums nearly 40 years ago are the same reasons Congress should abolish them today. By any standard, including their proponents' stated goals, the mandatory minimums enacted in the 1980s have failed. Specifically:

- *They have not discouraged drug use or abuse.* Drug use rates had already declined before Congress passed the 1986 and 1988 anti-drug laws. Between 1985 and 1988, drug use within the past 30 days declined from 12.1 percent to 7.7 percent[2]. As of 2007, drug use rates within the past 30 days had increased to 8.3 percent[3].
- *They have stripped courts of cost-effective, recidivism-reducing sentencing options like drug courts.* According to the Bureau of Justice Statistics, one-third of all federal drug offenders said they were using drugs at the time of arrest[4] and almost 80 percent of federal offenders admit to having used drugs at some time.[5] Unfortunately, according to BJS, less than 15 percent of federal offenders with drug problems receive treatment while in prison.[6]
- *They have failed to reduce drug trafficking.* Despite 50 years of experimenting with mandatory minimums, supporters cannot point to a single study that conclusively demonstrates any positive impact of mandatory minimum sentences on drug trafficking rates.
- *They are responsible for a prison population explosion.* The federal prison population has increased nearly five-fold since mandatory minimums were enacted in the mid-80s and mandatory guidelines became law.[7] The major cause is the increase in sentence length for drug trafficking from 23 months[8] before mandatory minimums to 83.2 months in 2008.[9] About 75 percent of the increase was due to mandatory minimums and 25 percent due to guideline increases above mandatory minimums.[10]
- *Their failure comes with billion-dollar direct costs.* Expanded use of prison sentences for drug crimes and longer sentences required by mandatory minimums have caused a dramatic increase in state and federal corrections costs. State corrections spending jumped from $6 billion in 1982 to over $50 billion in 2008.[11]
- *They impose substantial indirect costs.* Not only do longer prison sentences make it more difficult for prisoners to re-enter society successfully, but they also put a heavy burden on families and children who must live without a spouse or parent while that person is incarcerated.
- *They are not applied evenly.* In practice, mandatory minimum sentences have not been applied equally when viewed by race of the defendant. Further, two equally culpable defendants can receive vastly different sentences based on the value of the information they have to share with prosecutors.

In all of these ways, mandatory minimums have failed to perform as advertised. And, yet, I can't help but think that even if they were effective to some degree they would still be objectionable. Mandatory sentences offend a bedrock principle of justice best articulated in the federal sentencing statute. The core congressional command in the Sentencing Reform Act of 1984 directs courts to impose a sentence "sufficient, but not greater than necessary to comply" with the purposes of punishment.[12] This principle of parsimony has deep roots in American soil and in our sense of fundamental fairness. The law directs judges to exercise reasoned discretion, taking into account considerations such as the need to avoid unwarranted disparity, the history and characteristics of the defendant, and the seriousness of the offense, and then fashion a sentence for the particular individual who stands convicted. [13] Mandatory minimums prohibit courts from complying with that mandate.

Moreover, mandatory minimums challenge basic structures on which our government is founded. Federal mandatory minimum laws upset federalism by turning many heretofore state drug offenses into federal crimes. In addition, state and federal mandatory sentencing laws distort traditional roles by transferring judicial discretion to legislatures as well as prosecutors, who, by choice of charge, exercise undue and unreviewable influence over sentencing.

All of these problems have caused many former prosecutors, judges, and legal commentators to speak out against mandatory minimums. A report by the non-partisan Federal Judicial Center concluded with this statement about mandatory sentencing laws: "As instruments of public policy [mandatory minimums] do little good and much harm."[14] Today, mandatory minimum repeal enjoys widespread support from leaders in the criminal justice community. The Judicial Conference of the United States,[15] the American Bar Association,[16] the United States Sentencing Commission,[17] and the United States Conference of Mayors[18] are among those who oppose mandatory minimum sentencing.

President Obama also has spoken of the need for reform. Noting that his predecessor, former President George W. Bush, expressed skepticism about imposing long sentences for first- time drug offenders, then-candidate Obama said, "I agree with the President. The difference is, he hasn't done anything about it. When I'm President, I will. We will review these sentences to see where we can be smarter on crime and reduce the blind and counterproductive warehousing of non-violent offenders."

Attorney General Eric Holder seems to be making good on President Obama's commitment to sentencing policy review. At a recent sentencing symposium, Mr. Holder said that "[t]he desire to have an almost mechanical system of sentencing has led us away from individualized, fact-based determinations that I believe, within reason, should be our goal."

Last, but certainly not least, the American people support mandatory minimum reform. A 2008 poll found that fully 78 percent of Americans agree that courts, not Congress, should determine an individual's sentence, and 59 percent oppose mandatory minimums for nonviolent offenders.[19]

It's past time to put an end to mandatory minimums.

We are grateful to Chairman Scott for introducing legislation to enable courts to exercise discretion when the mandatory minimum is greater than necessary to comply with the purposes of punishment. We thank Congresswoman Waters for her bill that would eliminate all drug mandatory minimums and Mr. Poe for his that would eliminate mandatory minimums in certain cases. We look forward to working with all of you to eliminate one-size-fits-all sentencing laws.

End Notes

1 Families Against Mandatory Minimums, Correcting Course: Lessons From The 1970 Repeal Of Mandatory Minimums, *available at* http://www.famm.org/Repository/Files/8189_FAMM_BoggsAct_final.pdf (last visited July 13, 2009).

2 OFFICE OF NATIONAL DRUG POLICY, DRUG USE TRENDS (October 2002).

3 SUBSTANCE ABUSE AND MENTAL HEALTH SERVICES ADMINISTRATION, OFFICE OF APPLIED STUDIES (2008). Results from the 2007 National survey on Drug Use and HEalth: National findings (nsduh Series H34, DHHS Publication No. SMA 08-4343). Rockville, MD.

4 Bureau of Justice Statistics, Drug Use and Dependence, State and Federal Prisoners, 2004, at 5, *available at* http://www.ojp.usdoj.gov/bjs/pub/pdf/dudsfp04.pdf (last visited July 13, 2009).

[5] Id. at 2.

[6] *Id.* at 9.

[7] U.S. bureau of prisons, a brief history of the bureau of prisons, *available at* http://www.bop.gov/about/history.jsp (last visited July 10, 2009).

[8] United States Sentencing Commission, Fifteen Years of Guidelines Sentencing (Nov. 2004), at 48, *available at* http://www.ussc.gov/15_year/15year.htm (last visited July 13, 2009) [hereinafter Fifteen Year Review]; United States Sentencing Commission, Supplementary Report on the Initial Guidelines and Policy Statements (June 18, 1987), at 69-70.

[9] United States Sentencing Commission, 2008 Sourcebook of Federal Sentencing Statistics (2008), at Table 14, *available at* http://www.ussc.gov/ANNRPT/2008/SBTOC08.htm (last visited July 13, 2009)..

[10] Fifteen Year Review, at 54

[11] Pew Center on the States, One In 31: The Long Reach of the American Corrections 11 (Mar. 2009), *available at* http://www.pewcenteronthestates.org/uploadedFiles/PSPP_1in31_report_FINAL_WEB_3-26-09.pdf (last visited June 10, 2009).

[12] 18 U.S.C. § 3553(a) (2008).

[13] The list of sentencing considerations and the parsimony mandate are found in the sentencing statute at 18 U.S.C. § 3553(a)(1)-(7) (2008).

[14] Barbara S. Vincent & Paul Hofer, *The Consequences of Mandatory Minimum Prison Terms,* Federal Judicial Center (1994), at 32 (quoting Michael Tonry, ed., *Mandatory Penalties*, in 16 Crime & Justice: A REVIEW OF RESEARCH 243-44 (1990))

[15] *See, e.g.,* Judicial Conference of the United States, Report of the Proceedings of the Judicial Conference of the United States 16 (Mar. 13, 1990) (voting in favor of urging Congress to reconsider the wisdom of mandatory minimum sentences), *available at* http://www.uscourts.gov/judconf/90-Mar.pdf (last visited Nov. 5, 2008); *see also* Testimony of Honorable Paul Cassell before the House Judiciary Committee Subcommittee on Crime, Terrorism and Homeland Security (June 26, 2007), *available at* http://judiciary (last visited Nov. 5, 2008).

[16] *See* American Bar Association, Report # 121-A (Aug. 9-10, 2004), *available at* http://www.abanet.org/leadership (last visited Nov. 5, 2008).

[17] *See* U.S. Sentencing Commission, Special Report To The Congress: Mandatory Minimum Penalties In The Federal Criminal Justice System 25-33 (Aug. 1991) (describing how mandatory minimums undermine the purpose and goals of the federal sentencing guidelines, and concluding that "the intended purposes of mandatory minimums can be equally or better served by guidelines, without compromising the crime control goals to which Congress has evidenced its commitment."), *available at* http://www.ussc.gov/r_congress (last visited Nov. 5 2008).

[18] U.S. CONFERENCE OF MAYORS, 74TH ANNUAL MEETING ADOPTED RESOLUTIONS 47-48 (June 2-6, 2006), available at http://usmayors.org/resolutions/74th_conference (last visited Nov. 5, 2008).

[19] Families Against Mandatory Minimums/Strategy One poll on mandatory minimums (Aug. 2008), *available at* http://www.famm.org/Repository/Files/FAMM%20poll%20no%20embargo.pdf (last visited July 13, 2009).

In: An Examination of Sentencing Levels and Mandatory… ISBN: 978-1-61209-563-9
Editor: Catherine N. Bates

Chapter 9

STATEMENT OF MICHAEL J. SULLIVAN, PARTNER, ASHCROFT SULLIVAN, LLC, BEFORE THE SUBCOMMITTEE ON CRIME, TERRORISM AND HOMELAND SECURITY, HEARING ON "MANDATORY MINIMUMS AND UNINTENDED CONSEQUENCES"

Chairman Scott, Ranking Member Gohmert, and Members of the Committee, thank you for the opportunity to appear before you to discuss mandatory minimum sentencing policy.

Since the early days of our nation, Congress has recognized its important and legitimate role in the formulation of appropriate criminal sentences, and has prudently exercised this responsibility in setting fair and effective sentences, including minimum mandatory sentences, for certain serious offenses and/or offenders.

History has shown great leadership and foresight by legislative bodies at both the federal and state levels in understanding the important value of mandatory (minimum) sentences, as both a deterrent for potential offenders and a safety net against unbridled judicial sentencing discretion. This insight dates back to 1790 and is shown throughout the 19th and 20th centuries[1] and includes crimes such as murder, carjacking resulting in death, aggravated sexual assault, gun and drug dealing offenses, reentry after deportation, manufacturing and distribution of child pornography and national security type offenses. Throughout our history there are scores of examples of Congress proposing and enacting mandatory (minimum) sentences to address public safety and public policy concerns.

Mandatory minimum sentencing was first introduced as a comprehensive scheme at the federal level in 1984 with the creation of the United States Sentencing Commission. The principal, though not exclusive, purpose of the passage of the legislation creating the United States Sentencing Commission was to provide greater consistency and uniformity in federal sentencing.[2] Prior to the establishment of the United States Sentencing Commission and the development of a body of sentencing factors, oftentimes it was difficult to reconcile sentences from jurisdiction to jurisdiction or between similar conduct by defendants with comparable criminal histories. The goal beyond this important goal of uniformity in sentencing was to have a sentencing system that provided an appropriate punishment, helped to send the right deterrent message, ultimately leading to a reduction of crime and working toward improving a suspicious public's confidence in our criminal justice system. History has shown that the goals of uniformity, appropriate punishment, deterrence and building public confidence were achieved.

Congress' interest and commitment to fair and effective sentencing as an important public policy didn't stop with the passage and establishment of the United States Sentencing Commission. Congress recognized the important correlation between crime and punishment, the danger of drug dealers being armed, and the growing criminal use of guns as part of the drug dealing trade and passed the Comprehensive Crime Control Act of 1984. The Act established certain minimum sentences for using a firearm during the commission of drug trafficking offenses.[3] As part of that comprehensive legislation, Congress also drew a line in the sand around schools and playgrounds and said clearly, especially don't sell drugs there! President Ronald Reagan said in 1984 "That legislation . . . is the most comprehensive revision of federal criminal statutes to be enacted in many years."

Congress demonstrated its continued commitment to positively impacting public safety through crime reduction and greater uniformity in sentencing by enacting the Anti-Drug Abuse Acts of 1986[4] and 1988.[5] These effective, crime-reducing laws were enacted during a Democratic-controlled Congress and received strong bipartisan support.[6] This strong bipartisan support reflected the public's expectation that Congress should continue to pass laws that have certainty in consequences for those that fail to comply.

Congress was not finished with its work and support of mandatory minimums and passed other laws with mandatory minimums, including provisions of the 1990 Crime Control Act, which provided a 10-year mandatory sentence for organizing, managing, or supervising a continuing financial crimes enterprise.[7]

The mandatory minimum sentencing scheme for drug crimes oftentimes receives attention, scrutiny, and some criticism. This may be due to the victimization these crimes have on law abiding citizens, families, neighborhoods, and our health care systems together with the violence that is part of the drug dealing business.[8] However, many other crimes and criminal histories appropriately trigger minimum sentences at the federal and state levels. For example, we can look at certain gun violations, crimes against children, violent sexual offenses, civil rights violations, and even certain financial crimes and find that Congress and many state legislatures have had the wisdom to and are willing to shape public policy and sentencing outcomes with the enactment of mandatory minimum sentences.

The 108th Congress alone enacted "a flurry of new or enhanced mandatory minimum sentencing provisions." These included, the PROTECT Act ("Amber Alert"), the Unborn Victims of Violence Act, the Identity Theft Penalty Enforcement Act, the Intelligence Reform and Terrorism Prevention Act, the Anti-Terrorism and Port Security Act of 2003.[9]

The point is quite simple: mandatory minimums are an important legislative tool to clearly communicate to the American people the value that Congress puts on crime prevention, reduction of victimization and appropriate punishment. So there we have it, Congress has always played an important part, both substantively and as a leadership body, in a national crime and victimization reduction effort with remarkable results. The branch of government closest to the people they serve must continue to play this important public safety role. Many people closest to the criminal justice system – police, prosecutors, victims, community groups – recognize that the leadership of Congress in this area is as important today as any time in our nation's history. And, in light of the recent decisions by the United

States Supreme Court, beginning with *United States v. Booker*[10] and the cases that have followed *Booker* that have increased the opportunity for sentencing disparity, Congress' role is even more important.

The question that needs to be asked and answered is "Has the role that Congress played in sentencing, including the passage of mandatory minimum sentences, had an impact on public safety and crime?" The answer to that question can easily be found in crime statistics and is buttressed by anecdotal story after story from across our nation. Crime rates over the past 30 years certainly paint a picture of continuing success of reducing crime and victimization through sound public policy. As these numbers show, our nation has experienced a substantial reduction in violent crime over the past 30 years. This achievement was not by accident, but by design. The formula for success was to ensure an appropriate punishment at the federal level for serious criminal offenders. This strategy once showing success has been replicated across our nation by state legislatures. In addition, one only has to listen to their constituents to learn about parks and playgrounds reclaimed, young children being able to walk to school without fear, and law abiding citizens being able to exercise their God given right to peaceful enjoyment of their home and their neighborhood.

Let's look at the crime statistics, comparing where we were back in the early and mid-1980s that captured the nation and called upon Congress to do something, to the reduced crime levels of today that are a product of Congress' tough-on-crime sentencing policies since 1984.

- According to the Department of Justice, the proportion of drug defendants sentenced to a term of imprisonment increased from 72% in 1984 to 89% in 1999; nearly 2/3 of those sentenced were subject to a statutory minimum prison term [11]
- Though the number of drug offenders incarcerated has greatly increased, a 2007 FBI CIUS report shows the violent crime rate in America has greatly declined. The violent crime rate (per 100,000 inhabitants) was down 173.7 in 2007 compared to 1988. The year of lowest violent crime rate was 2004 with 463.2, followed by 2007 with 466.9. The highest was 1991 with 758.2. [12]
- the proportion of the sentence that drug offenders entering federal prison could expect to serve increased from 48% to 87%[13]. Mandatory minimum sentences are keeping serious offenders off our streets longer, keeping our communities safer.

In addition to these important goals being achieved -- uniformity in sentencing, certain offenses carrying certainty in punishment, and repeat violent offenders receiving enhanced punishment -- there has also been a collateral benefit of mandatory minimums. This collateral benefit deals with cooperation by the lower level offenders, providing critically important information to investigators and prosecutors that enhance investigations, identify more culpable and, in many instances, higher level players in the criminal organization. Mandatory minimums have allowed the government to make a case against the highest ranking members of national and international criminal organizations, from organized crime figures, to major drug traffickers, to those that manufacture child pornography. Nothing provides an incentive to cooperate with the government like the risk of a long mandatory sentence.

These hanging dark clouds of long prison sentences encourage offenders to help law enforcement to work their way up the criminal organization. Investigators and prosecutors across the country rely on the tools provided by Congress and state legislative bodies to open investigative windows into the organization and people of elaborate crime rings. Without the negotiation tool of mandatory minimum sentences, this crucial cooperation of lower level offenders might be impossible, and such access to the inside of the upper levels of the criminal organizations might be unattainable. This is particularly true as government prosecutors make cases against some of the most prolific, seemingly untouchable and very violent drug trafficking organizations. The heads of these organizations attempt to distance themselves from people and from the drugs. The mid-level offenders who often carry the large quantities of illicit drugs quickly see the value of cooperation in giving prosecutors information when facing long prison sentences. Statistics show that at the federal level, and I suspect at the state level as well, that more cooperation is provided to the government in drug investigations than any other type of crime.[14] Speaking from my personal experience as a former federal prosecutor, repealing mandatory minimums would make it much more challenging than it already is to target the leadership of these organizations by taking away the incentive to cooperate. The American public would suffer the harm of elevated crime rates in exchange for relaxed sentencing policies for serious criminals. [15]

Congress has heard of the myths associated with mandatory minimum sentences, such as the unfairness of the sentence and that our prisons are filled with users and low level first time offenders. That information is simply not true. Several years ago, there was an effort by Families Against Mandatory Minimums and a handful of judges who wanted complete authority over sentencing to repeal all the minimum mandatory drug trafficking sentences in Massachusetts. They made the same arguments as above. However, an examination of the Massachusetts State prison population revealed that those being sent to the state prison for drug trafficking offenses were not first time, low level offenders. They had long criminal records (over thirty arraignments and over twenty adjudications and guilty findings). The criminal record of those being sent to the state prison in Massachusetts for drug offenses looked very similar to those being sent to prison for other violent offenses; they both had long criminal records and had victimized scores of people and their communities.

The federal story is similar in that though our federal prison population has grown over the last 30 years, very few are there as first offenders and only for drug related crimes. These convicted drug offenders are not the street corner dealers, but serious players in the intricate drug dealing operations that threaten our communities, trafficking substantial amounts of illicit drugs and contributing significantly to the violent crime rates in our country. In order to qualify for a federal mandatory minimum sentence of 5 years, a first-time offender must be in possession of a minimum of 500 grams of cocaine,[16] which is the equivalent of 2,500 to 5,000 doses and an estimated street value of between $32,500 and $50,000 dollars.

- According to a 2001 study by the U.S. Department of Justice, in 1999, 62% of convicted drug defendants had committed a drug offense so serious they were subject to a statutory minimum prison term: 29% 60 months or less; 30% 61 to 120 months; 3% 121 months or more (including life). [17]
- According to 2008 U.S. Sentencing Commission data on prisoners under mandatory minimum sentences:
  - 6,905 (27.3%) drug offenders received mandatory minimums for 5-years; 9,882 (39.0%) received for 10-years; total = 16,787 [18]

- 10,359 (43.1%) drug offenders received mandatory minimum with no safety valve: 5,764 received mandatory minimum but safety valve (24.0%)[19]

Incarceration under a mandatory minimum sentence is infrequent for simple possession, accounting for approximately 2% – less than 800 – of all suspects merely investigated by U.S. prosecutors in 1999.[20] According to the testimony of Ricardo H. Hinojosa, Acting Chair of the U.S. Sentencing Commission, before the Subcommittee on May 21, 2009:

- In FY 2008, there were 105 federal cases for simple possession of crack cocaine, in which 58 offenders were subject to the statutory mandatory minimum penalty. 14.3% of crack cocaine offenders received the benefit of a safety valve provision compared to 43% of powder cocaine offenders[21]
- In FY 2007, there were 109 such cases, in which 49 offenders were subject to the statutory mandatory minimum penalty[22]

Consider a 1997 Bureau of Justice Statistics survey of federal prison inmates that shows how many drug offenders reported they had a substantial role in the drug conspiracy for which they were convicted. Of those incarcerated drug offenders,

- 16% reported they were either an importer or manufacturer of illicit drugs; and
- 25% reported they were responsible for distributing drugs to street-level drug dealers (total = 41%)[23]

The "safety valve"[24] implemented by Congress provides additional protection for first-time defendants without prior criminal history, who don't use the threat of violence in committing their drug offense, and who aren't the highly culpable offenders the mandatory minimum sentencing policy aims to target.

In closing, let me state that Congress should continue to examine our sentencing scheme. You should find opportunities to improve public safety through punishment and deterrence and you should be willing, especially in this post-*Booker* world, use minimum mandatory sentencing to accomplish the laudable goals that a Congress before you set out to achieve. Mr. Chairman, Ranking Member Gohmert, and Members of the Committee, thank you again for holding this very important hearing and allowing me to comment on the effectiveness of mandatory minimum sentencing. I will be glad to answer any question you may have.

End Notes

[1] United States Sentencing Commission, 1991 *Special Report to the Congress: Mandatory Minimum Penalties in the Federal Justice System* (as directed by section 1706 of Pub. L. 101-647) at 6-7 (hereinafter "US SC 1991 Report").
[2] *Id.* at 14-15.
[3] Pub. L. 98-473, 98 Stat. 1976 (1984).
[4] Pub. L. 99-570, 100 Stat. 3207 (1986).
[5] Pub L. 100-690, 102 Stat. 4181 (1988).
[6] The Anti-Drug Abuse Act of 1986 had strong bipartisan support: 207 Democratic and 94 Republican House co-sponsors of H.R.5484, and 15 Democratic and 14 Republican Senate co-sponsors of S.2878.
[7] Pub..L. 101-647, 104 Stat. 4789 (1990).

[8] Drug offenders charged with another offense were most often charged in tandem with a firearm offense (57% of offenders charged with a drug crime were charged in tandem with a firearm offense. Scalia, John. (2001). Office of Justice Programs, Bureau of Justice Statistics *Special Report: Federal Drug Offenders, 1999, with trends: 1984- 1999* (NCJ 187285) (hereinafter "BJS August 2001 Report"). Washington, DC: U.S. Department of Justice. Retrieved from Bureau of Justice Statistics reports online via DOJ access: http://www.ojp.usdoj.gov/bjs/pub/pdf/fdo99.pdf

[9] U.S. Congressional Research Service. Federal *Mandatory Minimum Sentencing Statutes: Legislative Proposals in the 108th Congress* (RS21 597; Dec. 17, 2004), by Charles Doyle.

[10] *United States v. Booker*, 125 S. Ct. 738 (2005).

[11] BJS August 2001 Report.

[12] *See* Table 1 of the Federal Bureau of Investigation, *Crime in the United States: 2007* (Sept. 2008). Washington, DC: U.S. Department of Justice. Available at: http://www.fbi.gov/ucr/cius2007/data/table_01.html; Retrieved: 07/09/2009.

[13] BJS August 2001 Report.

[14] According to the U.S. Department of Justice, 28% of convicted drug defendants received a reduced sentence for providing substantial assistance to prosecutors. BJS August 2001 Report.

[15] *See* David Risley, *Mandatory Minimum Sentences: an Overview.* (May 2000) (discussing desensitization of judges and resulting trends of sentencing leniency in areas of high drug crime concentration). Available at: http://www.drugwatch.org/Mandatory%20Minimum%20Sentences.htm; Retrieved: 07/09/2009.

[16] *See* U.S. Drug Enforcement Agency: *Federal Trafficking Penalties*. Available at: http://www.usdoj.gov/dea/agency/penalties Retrieved: 07/09/2009.

[17] BJS August 2001 Report.

[18] *See* Table 43 of the U.S. Sentencing Commission Datafile FY 2008 USSCFY08.

[19] *See* Table 44 of the U.S. Sentencing Commission Datafile FY 2008. USSCFY08.

[20] BJS August 2001 Report, at 3. *See* Table 2, *Drug suspects evaluated for prosecution by U.S. Attorneys, by statutory offense and drug type, 1999.*

[21] Hinojosa, Ricardo H. Statement to the House, Committee on the Judiciary. Subcommittee on Crime, Terrorism, and Homeland Security. *Unfairness in Federal Cocaine Sentencing: Is it time to Crack the 100 to 1 Disparity?,* Hearing, May 21, 2009. Available at: http://www.ussc.gov/testimony/Hinojosa_HouseTestimony_20090521.pdf; Accessed: 07/09/09.

[22] *Id.*

[23] BJS August 2001 Report, at 11.

[24] *See*, 18 U.S.C. § 3553(f).

In: An Examination of Sentencing Levels and Mandatory... ISBN: 978-1-61209-563-9
Editor: Catherine N. Bates

Chapter 10

STATEMENT OF NATIONAL BORDER PATROL COUNCIL OF THE AMERICAN FEDERATION OF GOVERNMENT EMPLOYEES AFL-CIO, BEFORE THE SUBCOMMITTEE ON CRIME, TERRORISM AND HOMELAND SECURITY, HEARING ON "MANDATORY MINIMUMS AND UNINTENDED CONSEQUENCES"

T. J. Bonner

The National Border Patrol Council appreciates the opportunity to share the views and concerns of the 17,000 front-line Border Patrol employees it represents regarding the unintended consequences of mandatory minimum sentences applied to law enforcement officers in the performance of their duties. Perhaps no case in recent memory demonstrates the need for reforming certain aspects of those laws than the unwarranted prosecution of Border Patrol Agents Ignacio Ramos and Jose Alonso Compean. That case raises a number of serious questions and concerns about the fundamental fairness of our system of justice, as well as whether or not its checks and balances adequately protect against abuse by overzealous prosecutors. Although our judicial system is unquestionably one of the best that has ever been developed, it is by no means perfect. When inevitable mistakes occur, they must be quickly identified and remedied in order to foster and maintain public confidence.

Since it is obviously impossible to establish a foolproof system of justice, it is important to incorporate safeguards into the existing one. A welcome and necessary improvement is contained in the "Ramos and Compean Justice Act of 2009." This legislative proposal would allow judges to downwardly depart from mandatory minimum sentences when necessary to prevent unjust sentences. For example, law enforcement officers who are found guilty of using a firearm to commit a crime of violence related to their employment would no longer be subject to the mandatory minimum penalties contained in 18 U.S.C. § 924(c) for using or carrying a firearm during and in relation to any crime of violence. This comports with the 1989 holding of the Supreme Court that "[t]he 'reasonableness' of a particular use of force must be judged from the perspective of a reasonable officer on the scene, rather than with the 20/20 vision of hindsight."[1] It is highly unlikely that Congress intended that those provisions of the Gun Control Act be applied to law enforcement officers who are using firearms — the tools of their trade — while acting within the scope of their authority. It is important to recognize that this legislative proposal would not shield rogue officers from the full consequences of their illegal actions, but would properly presume that the overwhelming majority of our Nation's law enforcement officers carry out their duties honorably under extremely difficult circumstances, and must often make split-second decisions with incomplete information. Forcing judges who preside over cases involving those issues to mechanically apply minimum sentences can easily result in gross miscarriages of justice.

A careful examination of the facts of the Ramos and Compean case reveals that these two agents were falsely accused and wrongfully prosecuted. Although this hearing primarily focuses on the unintended consequences of mandatory minimum sentences, a basic understanding of that case provides insight into how this travesty occurred and how to prevent recurrences. Accordingly, a synopsis of the relevant facts of that case is set forth in the attached appendix.

Although Ignacio Ramos and Jose Alonso Compean were released from prison by President George W. Bush's fmal act of executive clemency, nothing can compensate them for the twenty-five months of their lives that were lost serving unwarranted sentences, nor can the harsh suffering of these men and their families ever be erased. Moreover, the stigma of those unjust felony convictions continues to follow them around, severely diminishing their employment opportunities and curtailing other basic rights and freedoms enjoyed by most Americans. The adverse consequences of that prosecution extend far beyond that, however, and still have a negative impact on morale within the Border Patrol and numerous other law enforcement organizations. Many of these law enforcement officers are left wondering if the same fate will befall them if they defend themselves against an armed criminal. This is untenable in an occupation where even a moment's hesitation can spell disaster.

In sharp contrast to the disbarment and prosecution of former Durham County, North Carolina District Attorney Michael Nifong for wrongfully prosecuting three Duke University lacrosse players, former U.S. Attorney Johnny Sutton and his subordinates have never been held accountable for their actions. Until that occurs, other Federal prosecutors will be emboldened to levy reckless charges against law enforcement officers in order to make a name for themselves and/or advance hidden political agendas. The far-reaching ramifications of the prosecution of Ignacio Ramos and Jose Alonso Compean, as well as the integrity of our system of justice, demand a full and impartial investigation by an independent counsel with subpoena and prosecutorial jurisdiction, and appropriate punishment for all of those who are found guilty of wrongdoing. Such actions are long overdue, and the National Border Patrol Council respectfully urges Congress to commence that process immediately.

APPENDIX: SYNOPSIS OF THE RAMOS AND COMPEAN CASE

Although some of the relevant facts in the case involving Agents Ramos and Compean are in dispute, one thing is clear: There were only three eyewitnesses to the shooting that occurred on the afternoon of February 17, 2005 in Fabens, Texas — Border Patrol Agents

Ignacio Ramos and Jose Alonso Compean, and Osvaldo Aldrete-Davila, a Mexican national who was transporting 743 pounds of marijuana into the United States. No one else who was near the scene of the shooting could have possibly seen what transpired, as their view was completely blocked by the levee access road, which is eleven feet higher than the ground on which they stood.

As one might expect, the version of events recounted by Agents Ramos and Compean differs dramatically from the story told by the drug smuggler. The Border Patrol agents maintain that they fired in self-defense because Osvaldo Aldrete-Davila was pointing a weapon at them, and he contends that he was simply trying to flee back to Mexico. Since the drug smuggler absconded across the international boundary, we will never know with absolute certainty whether or not he was armed. It is possible, however, to glean some important clues from the few pieces of physical evidence that were able to be examined. The bullet that struck Osvaldo Aldrete-Davila did not exit his body, and a large fragment lodged in his right thigh near the skin and was subsequently recovered. Moreover, the wound channel became infected and was still quite visible when he was attended to by a doctor on March 16, 2005, about a month after he was shot.

The March 18, 2005 affidavit of the Department of Homeland Security's Office of Inspector General in support of the criminal complaint against Agents Ramos and Compean stated that "[o]n or about March 16, 2005, Colonel Winston J. Warme, MD, Orthopedics, William Beaumont Army Medical Center removed a 40 caliber Smith & Wesson jacketed hollow point projectile from the upper thigh of the victim. Colonel Warme, MD, advised that the bullet entered the lower left buttocks of the victim and passed through his pelvic triangle and lodged in his right thigh." At the trial, when Colonel Warme was asked if the "bullet was fired directly into the back of the person who was shot, or was it fired at an angle through his body," he responded that Aldrete-Davila's "body was on angle to the bullet," and that "the bullet went in on an angle." He also stated that "if [the person who was shot] were turning, as [the prosecutor] demonstrated, [the shooter] would have to be right behind the person." In other words, at the moment that the bullet struck him, Osvaldo Aldrete-Davila was running straight away from the Border Patrol agents, and his torso was twisted back toward them.

This supports the agents' claim that as the drug smuggler was running away, he turned back and pointed a weapon at them. Logically, the only object that someone fleeing from law enforcement officers would turn around and point at them would be a firearm. Long-standing experience has shown that almost all smugglers carry weapons while transporting large quantities of drugs. With the street value of his load of marijuana exceeding a million dollars, Osvaldo Aldrete-Davila had a very large investment to protect, and was almost certainly armed that day.

In light of these facts, the only way to conclude that Agents Ramos and Compean should have been prosecuted is if the word of a known drug smuggler is given more credence than the sworn statements of two law enforcement officers, and also if the physical evidence as well as the laws of physics are ignored. In this case, that is precisely what happened. The public statements of the U.S. Attorney's Office for the Western District of Texas make it clear that these Border Patrol agents were prosecuted because the former U.S. Attorney believed that they shot an unarmed suspect who was running away, destroyed evidence, engaged in a cover-up, and filed false official reports.

In support of the contention that Osvaldo Aldrete-Davila was unarmed, former U.S. Attorney Johnny Sutton pointed to the fact that all of the Border Patrol agents at the scene of the incident, including Agents Ramos and Compean, testified that they did not see the drug smuggler brandish a weapon as he slid into or climbed out of the drainage ditch. This does not prove that he was unarmed. It does, however, explain why none of the agents shot at him at that time. Osvaldo AldreteDavila did not produce a weapon until after he was alone with Agent Compean on the other side of the levee road, out of view of the agents who remained north of the drainage ditch.

It is also important to dispel the ridiculous notion put forth by former U.S. Attorney Sutton that the drug smuggler tried to surrender, and that if Agent Compean had simply placed handcuffs on him at that point, the incident would have ended peacefully. A careful analysis of the facts reveals that nothing could be farther from the truth. Osvaldo Aldrete-Davila could have pulled his van over to the side of the road and given up at any point after the Border Patrol vehicles following him activated their emergency lights, but he chose to ignore them and speed away. He could have obeyed the agents' commands to stop after he exited his vehicle north of the drainage ditch, but he chose to keep running. He could have stopped at the bottom of the drainage ditch, but chose to charge up the other side at full speed toward Agent Compean. None of these actions are consistent with those of someone who is desirous of surrendering. Agent Compean had every reason to believe that Osvaldo Aldrete-Davila was attempting to assault him, and acted appropriately when he tried to push him back down into the drainage ditch.

The alleged destruction of evidence consisted of Agent Compean picking up some of the empty cartridges and tossing them into the drainage ditch a few yards from where they were fired. If he were truly intent on "destroying evidence," he would have taken the shell casings as far away as possible and disposed of them. Rather than a sinister effort to conceal something, it is far more likely that in a state of confusion induced by post-traumatic stress disorder, he reverted to his firearms training, where agents are required to pick up their empty cartridges at the shooting range and place them in nearby containers after firing their weapons.

According to former U.S. Attorney Johnny Sutton, the failure by Agents Ramos and Compean to report the discharge of their weapons was a "cover-up," as Border Patrol policy requires agents to orally report such actions within one hour of the incident. If the shooting were justified, he reasoned, the agents would not have hesitated to make the required report. Again, the truth is far less dramatic. Both agents believed that everyone at the scene knew that shots had been fired. In fact, the April 12, 2005 Memorandum of Activity prepared by the Office of Inspector General of the Department of Homeland Security corroborates this, stating that its investigation disclosed that all nine of the other Border Patrol agents "were at the location of the shooting incident, assisted in destroying evidence of the shooting, and/or knew/heard about the shooting." Significantly, none of these other employees were ever charged with any crimes for their actions or omissions on that day, and only three of them were accused of administrative violations, and that was not until nearly two years after the incident. The primary charges in those actions revolved around their alleged false statements to investigators and lack of candor during the investigation. It is important to note that the failure to report the discharge of a firearm is an administrative infraction that, by the agency's own rules, is only punishable by a "written reprimand to 5-day suspension." It is also curious that the highest-ranking supervisor at the scene of the incident not only escaped any form ofpunishment, but has since received several promotions.

Finally, the allegation that Agents Ramos and Compean filed false official reports is based upon the mistaken belief that they should have mentioned the discharge of their weapons in the written report concerning the seizure of marijuana. The Border Patrol's Firearms Policy specifically precludes that, however, requiring that all "supervisory personnel or INS investigating officers are aware that employees involved in a shooting incident shall *not* be required or allowed to submit a written statement of the circumstances surrounding the incident. All written statements regarding the incident shall be prepared by the local INS investigating officers and shall be based upon an interview of the INS employee." [Emphasis in original] The rationale for this prohibition is explained in one of the preceding sections of the policy, which mandates that all "supervisory or investigative officers involved in the local INS investigation of the shooting incident are aware that any information provided by any employee under threat of disciplinary action by the Service or through any other means of coercion cannot be used against such employee in any type of action other than administrative action(s) taken by the Service consistent with *Garrity v. New Jersey,* 385 U.S. 493 (1966)."

It bears emphasizing that in order to prosecute these two Border Patrol agents, the U.S. Attorney's Office granted a high-ranking member of the notorious Juarez drug cartel full transactional immunity against prosecution for transporting large quantities of illicit narcotics in exchange for his perjured testimony. This is unprecedented, and sends a terrible message to other law enforcement officers, as well as to law-abiding citizens.

On September 24, 2005, shortly before the trial of Agents Ramos and Compean was scheduled to begin, Border Patrol agents observed Osvaldo Aldrete-Davila drive a van to a location near the same area of border where the February 17, 2005 incident occurred. Several individuals crossed from Mexico into the United States and began loading marijuana into the van. When the agents approached, Aldrete-Davila and the others fled into Mexico. Agents seized the van and discovered 1,040 pounds of marijuana inside.

Less than a month later, on October 23, 2005, the Border Patrol and Drug Enforcement Administration seized another 753 pounds of marijuana belonging to Osvaldo Aldrete-Davila in a van parked in the back of a residence near the border. The house's primary occupant identified Osvaldo Aldrete-Davila by name and physical description, and also picked him out of a photo lineup. Moreover, his brother in Mexico identified Aldrete-Davila over the phone as "the person who was shot by Border Patrol agents about six months ago."

All of this information was brought to the attention of the U.S. Attorney's Office for the Western District of Texas, which vigorously argued that it should not be allowed into evidence during the trial against Agents Ramos and Compean. Amazingly, the Judge agreed to conceal that vital information from the jury. She also agreed with the U.S. Attorney's Office that the level of violence along the border between the United States and Mexico had no bearing on the state of mind of Agents Ramos and Compean on the day of the incident, and the jury was not allowed to hear evidence concerning that issue either. (On an average day, three assaults are perpetrated against Border Patrol agents.) Similarly, testimony raising serious questions about the integrity of the Border Patrol agent who initially reported the shooting to the Office of Inspector General was not allowed in open court, and remains sealed. This individual, who was has been a close friend of Osvaldo Aldrete-Davila since childhood, remains employed as a Border Patrol agent, has never been disciplined for associating with a known drug smuggler and failing to report it, and in fact was praised by the former U.S. Attorney for the Western District of Texas.

Although former U.S. Attorney Johnny Sutton stated that he believed that the penalty levied against Agents Ramos and Compean was too harsh for the crime, this position is the height of hypocrisy. Federal prosecutors have extraordinary discretion concerning which charges to file in any given case. In the prosecution of Border Patrol Agents Ramos and Compean, for example, former U.S. Attorney Sutton originally charged them with violations of 18 U. S.C. § 113(a)(1), "assault with intent to commit murder," which carries a maximum penalty of 20 years imprisonment; 18 U.S.C. § 113(a)(3), "assault with a dangerous weapon, with intent to do bodily harm," which carries a maximum penalty of 10 years imprisonment; and 18 U.S.C. § 113(a)(6), "assault resulting in serious bodily injury," which also carries a maximum penalty of 10 years imprisonment. None of these charges have any mandatory minimum sentence associated with them. As the trial approached, former U.S. Attorney Sutton added several more charges: one count apiece of violating 18 U.S.C. § 924(c)(1)(A)(iii), "discharge of a firearm in relation to a crime of violence," which carries a mandatory minimum sentence of 10 years imprisonment; one count apiece of violating 18 U.S.C. § 1512(c)(2), "tampering with an official proceeding," which carries a maximum sentence of 20 years imprisonment; and two additional counts of the same charge against Jose Alonso Compean, which each carry an additional maximum sentence of 20 years imprisonment.

This stands in sharp contrast to a case filed two years ago by former U.S. Attorney Sutton against an individual in Del Rio, Texas who fired a high-powered (.30-06) rifle at Federal, State, and local law enforcement officers on the evening of January 28, 2007. While being handcuffed, the suspect remarked that he only stopped firing because he ran out of ammunition. This person was only charged with violating 18 U.S.C. § 111, "assaulting, resisting, or impeding certain officers or employees." That statute provides for an enhanced penalty of no more than 20 years imprisonment if a deadly or dangerous weapon is used in the assault, but carries no mandatory minimum sentence.

More than two years after the aforementioned September and October 2005 incidents involving the smuggling of large quantities of marijuana into the United States by Osvaldo AldreteDavila, he was finally indicted and arrested for those crimes. He entered a guilty plea, and was sentenced to nine and one-half years in prison. Aldrete-Davila subsequently appealed that sentence, and the U.S. Courts of Appeals for the Fifth Circuit denied the appeal on June 29, 2009.

End Notes

[1]Graham v. Connor, 490 U.S. 386, 396 (1989).

In: An Examination of Sentencing Levels and Mandatory… ISBN: 978-1-61209-563-9
Editor: Catherine N. Bates

Chapter 11

STATEMENT OF GROVER G. NORQUIST, PRESIDENT, AMERICANS FOR TAX REFORM, BEFORE THE SUBCOMMITTEE ON CRIME, TERRORISM AND HOMELAND SECURITY, HEARING ON "MANDATORY MINIMUMS AND UNINTENDED CONSEQUENCES"

Mr. Chairman, my name is Grover Norquist and I am the President of Americans for Tax Reform. Thank you for inviting me to testify today on the subject of mandatory minimum sentences.

Americans for Tax Reform is dedicated to reducing the influence of government in our lives. The first and most important way that ATR works toward this end is by reducing the burden of taxation on all taxpayers, but for years ATR has also fought the creeping federal regulatory burden and otherwise sought to promote individuals' control of their own lives rather than government.

We tend to view each and every federal program skeptically. We want to know if its benefits are worth the cost both in terms of money - that is, the taxes that are necessary to subsidize the program - and in terms of freedom - that is, is this an activity that free people should be doing for themselves or is this something only the government can do?

Taking the second consideration first, I think maintaining public safety and order is a legitimate function of government. But while fighting crime might be a responsibility of the state, my skepticism about government action extends even to popular-sounding anti- crime initiatives. I think it goes without saying that the Justice Department is no less interested in accumulating power than are the IRS, EPA or FDA. As a result, I don't think every law purportedly designed to protect us from terrorists or homegrown criminals is justifiable. Indeed, I have spoken out in the past against major provisions of the Patriot Act and against the use of secret evidence.

Against this backdrop, I would like to share my thoughts on mandatory minimum sentencing laws. I recognize that these laws might not constitute a government program *per se*, but their use certainly constitutes government policy.

To begin with, their pedigree makes them highly suspect. As with so many other federal programs, mandatory minimums were hatched by the Left, later embraced by the Right, and have been maintained by a bipartisan majority.

The Left's support for mandatory minimums was well-intentioned if ill-conceived. Their goal was to eliminate disparities in sentencing and thereby make the criminal justice system fairer. The idea that one judge might give two drug traffickers completely different sentences was questionable on its face. But what made it intolerable was that the disparity too often seemed to be a product of the color of the defendant's face. The Left's answer was to eliminate judicial discretion and force all judges to give the same sentence.

Conservatives later saw virtue in mandatory minimums not only as a tool for stopping a few errant liberal judges from handing down light sentences, but as a means to increase sentences across the board. Thus, the minimums established by Congress- especially in the 1980s during the height of the crack cocaine scare - were not really minimums at all, but rather uniformly tough sentences.

We should know by now to beware of easy solutions. As H.L. Mencken said, "There is always an easy solution to every human problem – neat, plausible, and wrong." Today, a generation later, it is increasingly clear that adoption of mandatory minimums, while a neat and plausible response to sentencing disparities, was the wrong solution.

First, the discretion exercised by judges was not extinguished but simply transferred to prosecutors. Prosecutors now have control over sentencing through their charging decisions. Unsurprisingly, politically-appointed and elected prosecutors are no less foolproof than judges. Both sides of the political aisle can point to examples of abuse in prosecutorial discretion, including, most recently, the decision to seek lengthy prison sentences for the Texas border agents. President Bush fixed that error before he left office by granting commutations to both men, but it would be preferable to have judges with the authority to review and check prosecutorial decisions.

The biggest problem from the perspective of the taxpayer, however, is that mandatory minimum sentencing policies have proven prohibitively expensive. In 2008, American taxpayers spent over $5.4 billion on federal prisons[1], a 925 percent increase since 1982.[2] This explosion in costs is driven by the expanded use of prison sentences for drug crimes and longer sentences required by mandatory minimums. Drug offenders are the largest category of offenders entering federal prisons each year. One third of all individuals sentenced in federal courts each year are drug offenders. And these convicts are getting long sentences. In 2008, more than two-thirds of all drug offenders receive a mandatory minimum sentence, with most receiving a ten-year minimum.

The jump in corrections costs at the state level has been equally dramatic. State corrections spending has ballooned from $6 billion in 1982 to over $50 billion in 2008. These skyrocketing costs are hitting states at a time when they are already being forced to cut back due to the bad economy.

The benefits, if any, of mandatory minimum sentences do not justify this burden to taxpayers. Illegal drug use rates are relatively stable, not shrinking. It appears that mandatory minimums have become a sort of poor man's Prohibition: a grossly simplistic and ineffectual government response to a problem that has been around longer than our government itself.

Yet all is not lost. Center-right governors like Rick Perry of Texas are trying new approaches. A couple of years ago, Texas started sending low-level, first-time felony drug users to mandatory drug treatment rather than prison. Before Governor Perry, it was

Republican Governor – John Engler of Michigan – who signed into law the first major repeal of state mandatory minimum sentences. Engler's action saved Michigan taxpayers $40 million in prison costs without jeopardizing public safety.

In closing, I want to note that questioning the wisdom of mandatory minimums has nothing to do with being soft on crime. I believe in strong and swift punishment when appropriate. I support the death penalty for murderers. But the government has a responsibility to use taxpayer money wisely. Viewed through the skeptical eye I train on all other government programs, I have concluded that mandatory minimum sentencing policies are not worth the high cost to America's taxpayers.

End Notes

[1] U.S. Dep't of Justice, FY 2009 Budget and Performance Summary, Federal Prison System, available at http://www.usdoj.gov/jmd/2009summary/html/127_bop.htm (last visited June 8, 2009).

[2] Bureau of Justice Statistics, U.S. Dep't of Justice, Justice Expenditure and Employment in the United States, 2003 (Apr. 2006), at 3, available at http://www.ojp.usdoj.gov/bjs/pub/pdf/jeeus03.pdf (last visited July 2, 2009).

In: An Examination of Sentencing Levels and Mandatory... ISBN: 978-1-61209-563-9
Editor: Catherine N. Bates

Chapter 12

STATEMENT OF LANNY A. BREUER, ASSISTANT ATTORNEY GENERAL, CRIMINAL DIVISION, UNITED STATES DEPARTMENT OF JUSTICE, BEFORE THE SUBCOMMITTEE ON CRIME, TERRORISM AND HOMELAND SECURITY, HEARING ON "UNFAIRNESS IN FEDERAL COCAINE SENTENCING: IS IT TIME TO CRACK THE 100 TO 1 DISPARITY?"

INTRODUCTION

Mr. Chairman, Ranking Member Gohmert, distinguished members of the Subcommittee —thank you for giving the Department of Justice the opportunity to appear before you today to share our views on the important issue of disparities in federal cocaine sentencing policy.

The Obama Administration firmly believes that our criminal and sentencing laws must be tough, predictable, fair, and not result in unwarranted racial and ethnic disparities. Criminal and sentencing laws must provide practical, effective tools for federal, state, and local law enforcement, prosecutors, and judges to hold criminals accountable and deter crime. The certainty of our sentencing structure is critical to disrupting and dismantling the threat posed by drug trafficking organizations and gangs that plague our nation's streets with dangerous illegal drugs and violence; it is vital in the fight against violent crime, child exploitation, and sex trafficking; and it is essential to effectively punishing financial fraud.

Ensuring fairness in the criminal justice system is also critically important. Public trust and confidence are essential elements of an effective criminal justice system – our laws and their enforcement must not only be fair, but they must also be perceived as fair. The perception of unfairness undermines governmental authority in the criminal justice process. It leads victims and witnesses of crime to think twice before cooperating with law enforcement, tempts jurors to ignore the law and facts when judging a criminal case, and draws the public into questioning the motives of governmental officials.

Changing these perceptions will strengthen law enforcement through increased public trust and cooperation, coupled with the availability of legal tools that are both tough and fair.

This Administration is committed to reviewing criminal justice issues to ensure that our law enforcement officers and prosecutors have the tools they need to combat crime and ensure public safety, while simultaneously working to root out any unwarranted and unintended disparities in the criminal justice process that may exist.

There is no better place to start our work than with a thorough examination of federal cocaine sentencing policy. Since the United States Sentencing Commission first reported 15 years ago on the differences in sentencing between crack and powder cocaine, a consensus has developed that the federal cocaine sentencing laws should be reassessed. Indeed, over the past 15 years, our understanding of crack and powder cocaine, their effects on the community, and the public safety imperatives surrounding all drug trafficking has evolved. That refined understanding, coupled with the need to ensure fundamental fairness in our sentencing laws, policy, and practice, necessitates a change. We think this change should be addressed in this Congress, and we know that many of you on this Committee have already introduced legislation to address the disparity between crack and powder cocaine. We look forward to working with you and other Members of Congress over the coming months to address this issue.

In committing ourselves to pursuing federal cocaine sentencing policy reform, we do not suggest in any way that our prosecutors or law enforcement agents have acted improperly or imprudently during the last 15 years. To the contrary, they have applied the laws as passed by Congress to address serious crime problems in communities across the nation.

Many in the law enforcement community now recognize the need to reevaluate current federal cocaine sentencing policy – and the disparities the policy creates. Law enforcement leaders have repeatedly and clearly indicated that the current federal cocaine sentencing policy not only creates the perception of unfairness, but also has the potential to misdirect federal enforcement resources. They have stressed that the most effective anti-drug enforcement strategy will deploy federal resources to disrupt and dismantle major drug trafficking organizations and violent drug organizations present in our neighborhoods.

For these and others reasons I will describe in the remainder of my testimony, we believe now is the time for us to re-examine federal cocaine sentencing policy – from the perspective of both fundamental fairness and public safety.

BACKGROUND

A. The Drug Trafficking Threat

Cocaine and other illegal drugs pose a serious risk to the health and safety of Americans. The National Drug Intelligence Center's 2009 National Drug Threat Assessment identifies cocaine as the leading drug threat to society. Cocaine is a dangerous and addictive drug, and its use and abuse can be devastating to families regardless of economic background or social status. Statistics on abuse, emergency room visits, violence, and many other indicators tell the story of tremendous harms caused by cocaine. We must never lose sight of these harms, their impact on our society, and our responsibility to reduce cocaine use and abuse.

Moreover, drug trafficking organizations and gangs have long posed an extremely serious public health and safety threat to the United States. The Administration is committed to rooting out these dangerous organizations. Whether it is Mexican or Colombian drug cartels moving large quantities of powder cocaine into and through the United States, or local gangs distributing thousands of individual rocks of crack in an American community, we will focus our resources on dismantling these enterprises – and disrupting the flow of money both here and abroad – to help protect the American public.

In the fight against illegal drugs, we also recognize that vigorous drug interdiction must be complemented with a heavy focus on drug abuse prevention and treatment. About 40 percent of offenders entering the federal prison system have a drug use disorder. The Violent Crime Control and Law Enforcement Act of 1994 requires the BOP, subject to the availability of appropriations, to provide appropriate substance abuse treatment for 100 percent of inmates who have a diagnosis for substance abuse or dependence and who volunteer for treatment. The Bureau's strategy includes early identification through a psychology screening, drug education, non-residential drug abuse treatment, intensive residential drug abuse treatment and community transition treatment.

Many state inmates also struggle with drug addiction. Many prisoners are unprepared to return to society. They not only re-offend, but they feed the lucrative black market for drugs. We cannot break this cycle of recidivism without increased attention to prevention and treatment, as well as comprehensive prisoner reentry programs.

It is only through a balanced approach – combining tough enforcement with robust drug prevention, treatment, and recovery support efforts such as reentry programs – that we will be successful in stemming both the demand and supply of illegal drugs in our country. Strong and predictable sentencing laws are part of this balanced approach.

B. The Enactment of the Current Cocaine Sentencing Scheme

In the 1 980s, crack cocaine was the newest form of cocaine to hit American streets. As this Committee well knows, in 1986, in the midst of this exploding epidemic, Congress passed the Anti-Drug Abuse Act, which set the current federal penalty structure for crack and powder cocaine trafficking.[1]

In doing so, Congress established the five- and ten-year mandatory minimum sentencing regime still in effect today. Under the law, selling five grams of crack cocaine triggers the same five-year mandatory minimum sentence as selling 500 grams of powder cocaine; those who sell 50 grams of crack are sentenced to the same ten-year mandatory minimum as those selling 5,000 grams of powder cocaine. Pursuant to its mandate to ensure that the federal sentencing guidelines are consistent with all federal laws, the U.S. Sentencing Commission in 1987 applied this same "100-to-1" ratio to the sentencing guidelines.

Leading up to the enactment of this law, Congress was confronted with heightened public attention on the scourge of illegal drugs and high profile drug overdose deaths, including that of Len Bias, a University of Maryland and National Collegiate Athletic Association basketball star drafted by the Boston Celtics in June 1986. Proposals for making crack penalties more severe than powder penalties ranged from the Reagan Administration's proposed 20-to-1 ratio to the late-Senator Chiles' 1000-to-1 disparity.

The legislative history does not provide definitive evidence for the rationale behind the adoption of the 100-to-1 ratio. What we do know from floor statements and reports on earlier versions of the enacted legislation is that during this debate, Congress sought to focus the tough five- and ten-year mandatory minimum penalties on "serious" and "major" traffickers—the traffickers who keep the street markets operating and the heads of drug trafficking organizations, responsible for delivering very large quantities of drugs. With stiff mandatory minimum penalties for crack cocaine set at levels as low as five grams, many have questioned whether these policy goals were achieved. An analysis by the Sentencing Commission using Fiscal Year 2005 data shows that 55 percent of federal crack defendants were street-level dealers. This compares with only 7.3 percent of powder defendants who were street-level dealers. Very few federal crack or powder offenders are "kingpins."

C. The Science of Cocaine: One Drug, Two Forms

Since the time Congress passed the crack cocaine penalties, much of the information on the different impact and effects of crack cocaine as compared to powder cocaine has come under scrutiny. We have since learned that powder cocaine and crack cocaine produce similar physiological and psychological effects once they reach the brain. Whether in its powder or crack form, both types of cocaine are addictive and both pose serious health risks.

According to the National Institute on Drug Abuse (NIDA), the key difference in cocaine's effects depends on how it is administered – by snorting, inhaling, or injecting. The intensity and duration of cocaine's effects – in any form – depend on the speed with which it is absorbed into the bloodstream and delivered to the brain. Smoking or injecting cocaine produces a quicker, stronger high than snorting it. For that reason, the user who is smoking or injecting the drug may need more of it sooner to stay high. Because powder cocaine is typically snorted, while crack is most often smoked, crack smokers can potentially become addicted faster than someone snorting powder cocaine. Notably, however, the NIDA has found that smoked cocaine is absorbed into the bloodstream as rapidly as injected cocaine, both of which have similar effects on the brain. Evidence does not support that crack is inherently more addictive than powder cocaine.

D. The Policy Debate

For nearly two decades, the 100-to-1 disparity has been the subject of dynamic debate and discussion among policymakers, academics, criminal justice organizations, and others.

The supporters of the current cocaine penalty structure believe that the disparity is justified because it accounts for the greater degree of violence and weapon possession or use associated with some crack offenses, and because crack can be potentially more addictive than powder, depending on the usual method of use.

This Administration shares these concerns about violence and guns used to commit drug offenses and other crimes associated with such offenses. We recognize that data suggests that weapons involvement and violence in the commission of cocaine- related offenses are generally higher in crack versus powder cases: a 2007 Sentencing Commission report found that weapons involvement for cocaine offenses was 27 percent for powder cocaine and 42.7

percent for crack. The same sample found that some form of violence occurred in 6.3 percent of powder cocaine crimes and in 10.4 percent of crack cocaine crimes.

Violence associated with any offense is a serious crime and must be punished; we think that the best way to address drug-related violence is to ensure the most severe sentences are meted out to those who commit violent offenses. However, increased penalties for this conduct should generally be imposed on a case-by-case basis, not on a class of offenders the majority of whom do not use any violence or possess a weapon. We support sentencing enhancements for those who use weapons in drug trafficking crimes, or those who use minors to commit their crimes, or those who injure or kill someone in relation to a drug trafficking offense. We also support charging separate weapons offenses to increase a sentence when an offender uses a weapon in relation to a drug trafficking offense.

But we cannot ignore the mounting evidence that the current cocaine sentencing disparity is difficult to justify based on the facts and science, including evidence that crack is not an inherently more addictive substance than powder cocaine. We know of no other controlled substance where the penalty structure differs so dramatically because of the drug's form.

Moreover, the Sentencing Commission has documented that the quantity-based cocaine sentencing scheme often punishes low-level crack offenders far more harshly than similarly situated powder cocaine offenders. Additionally, Sentencing Commission data confirms that in 2006, 82 percent of individuals convicted of federal crack cocaine offenses were African American, while just 9 percent were White. In the same year, federal powder cocaine offenders were 14 percent White, 27 percent African American, and 58 percent Hispanic. The impact of these laws has fueled the belief across the country that federal cocaine laws are unjust. We commend the Sentencing Commission for all of its work on this issue over the last 15 years. The Sentencing Commission reports are the definitive compilation of all of the data reflecting federal cocaine sentencing policy. We cannot ignore their message.

MOVING FORWARD: A TIDE OF CHANGE

Since 1995, at Congress's request, the Commission has called for legislation to substantially reduce or eliminate the crack/powder sentencing disparity. Most recently, in 2007, the Commission called the crack/powder disparity an "urgent and compelling" issue that Congress must address. Both chambers of Congress have held multiple hearings on the topic, and legislation to substantially reduce or eliminate the disparity has been introduced by members of both political parties, several of whom sit on this Committee.

In addition, the overwhelming majority of states do not distinguish between powder cocaine and crack cocaine offenses.

For the reasons outlined above, this Administration believes that the current federal cocaine sentencing structure fails to appropriately reflect the differences and similarities between crack and powder cocaine, the offenses involving each form of the drug, and the goal of sentencing serious and major traffickers to significant prison sentences. We believe the structure is especially problematic because a growing number of citizens view it as fundamentally unfair. The Administration believes Congress's goal should be to completely eliminate the sentencing disparity between crack cocaine and powder cocaine.

Last month the Attorney General asked the Deputy Attorney General to form and chair a working group to examine federal sentencing and corrections policy. The group's comprehensive review will include possible recommendations to the President and Congress for new sentencing legislation affecting the structure of federal sentencing. In addition to studying issues related to prisoner reentry, Department policies on charging and sentencing, and other sentencing-related topics, the group will also focus on formulating a new federal cocaine sentencing policy; one that completely eliminates the sentencing disparity between crack and powder cocaine but also fully accounts for violence, chronic offenders, weapon possession and other aggravating factors associated – in individual cases – with both crack and powder cocaine trafficking. It will also develop recommendations for legislation, and we look forward to working closely with Congress and the Sentencing Commission on this important policy issue and finding a workable solution.

Until a comprehensive solution – one that embodies new quantity thresholds and perhaps new sentencing enhancements – can be developed and enacted as legislation by Congress and as amended guidelines by the Sentencing Commission, federal prosecutors will adhere to existing law. We are gratified that the Sentencing Commission has already taken a small step to ameliorate the 100:1 ratio contained in existing statutes by amending the guidelines for crack cocaine offenses. We will continue to ask federal courts to calculate the guidelines in crack cocaine cases, as required by Supreme Court decisions. However, we recognize that federal courts have the authority to sentence outside the guidelines in crack cases or even to create their own quantity ratio. Our prosecutors will inform courts that they should act within their discretion to fashion a sentence that is consistent with the objectives of 18 U.S.C. § 3553(a) and our prosecutors will bring the relevant case-specific facts to the courts' attention.

CONCLUSION

As the history of this debate makes clear, there has been some disagreement about whether federal cocaine sentencing policy should change, and, if so, how it should change. This Administration and its components, including the Justice Department and the Office of National Drug Control Policy, look forward to working with this Committee and members of Congress in both chambers to develop sentencing laws that are tough, smart, fair, and perceived as such by the American public. We have already begun our own internal review of sentencing and the federal cocaine laws. Our goal is to ensure that our sentencing system is tough and predictable, but at the same time promotes public trust and confidence in the fairness of our criminal justice system. Ultimately, we all share the goals of ensuring that the public is kept safe, reducing crime and substance abuse, and minimizing the wide-reaching, negative effects of illegal drugs.

Thank you for the opportunity to share the Administration's views, and I welcome any questions you may have.

End Notes

[1] In 1988, Congress also established a five gram, five-year mandatory minimum sentence for simple possession of crack cocaine, the only federal mandatory minimum penalty for a first offense of simple possession of a controlled substance. Anti-Drug Abuse Act of 1988, P.L., 100-690.

In: An Examination of Sentencing Levels and Mandatory... ISBN: 978-1-61209-563-9
Editor: Catherine N. Bates

Chapter 13

STATEMENT OF RICARDO H. HINOJOSA, ACTING CHAIR, UNITED STATES SENTENCING COMMISSION, BEFORE THE SUBCOMMITTEE ON CRIME, TERRORISM AND HOMELAND SECURITY

Chairman Scott, Ranking Member Gohmert, and members of the Subcommittee, I appreciate the opportunity to appear before you on behalf of the United States Sentencing Commission to discuss federal cocaine sentencing policy.

The Commission has considered cocaine sentencing issues over a number of years[1] and has worked closely with Congress to address the sentencing disparity that exists between the penalties for powder cocaine and crack cocaine offenses. The Commission amended the federal sentencing guidelines in 2007 to partially address the sentencing disparity and, pursuant to its authority under 28 U.S.C. § 994(u),[2] gave retroactive effect to that amendment effective March 3, 2008. The Commission continues to be of the view, however, that any comprehensive solution to the problem of federal cocaine sentencing policy requires revision of the current statutory penalties and therefore must be legislated by Congress. The Commission urges Congress to take legislative action on this important issue.

Part I of this statement briefly summarizes the statutory and guideline penalty structure for crack cocaine offenses. Part II provides an analysis of federal cocaine sentences, including information on differences in average sentence length between crack cocaine and powder cocaine offenses. Part III provides a brief update on case law concerning crack cocaine sentencing and data on recent cocaine sentencing practices. Part IV provides information concerning the retroactive application of the 2007 crack cocaine guideline amendment. Part V sets forth the Commission's recommendations for statutory penalty revisions.

I. STATUTORY AND GUIDELINE PENALTY STRUCTURE

The Anti-Drug Abuse Act of 1986[3] established the basic framework of statutory mandatory minimum penalties currently applicable to federal drug trafficking offenses. The quantities triggering those mandatory minimum penalties differ for various drugs and in some cases, including cocaine, for different forms of the same drug.

In establishing the mandatory minimum penalties for cocaine, Congress differentiated between two principal forms of cocaine: cocaine hydrochloride (commonly referred to as "powder cocaine") and cocaine base (commonly referred to as "crack cocaine"). Because of congressional concern at that time about the dangers associated with crack cocaine,[4] the 1986 Act provided significantly higher punishment for crack cocaine offenses based on the quantity of the drug involved in the offense.

As a result of the 1986 Act, federal law requires a five-year mandatory minimum penalty for a first-time trafficking offense involving at least five grams of crack cocaine, or at least 500 grams of powder cocaine, and a ten-year mandatory minimum penalty for a first-time trafficking offense involving at least 50 grams of crack cocaine, or at least 5,000 grams of powder cocaine. Because it takes 100 times more powder cocaine than crack cocaine to trigger the same mandatory minimum penalty, this penalty structure is commonly referred to as the "100-to-1 drug quantity ratio." In addition, unlike for any other drug, in 1988 Congress enacted a five-year statutory mandatory minimum penalty for simple possession of at least five grams of crack cocaine.[5]

When Congress passed the 1986 Act, the Commission was in the process of developing the initial sentencing guidelines. The Commission responded to the legislation by generally incorporating the statutory mandatory minimum sentences into the guidelines and extrapolating upward and downward to set guideline sentencing ranges for all drug quantities. Offenses involving at least five grams of crack cocaine or at least 500 grams of powder cocaine, as well as all other drug offenses carrying a five- year mandatory minimum penalty, were assigned a base offense level of 26, corresponding to a sentencing guideline range of 63 to 78 months for a defendant in Criminal History Category I. Similarly, offenses involving at least 50 grams of crack cocaine or at least 5,000 grams of powder cocaine, as well as all other drug offenses carrying a 10-year mandatory minimum penalty, were assigned a base offense level of 32, corresponding to a sentencing guideline range of 121 to 151 months for a defendant in Criminal History Category I. Crack cocaine offenses and powder cocaine offenses involving quantities above and below the mandatory minimum penalty threshold quantities were set proportionately using the same 100-to-1 drug quantity ratio.

The Commission's 2007 crack cocaine guideline amendment reduced by two levels the base offense levels assigned to the various quantities of crack cocaine. Consequently, for crack cocaine offenders, the base offense levels now correspond to guideline ranges that include rather than exceed the five-year and ten-year mandatory minimum terms of imprisonment.[6] Offenses involving quantities of crack cocaine above and below the mandatory minimum threshold quantities similarly were adjusted downward by two levels.

The Commission promulgated the 2007 crack cocaine guideline amendment after an extensive review of the issues associated with federal cocaine sentencing policy. Consistent with previous Commission conclusions that the 100-to-1 drug quantity ratio should be modified[7] but recognizing Congress's authority to establish federal cocaine sentencing policy through statutory mandatory minimum penalties, the Commission tailored the 2007 crack cocaine guideline amendment to fit within the current statutory penalty scheme.

II. Analysis of Federal Cocaine Sentences

A. Federal Cocaine Offenses and Offenders

1. Number of Offenses

Powder cocaine and crack cocaine offenses together historically have accounted for nearly half of the federally sentenced drug trafficking offenders. As indicated in Figure 1, of 24,605 total drug trafficking cases in fiscal year 2008, there were 5,913 crack cocaine cases (24.0% of all drug trafficking cases) and 5,769 powder cocaine cases (23.4% of all drug trafficking cases). Of 24,748 total drug trafficking cases in fiscal year 2007, there were 5,248 crack cocaine cases (21.2% of all drug trafficking cases) and 6,172 powder cocaine cases (24.9% of all drug trafficking cases).[8]

2. Demographics

As indicated in Table 1, Black offenders continue to comprise the majority of federal crack cocaine trafficking offenders, but that has decreased from 91.4 percent in fiscal year 1992 to 80.6 percent in fiscal year 2008. White offenders comprised 10.2 percent of crack cocaine offenders in fiscal year 2008, compared to 3.2 percent in 1992. Hispanic offenders comprised 8.2 percent in fiscal year 2008, compared to 5.3 percent in 1992.

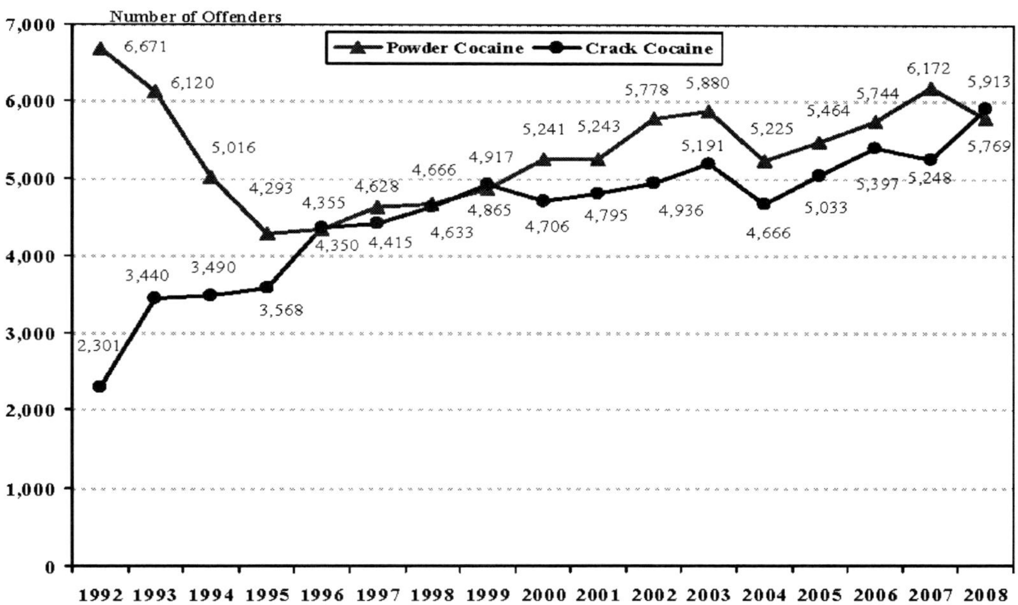

Only cases sentenced under USSG §2D1.1 (Drug Trafficking) with a primary drug type of powder cocaine or crack cocaine are included in this figure. This figure excludes cases with missing information for the variables required for analysis. Note that total percentages may not add up to exactly 100 percent due to rounding.

Source: U.S. Sentencing Commission, 1992-2008 Datafiles, MONFY92 –USSCFY08.

Figure 1. Trend in Number of Powder Cocaine and Crack Cocaine Offenders FY1992-FY2008.

Table 1. Demographic Characteristics of Federal Cocaine Offenders Fiscal Years 1992, 2000 & 2008

	Powder Cocaine						Crack Cocaine					
	1992		2000		2008		1992		2000		2008	
	N	%	N	%	N	%	N	%	N	%	N	%
Race/Ethnicity												
White	2,113	32.3	932	17.8	942	16.4	74	3.2	269	5.6	605	10.2
Black	1,778	27.2	1,596	30.5	1,734	30.2	2,096	91.4	4,069	84.7	4,753	80.6
Hispanic	2,601	39.8	2,662	50.8	3,018	52.5	121	5.3	434	9.0	484	8.2
Other	44	0.7	49	0.9	57	1.0	30.1		33	0.7	57	1.0
Total	6,536	100	5,239	100	5,751	100	2,294	100	4,805	100	5,899	100
Citizenship												
U.S. Citizen	4,499	67.7	3,327	63.9	3,636	63.1	2,092	91.3	4,482	93.4	5,702	96.4
Non-Citizen	2,147	32.3	1,881	36.1	2,127	36.9	199	8.7	318	6.6	211	3.6
Total	6,646	100	5,208	100	5,763	100	2,291	100	4,800	100	5,913	100
Gender												
Female	787	11.8	722	13.8	546	9.5	270	11.7	476	9.9	512	8.7
Male	5,886	88.2	4,518	86.2	5,222	90.5	2,032	88.3	4,330	90.1	5,401	91.3
Total	6,673	100	5,240	100	5,768	100	2,302	100	4,806	100	5,913	100
Average Age	Average=34		Average=34		Average=35		Average=28		Average=29		Average=31	

This table excludes cases missing information for the variables required for analysis.
Total percentages may not add up to exactly 100 percent due to rounding.
Source: U.S. Sentencing Commission, 1992, 2000, and 2008 Datafiles, MONFY92, USSCFY00, and USSCFY08.

Hispanic offenders comprise the majority of powder cocaine offenders, having increased from 39.8 percent in fiscal year 1992 to 52.5 percent in fiscal year 2008. Black offenders comprised 30.2 percent of powder cocaine offenders in fiscal year 2008, compared to 27.2 percent in fiscal year 1992. White offenders comprised 16.4 percent of powder cocaine offenders in fiscal year 2008, compared to 32.3 percent of powder cocaine offenders in fiscal year 1992.

B. Average Sentence Length

Federal crack cocaine offenders consistently have received longer sentences than powder cocaine offenders. As indicated in Figures 2 and 3, the difference in average sentence length between these two groups of offenders was greater in 2007 than it was in 1992. In fiscal year 1992, the average sentence length for crack cocaine offenders was 124 months compared to 99 months for powder cocaine offenders, amounting to a difference of 25 months, or 25.3 percent. That difference widened to 43 months, or 50.0 percent, in fiscal year 2007, when the average sentence length for crack cocaine offenders was 129 months compared to 86 months for powder cocaine offenders.

In fiscal year 2008, the difference in average sentence length between crack cocaine and powder cocaine offenses narrowed. This occurred not only because of the implementation of the 2007 crack cocaine guideline amendment but also because of an increase in the average sentence length for powder cocaine offenders. In fiscal year 2008, the average sentence length for crack cocaine offenders was 115 months, compared to 91 months for powder cocaine offenders, making the average sentence length for crack cocaine offenders 26.4 percent, or 24 months, longer than the average sentence length for powder cocaine offenders. However, while the difference in average sentence length narrowed, there remains a difference.

C. Reasons for Differences in Average Sentence Length

1. Statutory Mandatory Minimum Sentences

Most of the difference in average sentence length between crack cocaine and powder cocaine offenses is attributable to the current quantity-based statutory mandatory minimum penalties and the manner in which those penalties are incorporated into the guidelines. In fiscal year 2008, the median drug weight for powder cocaine offenses was 7,000 grams, an amount 135 times greater than the median drug weight for crack cocaine offenses, which was 52 grams. In fiscal year 2007, the median drug weight was 6,370 grams for powder cocaine offenses compared to 53 grams for crack cocaine offenses.

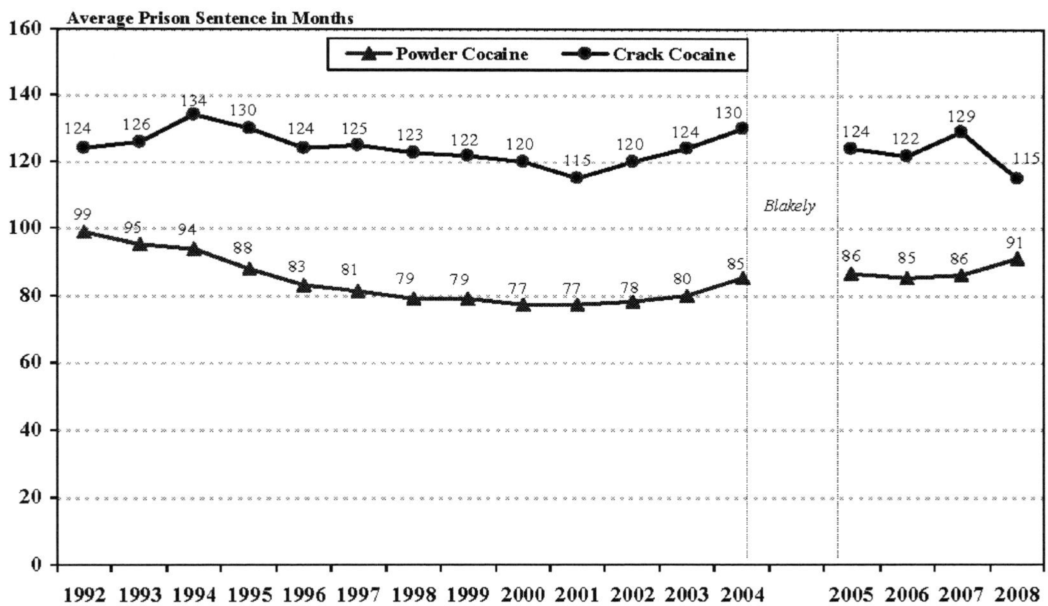

Only cases sentenced under USSG §2D1.1 (Drug Trafficking) with a primary drug type of powder cocaine or crack cocaine are included in this figure. Cases with sentences of probation or any time of confinement as defined in USSG §5C1.1 are not included in this figure. Cases with sentences greater than 470 months were included in the sentence average computation as 470 months. This figure excludes cases with missing information for the variables required for analysis. Note that total percentages may not add up to exactly 100 percent due to rounding.

Source: U.S. Sentencing Commission, 1992-2008 Datafiles, MONFY92–USSCFY08, 2004 Pre-Blakely Only Cases (October 1, 2003–June 24, 2004), and 2005 Post-BookerOnly Cases (January 12, 2005 – September 30, 2005).

Figure 2. Trend in Prison Sentences for Powder Cocaine and Crack Cocaine Offenders. FY1992-FY2008.

Table 2. Guideline Sentencing Characteristics, Criminal History, and Position Relative to the Guideline Range for Crack Cocaine Offenders[1]

	Fiscal Year 2007		Fiscal Year 2008	
Average Base Offense Level	**30**		**28**	
Median Crack Cocaine Weight in Grams	**53**		**52**	
Average Prison Sentence (Months)	**130**		**116**	
	N	**%**	**N**	**%**
TOTAL	**5,037**		**5,601**	
Weapon Enhancment				
Weapon SOC (USSG § 2D1.1(b)(1))	994	19.7	1,025	18.3
18 U.S.C. § 924(c) Conviction	543	10.8	548	9.8
Safety Valve §5C1.2[2]	683	13.6	800	14.3
Guideline Role Adjustment				
Aggravating Role §3B1.1	233	4.6	260	4.6
Mitigating Role §3B1.2	286	5.7	287	5.1
Criminal History Category	**N**	**%**	**N**	**%**
I	1,052	20.9	1,242	22.2
II	596	11.8	685	12.2
III	1,015	20.2	1,093	19.5
IV	601	11.9	678	12.1
V	383	7.6	474	8.5
VI	1,390	27.6	1,429	25.5
Total	**5,037**	**100.0**	**5,601**	**100.0**
Sentence Relative to Guideline Range	**N**	**%**	**N**	**%**
Within Range	2,946	56.3	3,306	56.1
Above Range	22	0.4	39	0.7
Government Sponsored	1,596	30.5	1,637	27.8
Non-Government Below Range	673	12.9	916	15.5
Total	**5,237**	**100.0**	**5,898**	**100.0**

[1] This tables includes only cases sentenced under §2D1.1 (Drug Trafficking) where crack cocaine was the primary drug type.

Total percentages may not add up to exactly 100 percent due to rounding. This table excludes cases with missing information for the variables required for analysis.

[2] Safety valve includes cases that received either a two-level reduction pursuant to USSG §2D1.1(b)(11) and USSG §5C1.2, or relief from the statutory mandatory minimum sentence pursuant to 18 U.S.C. § 3553(f), or both.

Source: U.S. Sentencing Commission, 2007-2008 Datafiles, USSCFY07-USSCFY08.

Table 2A. Guideline Sentencing Characteristics, Criminal History, and Position Relative to the Guideline Range for Powder Cocaine Offenders[1]

	Fiscal Year 2007		Fiscal Year 2008	
Average Base Offense Level	**30**		**30**	
Median Crack Cocaine Weight in Grams	**6,370**		**7,000**	
Average Prison Sentence (Months)	**86**		**91**	
TOTAL	**5,888**		**5,578**	
Weapon Enhancment				
Weapon SOC (USSG § 2D1.1(b)(1))	583	9.9	632	11.3
18 U.S.C. § 924(c) Conviction	274	4.7	314	5.6
Safety Valve §5C1.2[2]	2,633	44.7	2,365	42.4
Guideline Role Adjustment				
Aggravating Role §3B1.1	451	7.7	453	8.1
Mitigating Role §3B 1.2	1,193	20.3	1,116	20.0
Criminal History Category	**N**	**%**	**N**	**%**
I	3,579	60.8	3,349	60.0
II	688	11.7	646	11.6
III	736	12.5	671	12.0
IV	298	5.1	301	5.4
V	144	2.4	142	2.6
VI	443	7.5	469	8.4
Total	**5,888**	**100.0**	**5,578**	**100.0**
Sentence Relative to Guideline Range	**N**	**%**	**N**	**%**
Within Range	3,236	52.7	2,879	50.1
Above Range	29	0.5	33	0.6
Government Sponsored	2,196	35.7	2,048	35.6
Non-Government Below Range	683	11.1	789	13.7
Total	**6,144**	**100.0**	**5,749**	**100.0**

1 This tables includes only cases sentenced under §2D1.1 (Drug Trafficking) where powder cocaine was the primary drug type. Total percentages may not add up to exactly 100 percent due to rounding. This table excludes cases with missing information for the variables required for analysis.

2 Safety valve includes cases that received either a two-level reduction pursuant to USSG §2D1.1(b)(11) and USSG §5C1.2, or relief from the statutory mandatory minimum sentence pursuant to 18 U.S.C. § 3553(f), or both.

Source: U.S. Sentencing Commission, 2007-2008 Datafiles, USSCFY07-USSCFY08.

These quantities resulted in crack cocaine and powder cocaine offenders being convicted under statutes carrying a mandatory minimum sentence at virtually equal rates. In fiscal year 2008, 80.6 percent of crack cocaine offenders were convicted of a statute carrying a mandatory minimum term of imprisonment, compared to 80.0 percent of powder cocaine offenders.

Exposure to statutory mandatory minimum sentences further contributes to the difference in average sentence length because crack cocaine offenders are less likely to receive the benefit of statutory and guideline "safety valve" mechanisms that allow certain low-level offenders to be sentenced without regard to the statutory mandatory minimums. As indicated in Tables 2 and 2A, in fiscal year 2008, 14.3 percent of crack cocaine offenders received the benefit of a safety valve provision as set forth at 18 U.S.C. § 3553(f)[9] or through the federal sentencing guidelines[10] compared to 42.4 percent of powder cocaine offenders. In fiscal year 2007, 13.6 percent of crack cocaine offenders received the benefit of a safety valve provision compared to 44.7 percent of powder cocaine offenders. The difference in rates of safety valve application between crack cocaine and powder cocaine offenders is in part attributable to differences in their criminal history scores and the extent to which weapons are involved in the offense, as discussed below.[11]

2. Aggravating and Mitigating Factors

In addition to drug quantity, the current penalty structure for drug offenses accounts for certain aggravating and mitigating factors, such as weapon involvement and role in the offense. Differences in the prevalence of these factors in crack cocaine and powder cocaine offenses also contribute to the difference in average sentence length for these offenses.

a. Weapon Involvement

Some of the difference in average sentence length is attributable to the higher rate at which a guideline[12] or statutory[13] weapon enhancement applies in crack cocaine offenses compared to powder cocaine offenses. Although a weapon enhancement applies in a minority of both crack cocaine and powder cocaine offenses, as indicated in Tables 2 and 2A, such an enhancement applies more often in crack cocaine offenses.

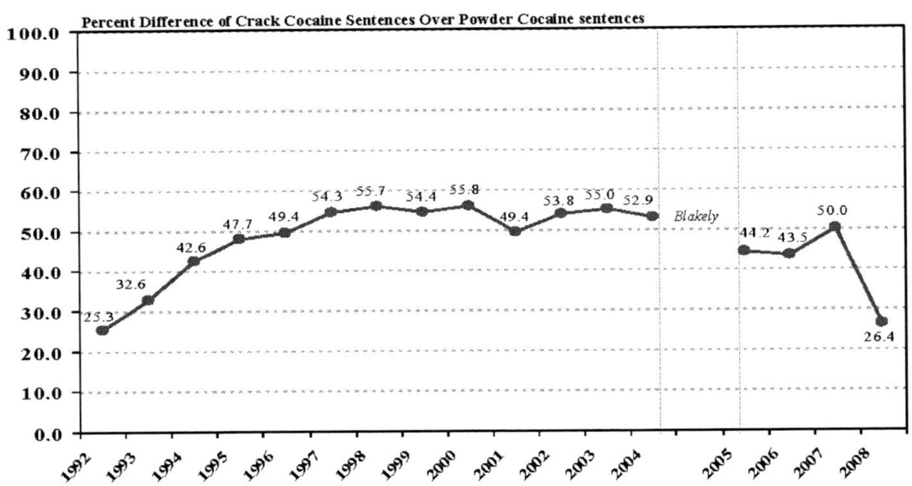

Only cases sentenced under USSG §2D1.1 (Drug Trafficking) with a primary drug type of powder cocaine or crack cocaine are included in this figure. Cases with sentences of probation or any time of confinement as defined in USSG §5C1.1 are not included in this figure. Cases with sentences greater than 470 months were included in the sentence average computation as 470 months. This figure excludes cases with missing information for the variables required for analysis. The figure shows, for each year, the percentage difference between prison sentences for crack cocaine and powder cocaine. For example, in Fiscal Year 1992, crack cocaine sentences were 25.3 percent greater than powder cocaine sentences. The percentage was calculated by dividing the difference between the average crack cocaine sentence and the average powder cocaine sentence by the average powder cocaine sentence. Note that total percentages may not add up to exactly 100 percent due to rounding.

Source: U.S. Sentencing Commission, 1992-2008 Datafiles, MONFY92 – USSCFY08, 2004 Pre-Blakely Only Cases (October 1, 2003 –June 24, 2004), and 2005 Post-Booker Only Cases (January 12, 2005 –September 30, 2005).

Figure 3. Trend in Proportional Differences Between Average Cocaine Sentences FY1992-FY2008.

In fiscal year 2008, 28.1 percent of crack cocaine offenders either received the guideline weapon enhancement (18.3%) or were convicted pursuant to 18 U.S.C. § 924(c) (9.8%). By comparison, 16.9 percent of powder cocaine offenders either received the guideline weapon enhancement (11.3%) or were convicted pursuant to 18 U.S.C. § 924(c) (5.6%). In fiscal year 2007, 30.5 percent of crack cocaine offenders either received the guideline weapon enhancement (19.7%) or were convicted pursuant to 18 U.S.C. § 924(c) (10.8%). By comparison, 14.6 percent of powder cocaine offenders either received the weapon enhancement (9.9%) or were convicted pursuant to 18 U.S.C. § 924(c) (4.7%).

b. Role in the Offense

Some of the difference in average sentence length is attributable to the relative infrequency with which crack cocaine offenders receive a mitigating role adjustment under the guidelines compared to powder cocaine offenders.[14] In fiscal year 2008, 5.1 percent of crack cocaine offenders received a mitigating role adjustment compared to 20.0 percent of powder cocaine offenders. In fiscal year 2007, 5.7 percent of crack cocaine offenders received a mitigating role adjustment compared to 20.3 percent of powder cocaine offenders.

With respect to aggravating role,[15] in fiscal year 2008, 4.6 percent of crack cocaine offenders received an aggravating role adjustment compared to 8.1 percent of powder cocaine offenders. In fiscal year 2007, 4.6 percent of crack cocaine offenders received an aggravating role adjustment compared to 7.7 percent of powder cocaine offenders.

3. Criminal History

In addition to offense severity (as measured by drug quantity and applicable aggravating and mitigating factors), criminal history is a major component in determining an offender's sentence under the federal sentencing guidelines. Some of the difference in average sentence length is attributable to the fact that crack cocaine offenders generally have more extensive criminal history than powder cocaine offenders. In both fiscal years 2008 and 2007, the average criminal history category for crack cocaine offenders was Criminal History Category IV, compared to Criminal History Category II for powder cocaine offenders. Tables 2 and 2A show the distribution of crack cocaine offenders and powder cocaine offenders by criminal history category in both fiscal years 2007 and 2008.[16]

As discussed in Part IIC, the difference in criminal history between crack cocaine and powder cocaine offenders contributes to the relatively low rates at which crack cocaine offenders qualify for statutory and guideline "safety valve" provisions compared to powder cocaine offenders. An offender in a criminal history category higher than Criminal History Category I cannot receive the benefit of these provisions. In fiscal year 2008, 77.8 percent of crack cocaine offenders were in a criminal history category higher than Criminal History Category I, compared to 40.0 percent of powder cocaine offenders. In fiscal year 2007, 79.1 percent of crack cocaine offenders were in a criminal history category higher than Criminal History Category I, compared to 39.2 percent of powder cocaine offenders.

III. Recent Crack Cocaine Sentencing Case Law and Cocaine Sentencing Practices

A. Supreme Court Case Law

The sentencing disparity between crack cocaine and powder cocaine offenses has been the subject of recent Supreme Court case law. In *Kimbrough v. United States,*[17] the Court relied on the Commission's conclusion that the disparity between the treatment of crack cocaine and powder cocaine offenses "fails to meet the sentencing objectives set forth by Congress in both the Sentencing Reform Act and the 1986 Act"[18] in holding that a sentencing judge may consider that disparity when determining an appropriate sentence in a crack cocaine case. In *Spears v. United States,*[19] the Supreme Court clarified in a *per curiam* decision that, under its holding in *Kimbrough,* district courts have "authority to vary from the crack cocaine Guidelines based on *policy* disagreements with them, and not simply based on an individualized determination that they yield an excessive sentence in a particular case."[20] Thus, a sentencing judge may categorically reject the existing guidelines ratio and "apply a different ratio which, in his judgment, corrects the disparity." [21]

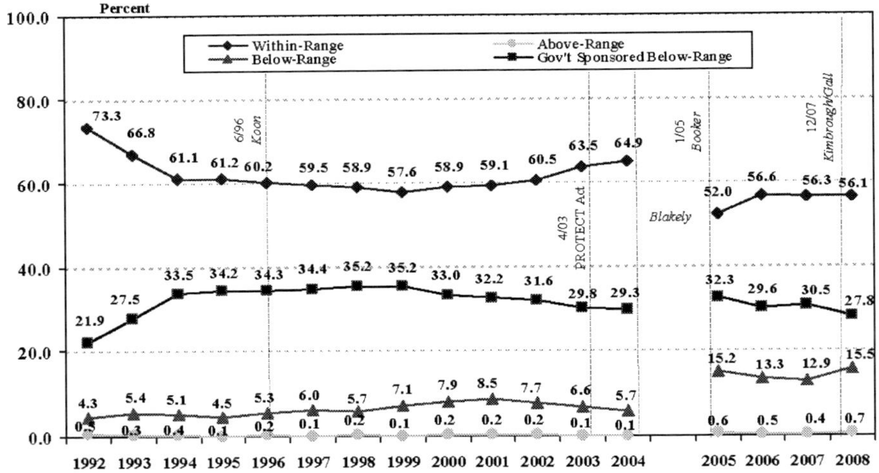

Only cases sentenced under USSG §2D1.1 (Drug Trafficking) with a primary drug type of crack cocaine are included in this figure. Government Sponsored Below-Range is comprised of: USSG §5K1.1 Departures Only (FY92-FY02), USSG §5K1.1 and Other Government Sponsored Departures (FY03), USSG §5K1.1, USSG §5K3.1 and Other Government Sponsored Departures (FY04) and USSG §5K1.1, USSG §5K3.1 and Other Government Sponsored Departures/ Variances (FY05-FY08). This figure excludes cases with missing information for the variables required for analysis. Note that total percentages may not add up to exactly 100 percent due to rounding.

Source: U.S. Sentencing Commission, 1992-2008 Datafiles, MONFY92 USSCFY08, 2004 Pre-Blakely Only Cases (October 1, 2003 June 24, 2004), and 2005 Post-Booker Only Cases (January 12, 2005 September 30, 2005).

Figure 4. Rates of Within-Range and Out-of-Range Sentences for Crack Cocaine Offenses FY1992 to FY2008.

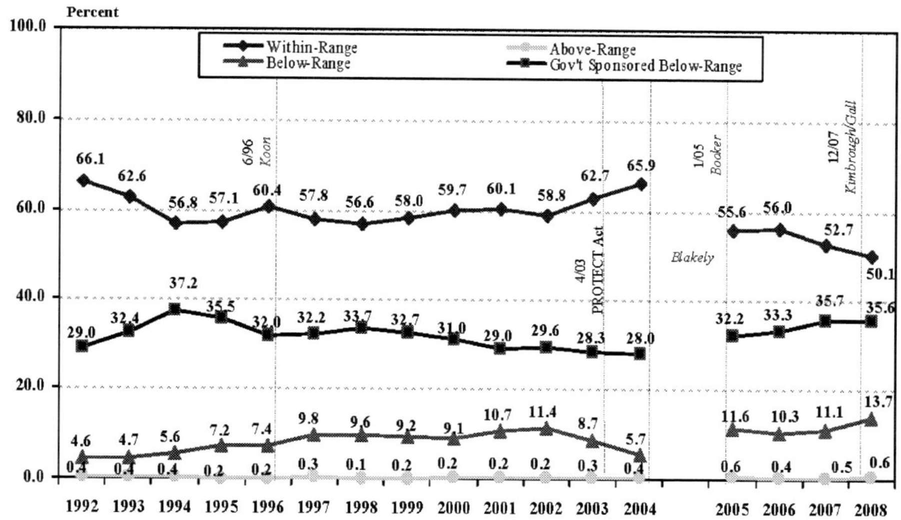

Only cases sentenced under USSG §2D1.1 (Drug Trafficking) with a primary drug type of powder cocaine are included in this figure. Government Sponsored Below-Range is comprised of: USSG §5K1.1 Departures Only (FY92-FY02), USSG §5K1.1 and Other Government Sponsored Departures (FY03), USSG §5K1.1, USSG §5K3.1 and Other Government Sponsored Departures (FY04) and USSG §5K1.1, USSG §5K3.1 and Other Government Sponsored Departures/Variances (FY05-FY08). This figure excludes cases with missing information for the variables required for analysis. Note that total percentages may not add up to exactly 100 percent due to rounding.

Source: U.S. Sentencing Commission, 1992-2008 Datafiles, MONFY92–USSCFY08, 2004 Pre-Blakely Only Cases (October 1, 2003–June 24, 2004), and 2005 Post-BookerOnly Cases (January 12, 2005–September 30, 2005).

Figure 5. Rates of Within-Range and Out-of-Range Sentences for Powder Cocaine Offenses FY1992 to FY2008.

Of the 959 crack cocaine cases sentenced after *Spears* that have been received, coded, and analyzed by the Commission as of April 24, 2009, five cases specifically cite *Spears* in the court's written statement of reasons for the sentence imposed. Of those five cases, the court applied a 20-to-1 drug quantity ratio in two of the cases and a 1-to-1 drug quantity ratio in one of the cases. In the remaining two cases, the court cited *Spears* but did not apply a different ratio, although one of those cases referred to the applicable ratio as excessive.

In two additional cases, the court cited *Spears* and applied a different drug quantity ratio. In one of those cases, the court applied a 10-to-1 drug quantity ratio[22] and in the other, the court applied a 1-to-1 drug quantity ratio.[23]

B. Sentencing Practices

As indicated in Figure 4, during the immediate years preceding *United States v. Booker*,[24] which rendered the sentencing guidelines advisory, courts imposed non- government sponsored, below-range sentences in 7.7 percent, 6.6 percent, and 5.7 percent of the crack cocaine cases sentenced in fiscal years 2002, 2003, and 2004, respectively. By comparison, courts imposed non-government sponsored, below-range sentences in 15.2 percent, 13.3 percent, and 12.9 percent of the crack cocaine cases sentenced in fiscal years 2005, 2006, and 2007, respectively. Furthermore, in fiscal year 2008, approximately 10 months of which were post -*Kimbrough*, the rate of non- government sponsored, below-range sentences increased to 15.5 percent of crack cocaine cases sentenced that year.

Courts increasingly are sentencing powder cocaine offenders to sentences below the applicable sentencing guideline range but less often than for crack cocaine offenders. As indicated in Figure 5, courts imposed non-government sponsored, below-range sentences in 11.4 percent, 8.7 percent, and 5.7 percent of the powder cocaine cases sentenced in fiscal years 2002, 2003, and 2004, respectively. By comparison, courts imposed non-government sponsored, below-range sentences in 11.6 percent, 10.3 percent, and 11.1 percent in fiscal years 2005, 2006, and 2007, respectively. In fiscal year 2008, the rate of non-government sponsored, below-range sentences increased to 13.7 percent of the powder cocaine cases sentenced that year.[25]

When analyzed by periods marked by the dates of the Supreme Court's decisions in *Booker*, *Kimbrough*, and *Spears,* the data suggest that the Supreme Court's decisions have had some impact on federal crack cocaine sentencing practices. Courts imposed non-government sponsored, below-range sentences in 6.9 percent of the 11,649 crack cocaine cases sentenced in the three-year period immediately before enactment of the Prosecutorial Remedies and Other Tools to end the Exploitation of Children Today (PROTECT) Act[26] (October 1, 2000-April 30, 2003). By comparison, courts imposed non-government sponsored, below-range sentences in 13.3 percent of the 15,044 crack cocaine cases sentenced in the post-*Booker* period (January 12, 2005 to December 9, 2007) and 16.0 percent of the 5,998 crack cocaine cases sentenced during the post-*Kimbrough* period (December 10, 2007 to January 20, 2009).

Although too few cases have been sentenced post-*Spears* to draw any conclusions about the impact of that decision, the rate of non-government sponsored, below-range sentences increased to 18.4 percent, or 176 of the 959 crack cocaine cases sentenced during the post-*Spears* period (on or after January 21, 2009) that have been received, coded, and analyzed by the Commission.[27]

IV. Retroactivity of 2007 Crack Cocaine Guideline Amendment

As discussed in Part I, the Commission promulgated a guideline amendment in 2007 that reduced by two levels the base offense levels assigned to the various quantities of crack cocaine. The Sentencing Reform Act, at 28 U.S.C. § 994(u), authorizes the Commission to determine whether a guideline amendment that reduces the sentencing range may be retroactively applied. Pursuant to that authority, the Commission voted to give retroactive effect to the 2007 crack cocaine guideline amendment effective March 3, 2008. As a result, courts were authorized under 18 U.S.C. § 3582(c)(2) to consider motions for reduced sentence based on the 2007 crack cocaine guideline amendment.[28]

In addition to voting to give the crack cocaine guideline amendment retroactive effect, the Commission amended the relevant policy statement, § 1B1.10 (Reduction in Term of Imprisonment as a Result of Amended Guideline Range), to provide limitations and guidance to the courts on determining whether, and to what extent, to grant a motion for reduced sentence pursuant to 18 U.S.C. § 3582(c)(2).[29] In particular, the Commission amended the policy statement to clarify that the court shall not reduce the defendant's term of imprisonment to a term less than the minimum of the amended guideline range, except in certain limited circumstances. In addition, the Commission amended the policy statement to require courts to consider the nature and seriousness of the danger to the community that may be posed by such a reduction and to permit consideration of an offender's post-sentencing conduct.

Prior to voting on retroactivity, the Commission also prepared a retroactivity analysis that predicted that 19,500 offenders sentenced between 1991 and 2007 might be eligible to seek a reduction. [30] The retroactivity analysis further predicted that the average sentence reduction would be approximately 27 months.[31]

The Commission has received, coded and analyzed court documentation concerning motions for reduced sentence pursuant to 18 U.S.C. § 35 82(c)(2) that were decided through March 5, 2009, which represents one year of retroactive application. During that one-year period, the courts decided 19,239 motions.[32] Of the 19,239 motions, 13,408 (69.7%) were granted. Of the 13,408 motions granted, information regarding the extent of the reduction granted was available in 11,951 cases. Of those 11,951 cases, the average sentence was reduced on average by 24 months – or 17.0 percent – from 140 months to 116 months.[33]

Of the 19,239 motions, 5,831 (30.3%) were denied.[34] Of the 5,831 motions denied, 706 (11.0%) involved offenders who were ineligible for a reduction under USSG §1B1.10 because the offense did not involve crack cocaine, and 4,175 (64.9%) involved offenders who were otherwise ineligible. Of these 4,175 denials, 1,536 were denied because a statutory mandatory minimum controlled the sentence (representing 23.9% of all denials), and 1,453 were denied because applicable career offender or armed career criminal statutory and/or guideline provisions controlled the sentence (representing 22.6% of all denials).[35] Of the 5,831 motions denied, 970 (15.1%) involved offenders who were eligible for a reduction but whose motions were denied on the merits, most often (445, or 6.9% of all denials) because the offender had already benefitted from a departure or variance at the initial sentencing.[36]

V. RECOMMENDATIONS

The Commission continues to believe that there is no justification for the current statutory penalty scheme for powder cocaine and crack cocaine offenses. The Commission is of the view that any comprehensive solution to this problem requires revision of the current statutory penalties and therefore must be legislated by Congress. The Commission remains committed to its recommendation in 2002 that any statutory ratio be no more than 20-to-1. Specifically, consistent with its May 2007 Report, the Commission recommends that Congress:

- Increase the five-year and ten-year statutory mandatory minimum threshold quantities for crack cocaine offenses to focus the penalties more closely on serious and major traffickers as described generally in the legislative history of the 1986 Act.

- Repeal the mandatory minimum penalty provision for simple possession of crack cocaine under 21 U.S.C. § 844.
- Reject addressing the 100-to-1 drug quantity ratio by decreasing the five- year and ten-year statutory mandatory minimum threshold quantities for powder cocaine offenses, as there is no evidence to justify such an increase in quantity-based penalties for powder cocaine offenses.

The Commission further recommended in its May 2007 Report that any legislation implementing these recommendations also provide emergency amendment authority for the Commission to incorporate the statutory changes in the federal sentencing guidelines. [37] Emergency amendment authority would enable the Commission to minimize the lag between any statutory and guideline modifications for cocaine offenders.

The Commission believes that the federal sentencing guidelines continue to provide the best mechanism for achieving the principles of the Sentencing Reform Act of 1984, including the consideration of all of the factors set forth at 18 U.S.C. § 3553(a). The Commission recommends to Congress that its concerns about the harms associated with cocaine drug trafficking are best captured through the sentencing guideline system.

CONCLUSION

The Commission is committed to working with Congress to address the statutorily mandated disparities that still exist in federal cocaine sentencing. The Commission also is committed to working with Congress on all other issues related to maintaining just and effective national sentencing policy in a manner that preserves the bipartisan principles of the Sentencing Reform Act of 1984. Thank you for the opportunity to appear before you today, and I look forward to answering your questions.

End Notes

[1] *See* United States Sentencing Commission (hereinafter "USSC" or "Commission"), *Report On Cocaine and Federal Sentencing Policy* ("May 2007 Report"), US SC, 2002 Report to Congress: Cocaine and Federal Sentencing Policy (May 2002); USSC, 1997 *Special Report to Congress: Cocaine and Federal Sentencing Policy* (as directed by section 2 of Pub. L. 104–38) (April 1997); USSC, *1995 Special Report to Congress: Cocaine and Federal Sentencing Policy* (as directed by section 280006 of Pub. L. 103–322) (February 1995).

[2] 28 U.S.C. § 994(u) provides that "[i]f the Commission reduces the term of imprisonment recommended in the guidelines applicable to a particular offense or category of offenses, it shall specify in what circumstances and by what amount the sentences of prisoners serving terms of imprisonment for the offense may be reduced." *See also* USSG, App. C, Amendment 713 (March 3, 2008).

[3] Pub. L. 99–570, 100 Stat. 3207 (1986) (hereinafter "1986 Act").

[4] *See* USSC, *2002 Report to Congress: Cocaine and Federal Sentencing Policy* (May 2002) at 7-10 for a discussion of the legislative history of the 1986 Act as it pertains to crack cocaine.

[5] *See* 21 U.S.C. § 844.

[6] USSG, App. C, Amendment 706 (Nov. 1, 2007). Specifically, the 2007 crack cocaine guideline amendment reduced the base offense level for offenses involving at least five grams of crack cocaine by two levels, from level 26 to level 24, which corresponds to a sentencing guideline range of 51 to 63 months for a defendant in Criminal History Category I. The base offense level for offenses involving at least 50 grams of crack cocaine similarly was reduced by two levels, from level 32 to level 30, which corresponds to a sentencing guideline range of 97-121 months for a defendant in Criminal History Category I. If a statutory mandatory minimum

applies, the applicable guideline range is 60 to 63 months in a case in which the five-year mandatory minimum applies, and 120 to 121 months in a case in which the ten-year mandatory minimum applies. *See* USSG §5G1.1 (Sentencing on a Single Count of Conviction).

[7] *See supra* note 1.

[8] In fiscal year 2008, there were 105 federal cases for simple possession of crack cocaine, in which 58 offenders were subject to the statutory mandatory minimum penalty. In fiscal year 2007, there were 109 such cases, in which 49 offenders were subject to the statutory mandatory minimum penalty.

[9] The "safety valve" at 18 U.S.C. § 3553(f) provides a mechanism by which only drug offenders who meet certain statutory criteria may be sentenced without regard to the otherwise applicable drug mandatory minimum provisions. Enacted in 1994, the safety valve provision was created by Congress to permit offenders "who are the least culpable participants in drug trafficking offenses, to receive strictly regulated reductions in prison sentences for mitigating factors" recognized in the federal sentencing guidelines.

[10] The Commission uses "safety valve" to refer to cases that receive either the two-level reduction pursuant to USSG §2D1 .1 (b)(1 1) and USSG §5C1 .2, or relief from the statutory mandatory minimum sentence pursuant to 18 U.S.C. § 3553(f), or both.

[11] Among the requirements to receive "safety valve" relief from the statutory mandatory minimum sentence, the defendant must not have more than one criminal history point, as determined under the sentencing guidelines, and the defendant must not have used violence or credible threats of violence or must not have possessed a firearm or other dangerous weapon (or induce another participant to do so) in connection with the offense. *See* 18 U.S.C. § 3553(f)(1).

[12] The guidelines provide a two-level enhancement (an approximate 25% increase in penalty) at §2D1 .1 (b)(1) if a dangerous weapon (including a firearm) was possessed.

[13] *See* 18 U.S.C. § 924(c).

[14] Pursuant to USSG §3B 1.2 (Mitigating Role), a two- to four-level reduction in offense level applies in a case in which the offender's role in the offense was minimal or minor (or between minimal and minor).

[15] Pursuant to USSG §3B 1.1 (Aggravating Role), a two- to four-level increase in offense level applies in a case in which the offender was an organizer, leader, manager, or supervisor of the criminal activity.

[16] Of the 1,429 crack cocaine offenders who were in Criminal History Category VI in fiscal year 2008, 951 were career offenders. Of these 951 career offenders, 535 would have been in a lower criminal history category but for their career offender status. Of the 469 powder cocaine offenders who were in Criminal History Category VI in fiscal year 2008, 356 were career offenders. Of these 356 career offenders, 251 would have been in a lower criminal history category but for their career offender status.

[17] U.S. ___, 128 S. Ct. 558 (2007).

[18] *Id.* at 568 (internal quotations omitted).

[19] U.S. ___, 129 S. Ct. 840 (2009) (per curiam).

[20] *Id.* at 843-44 (emphasis in original).

[21] *Id.* at 843.

[22] *See United States v. Edwards*, 2009 WL 424464 (N.D. Ill. February 17, 2009).

[23] *See United States v. Gully*, No. CR 08-3005-MWB, slip op. (N.D. Iowa May 18, 2009).

[24] 543 U.S. 220 (2005).

[25] In addition, powder cocaine offenders also received government sponsored, below-range sentences more frequently than crack cocaine offenders. In fiscal years 2007 and 2008, the rate of government sponsored, below-range sentences for crack cocaine offenders was 30.5 percent and 27.8 percent, respectively, compared to 35.7 percent and 35.6 percent, respectively, for powder cocaine offenders.

[26] Pub. L. 108–21.

[27] Of those 959 cases, 500 cases (52.1%) were sentenced within the applicable guideline range, 273 cases (28.5%) were sentenced below the applicable guideline range pursuant to a government motion, and 10 cases (1.0%) were sentenced above the applicable guideline range.

[28] 18 U.S.C. § 3582(c)(2) provides "in the case of a defendant who has been sentenced to a term of imprisonment based on a sentencing range that has subsequently been lowered by the Sentencing Commission pursuant 28 U.S.C. 994(o), upon motion of the defendant or the Director of the Bureau of Prisons, or on its own motion, the court may reduce the term of imprisonment, after considering the factors set forth in section 3 553(a) to the extent that they are applicable, if such a reduction is consistent with applicable policy statements issued by the Sentencing Commission."

[29] USSG, App. C, Amendment 712 (Mar. 3, 2008).

[30] *See* US SC, *Analysis of the Impact of the Crack Cocaine Amendment If Made Retroactive* (Oct. 3, 2007), *available at* http://www.ussc.gov/general/Impact_Analysis_20071003_3b.pdf (hereinafter "Retroactivity Analysis").

[31] Retroactivity Analysis at 23. These predictions were based on a number of assumptions. For a discussion of the assumptions and model used, *see generally* Retroactivity Analysis.

[32] US SC, *Preliminary Crack Cocaine Retroactivity Data Report*, Table 1 (March 2009) (hereinafter "March 2009 Retroactivity Report").

[33] *Id.* at Table 8.

[34] *Id.*

[35] March 2009 Retroactivity Report at Table 9. In some cases, courts cite multiple reasons for denying a motion for reduction in sentence. Reasons for ineligibility include that the offender was sentenced at the statutory mandatory minimum, the offender was sentenced as a career offender or armed career offender, or that the case involved too high a drug quantity to benefit from a reduction. *Id.*

[36] *Id.*

[37] "Emergency amendment authority" allows the Commission to promulgate guideline amendments outside of the ordinarily applicable amendment cycle provided by 28 U.S.C. § 994(a) and (p).

In: An Examination of Sentencing Levels and Mandatory… ISBN: 978-1-61209-563-9
Editor: Catherine N. Bates

Chapter 14

TESTIMONY OF JOSEPH I. CASSILLY, STATE'S ATTORNEY HARTFORD COUNTY, BEL AIR, MARYLAND AND PRESIDENT, NATIONAL DISTRICT ATTORNEYS ASSOCIATION, BEFORE THE SUBCOMMITTEE ON CRIME, TERRORISM AND HOMELAND SECURITY, HEARING ON "RESTORING FAIRNESS TO FEDERAL SENTENCING: ADDRESSING THE CRACK-POWDER DISPARITY"

I am testifying on behalf of the National District Attorneys Association, the oldest and largest organization representing State and local prosecutors. I have attached a resolution adopted by NDAA regarding the sentencing disparity between crack and powder cocaine. NDAA agrees that some adjustment is warranted, but just as the 100:1 disparity cannot be justified by empirical data we believe that the proposed 1:1 realignment of Federal penalties for crack versus powder cocaine also lacks any empirical or clinical evidence. A random adjustment will have severe negative consequences on the efforts of this nation's prosecutors to remove the destructive effects of crack and violence from our communities.

I have been a criminal prosecutor for over 31 years. My prosecutors and I work on one of the most active and successful task forces in Maryland and cooperate with federal agents and prosecutors from the Office of the U. S. Attorney for Maryland.

The cooperation of Federal and State prosecutors and law enforcement that has developed over the years is due in large part to the interplay of Federal and State laws. Maryland state statutes differentiate sentences between crack and powder cocaine offenders on a 9:1 ratio based on the amount that would indicate a major dealer. There is not in reality a 100:1 difference in the sentences given to crack versus powder offenders. A DOJ report states, "A facial comparison of the guideline ranges for equal amounts of crack and powder cocaine reveals that crack penalties range from 6.3 times greater to approximately equal to powder sentences."

In recent years local prosecutors have brought hundreds of large quantity dealers for Federal prosecution, primarily because of the discretion of Federal prosecutors in dealing with these cases. This discretion allows for pleas to lesser amounts of cocaine or the option of not seeking sentence enhancements. The end result is that the majority of these cases are ultimately resolved by a guilty plea to a sentence below the statutory amount.

The practical effect of guilty pleas is that serious violent criminals are immediately removed from our communities, they spend less time free on bail or in pre-trial detention, civilian witnesses are not needed for trial or sentencing hearings and are therefore not subject to threats and intimidation and undercover officers are not called as witnesses: all of which would happen if we were forced to proceed with these cases in courts. Yet meaningful sentences are imposed, which punish the offender but also protect the community. The plea agreements often call for testimony against higher ups in the crack organization. It is critical that Federal sentences for serious crack dealers remain stricter than State laws if this coordinated interaction is to continue.

Let me dispel myths about controlled substance prosecutions that are propagated by those who would de-criminalize the devastation caused by illegal drugs.

1. There is a difference between the affect of crack versus powder cocaine on the user [1] In a study entitled "Crack Cocaine and Cocaine Hydrochloride: Are the Differences Myth or Reality?" by D. K. Hatsukami and M.W. Fischman, Department of Psychiatry, Division of Neurosciences, University of Minnesota, Minneapolis it is stated,

> "The physiological and psychoactive effects of cocaine are similar regardless of whether it is in the form of cocaine hydrochloride or crack cocaine (cocaine base). However, evidence exists showing a greater abuse liability, greater propensity for dependence, and more severe consequences when cocaine is smoked (cocaine-base) ... compared with intranasal use (cocaine hydrochloride). The crucial variables appear to be the immediacy, duration, and magnitude of cocaine's effect, as well as the frequency and amount of cocaine used rather than the form of the cocaine."

   Smoked cocaine results in the quickest onset and fastest penetration. Generally, smoked cocaine reaches the brain within 20 seconds; the effects last for about 30 minutes, at which time the user to avoid the effects of a "crash" re-uses. The Drug Enforcement Administration's (DEA) intelligence indicates that a crack user is likely to consume anywhere from 3.3 to 16.5 grams of crack a week, or between 13.2 grams and 66 grams per month.

   Intranasally administered cocaine has a slower onset. The maximum psychotropic effects are felt within 20 minutes and the maximum physiological effects within 40 minutes. The effects from intranasally administered cocaine usually last for about 60 minutes after the peak effects are attained. A typical user snorts between two and three lines at a time and consumes about 2 grams per month.

   Using these amounts, the cost per user per month for crack cocaine is between $1,300 and $6,600 as compared to a cost for powder cocaine of $200 per month; a 6.5 to 33:1 ratio in cost.

2. There is a difference in the associated crimes and the effect on the community caused by crack as opposed to powder cocaine.

The inability to legitimately generate the large amount of money needed by a crack addict leads to a high involvement in crimes that can produce ready cash such as robbery and prostitution. Studies show crack cocaine use is more associated with systemic violence than powder cocaine use. One study found that the most prevalent form of violence related to crack cocaine abuse was aggravated assault. In addition, a 1998 study identified crack as the drug most closely linked to trends in homicide rates. Furthermore, crack is much more associated with weapons use than is powder cocaine: in FY2000, weapons were involved in more than twice as many crack convictions as powder.

One of the best-documented links between increased crime and cocaine abuse is the link between crack use and prostitution. In this study, 86.7% of women surveyed were not involved in prostitution in the year before starting crack use; one-third become involved in prostitution in the year after they began use. Women who were already involved in prostitution dramatically increased their involvement after starting to use crack, with rates nearly four times higher than before beginning crack use.

One complaint about the sentencing disparity is that it discriminates against black crack dealers versus white powder dealers. Unfortunately, what most discriminates against our black citizens is the violence, degradation and community collapse that is associated with crack use and crack dealers and their organizations. It is the black homeowners who most earnestly plead with me, as a prosecutor, for strict enforcement and long prison sentences for crack offenders. The stop snitching video was made by black crack dealers in Baltimore to threaten black citizens with retaliation and death for fighting the dealers. A black family of five was killed by a fire bomb which was thrown into their home at the direction of crack dealers because they were reporting crack dealers on the street in front of their house. Those areas with the highest violent crime rates are the same areas with the highest crack cocaine use.

Congress should consider that many persons serving federal crack sentences have received consideration from the prosecutors in return for a guilty plea. (i.e. pleas to lesser amounts of cocaine or the option of not seeking sentence enhancements) Many criminals who could be affected by a retroactive application of a new sentencing scheme have already received the benefits of lower sentences and would get a second reduction. New sentencing hearings would mean that citizens from the communities that crack dealers once ruined would have to come forward to keep the sentences from being cut.

The nation's prosecutors urge Congress to adopt a sentencing scheme with regard to the destruction caused by crack cocaine to our communities. If there is a need to reduce the disparity between crack and powder cocaine then perhaps the solution is to increase sentences for powder cocaine.

End Notes

[1] Most of the following comments are taken from reports of the United States Sentencing Commission or of the Department of Justice.

In: An Examination of Sentencing Levels and Mandatory... ISBN: 978-1-61209-563-9
Editor: Catherine N. Bates

Chapter 15

TESTIMONY OF WILLIE M. AIKENS, BEFORE THE SUBCOMMITTEE ON CRIME, TERRORISM AND HOMELAND SECURITY, HEARING ON "UNFAIRNESS IN FEDERAL COCAINE SENTENCING: IS IT TIME TO CRACK THE 100 TO 1 DISPARITY?"

Thank you Chairman Scott and members of the Subcommittee for inviting me to testify before you today. My name is Willie M. Aikens and I am here to tell my story about the direct effects of crack cocaine on my life. I will also testify about how the mandatory minimums and especially the sharp disparity between the penalties for crack and powder cocaine have touched me, my family, and friends I left behind in the Federal Prison System.

I grew up in Seneca, South Carolina without ever seeing or knowing who my biological father was. My stepfather was very abusive and was an alcoholic, and so was my first cousin who lived in the same house as me. They both died in 1968 from alcohol related deaths, so at an early age I saw the devastating effects of drugs and alcohol. Later on in life I didn't believe the same thing could happen to me, though it did. I didn't let any of this stop me from pursuing my goal of being an athlete. I truly believe playing sports kept me out of trouble. I went on to finish high school and I earned a football scholarship to South Carolina State College. Since baseball was my favorite sport, I asked the coaches if I could play baseball and they all agreed.

While at South Carolina State College I went on to do well in football and baseball. After my freshman year, I dropped out of college and was drafted by the California Angels in the first round. The Angels offered me a good signing bonus, so I took it. I went on to play three years in the minor league system before I was promoted to the Major Leagues. I had my first taste of the big show in 1977. I also had my first taste of powder cocaine that same year. This was my first encounter with drugs. I played for the Angels until 1979, and then I was traded to the Kansas City Royals.

My first year in Kansas City was a great one. My team had an outstanding season and we went on to play in the 1980 World Series. I also was introduced to cocaine once again and my usage increased because of my social lifestyle. I used cocaine after each game of the 1980 World Series as a member of the Kansas City Royals. We lost the series to the Philadelphia

Phillies, but I became the first player in Major League history to have more than one multiple homer game. I hit two home runs in game 1 and two home runs in game 2. That had never been done before and still today no one else has done it.

During my second year in Kansas City, I was using cocaine regularly along with several other Royals players. Our supplier was a guy who was a Royals fan, and we all would go over to his house at least five days out of the week. This guy would follow us on road trips to watch us play and he would bring cocaine along too. Most of the guys on my team who used drugs knew other players on other teams that used drugs also, so we always had a way of getting cocaine. This began in 1981 and went on until 1983, when our supplier got busted with four ounces of powder cocaine. The FBI had been watching him and they put a wire tap on his telephone. Three of my teammates, Vida Blue, Willie Wilson and Jerry Martin, and I had made telephone calls to this guy. We got indicted for attempting to procure cocaine over the telephone and we eventually pled guilty to misdemeanor drug charges. At our sentencing hearing none of us thought jail time was a possibility, but the judge sentenced us to three months in prison. We were the first active Major Leaguers to serve jail time for drugs. All four of us were suspended for the entire 1984 season, though the suspensions were later reduced and we were allowed to return to our teams in May 1984. Even though I had my best season in 1983, my attitude with my manager was bad, and I have no doubt that my cocaine usage was the direct cause. After the 1983 season, I was traded to the Toronto Blue Jays and my baseball career went downhill. After playing two years in Toronto, I got released and could never find a job playing baseball again in the United States. I ended up playing in Mexico for the next six years and I started back using drugs again in 1987. While playing in Mexico two beautiful daughters were born to me.

I retired from baseball in 1990, and returned to Kansas City. For the next four years I became a recluse in my own home, going out mainly to buy cocaine. I had started smoking cocaine in Mexico, so I knew all the ins and outs of preparing the drug. I went through two bank accounts of over three- hundred thousand dollars and didn't think twice about what I was doing. I was living a destructive lifestyle and was enjoying every bit of it. Finally in 1994, all of this came to a stop.

One day out of nowhere this girl arrived at my house in a car looking for Cherry Street. I was in my yard on my way to buy some cocaine. I took her to Cherry Street, but she didn't turn off there, she kept following me. I pulled into this gas station and asked her why she didn't go to Cherry Street. She didn't give me an answer. I started rapping to her, asking her if she had a boyfriend. She said sort of, so I asked her for her telephone number. I ended up giving her my number and within the next week she called me. I asked her if she did drugs. She said she sat around on weekends and played cards with her girlfriends and got high. She told me she was looking for someone to get her drugs. I told her I knew someone who had all the drugs she wanted. That was exactly what she wanted to hear.

It turned out that she was an undercover officer for the Kansas City Police department, which had started their investigation of me because of anonymous telephone calls. The first time I sold drugs to her was in December 1993. I had just purchased 7 grams of powder cocaine to use for myself. She called me over the telephone and wanted an eight ball, which was three and a half grams. I told her to come on by. She wanted rock cocaine, so I cooked it for her. About two weeks later she called me again and wanted to buy 7 grams of cocaine. I told her over the telephone that if she wanted the drugs, we would have to go to my dealer's house to purchase them. She came and picked me up. After arriving at the dealer's house she gave me the money and I purchased 7 grams of powder cocaine. She wanted rock cocaine or crack, so we drove back to my condo and I cooked it for her again. She called me twice more and each time we went to my dealer's house and purchased powder cocaine. After this last transaction, the city police kicked in my door at my condo one week later. After four purchases of crack cocaine, she finally had 50 grams or more, which put me in the mandatory minimum ten years guidelines. The Kansas City police turned my case over to the federal authorities for prosecution to make sure I got the longest sentence possible

I took my case to trial and lost. My lawyer used the entrapment defense at my trial. Because the undercover officer knew crack cocaine carried a stiffer penalty, we wanted the jurors to see that crack was involved in my case only because the officer had asked me to cook it. She testified at my trial that she knew crack cocaine carried a harsher penalty and that was the reason why she wanted it cooked. I was convicted on four counts of distribution of crack cocaine, one count of the use of a weapon during the commission of a crime and one count of obstruction of justice. I received a sentence of 20 years and 8 months, the highest sentence that the judge could give me under the sentencing guidelines. My release date was May, 2012. I didn't believe the next fourteen years of my life would be behind prison's walls. If I had been charged with a similar amount of powder cocaine, my sentence on the drug charges would have been at most 27 months.

During those fourteen years of incarceration I rededicated my life to Jesus Christ. In other words, I became a born again Christian. I came to realize that being taken off the streets at that time saved my life. It didn't take fourteen years to change me, but it did take being incarcerated to leave that lifestyle behind. I drank and drugged for four straight years in my condo and I had no plans of changing my lifestyle when I got caught. So, I give all honor and praise to God for saving my life. While I was in prison, I completed three different drug rehabilitation programs, which helped me realize that I had an addiction problem, which led to my criminal activity. I came to realize that the foundation of my problems was my drug usage, not the undercover officer setting me up. I came in contact with so many other people that had the same problem I had. I also came in contact with a lot of people that had life sentences because they were convicted of selling crack cocaine. Many of them were first time offenders, had no criminal record and had no violence in their case. My case was very sad, but theirs was sadder. These people were never going home.

After I had spent fourteen years of my life in prison, Congress finally allowed the Sentencing Commission to reduce the crack cocaine guidelines. The Sentencing Commission also recommended that the amended guidelines be made retroactive. In March of 2008, that became a reality. Many people sentenced for crack cocaine now became eligible for a two level reduction on the guidelines. I benefited from this change in the law, and the court gave me almost five years off my sentence. Instead of being released in 2012, I was eligible for release immediately. I got out of prison last June.

Since my release from prison I have developed a relationship with my daughters. I have found a job working construction in Kansas City and I am in the process of getting back into professional baseball. I have been clean and sober for fifteen years and I have a strong spiritual foundation. I am writing a book and I am doing speaking engagements in and around the Kansas City area about the dangers of drugs and alcohol. God has truly blessed my life.

In closing I would like to add that I didn't come to Washington, DC to testify for myself. I came to Washington, DC for all the people I left behind in prison. I made a promise to those people that if God allowed me to leave prison before them, then I would do everything in my power to help them. That is the main reason why I am sitting in this chair today. We have so many sad cases of drug addicts being locked up and the keys being thrown away. We have so many families that are suffering right now because a son, a father, a mother, a brother and sister will never come home from prison. Look at me and look at the progress that I have made in my life because I was given another chance to live my life as a free man. I believe many more people will do the same thing if they are given a chance. These mandatory minimum laws and the crack cocaine disparity with powder cocaine need to be eliminated. Cocaine is cocaine regardless of the form it comes in. Put the power of sentencing back into the hands of the judges and let them decide what sentence is fair.

I am praying that this will be the last time the Subcommittee will meet regarding these unfair laws. The mandatory minimum laws and the crack cocaine vs powder cocaine disparity need to be changed. I could have gotten probation for 64 grams of powder cocaine, and the most I would have gotten is two years in prison. The fact that it was crack cocaine added ten years to my sentence, which is totally wrong.

Thank you for hearing me.

In: An Examination of Sentencing Levels and Mandatory… ISBN: 978-1-61209-563-9
Editor: Catherine N. Bates

Chapter 16

STATEMENT OF BOB BUSHMAN, VICE PRESIDENT, NATIONAL NARCOTIC OFFICERS' ASSOCIATIONS' COALITION, BEFORE THE SUBCOMMITTEE ON CRIME, TERRORISM AND HOMELAND SECURITY, HEARING ON "UNFAIRNESS IN FEDERAL COCAINE SENTENCING: IS IT TIME TO CRACK THE 100 TO 1 DISPARITY?"

Chairman Scott and Congressman Gohmert, thank you for inviting me to share the views of the National Narcotic Officers' Associations' Coalition (NNOAC). My name is Bob Bushman and I have been a law enforcement officer in Minnesota for 30 years. I am Vice President of the NNOAC, which represents 44 state associations with more than 69,000 law enforcement officers nationwide.

The NNOAC has worked with this committee to support several critical public safety measures over the past decade, and we are pleased that many, including both the Byrne Justice Assistance Grant (JAG) Reauthorization Act and the Second Chance Act that were signed into law last year, have resulted from those collaborative efforts.

Technically, what our N NOAC members do is enforce the laws against crime and illegal drugs that legislative bodies, like Congress, put on the books.

In human terms, the people we represent are dedicated law enforcement officers. As we testify here today, many police officers, sheriff's deputies, and state and federal agents are working in neighborhoods throughout our country, protecting our communities from predators who profit greatly by selling and distributing poisons to our kids with the knowledge that these poisons will make them addicts, expose them to violence, and in some instances, even kill them. These predators purposely harm not only the user, but the user's family, and the community as well. And, in most instances, our members are the only ones that stand in their way.

I remember the devastation I saw in the 1980s and 90s as a cop working crack cases in our Twin Cities. It was unlike anything I or my partners had ever seen. The highest homicide rates most cities have ever experienced occurred during the crack epidemic of the late 80s and early 90s. Our country experienced a painful "wake-up call" and acted decisively to get a handle on the problem. The crack trade was responsible for dramatic increases in violent crime and, consequently, it consumed police resources in many of our most urban areas. The negative impact on public safety was staggering. Drive-by shootings, gang wars and home invasions were common occurrences. Citizens – through their elected representatives and leaders – demanded tough measures to bring the situation under control. The current laws related to sentencing of crack offenders were a direct response to the desperate pleas of the law abiding citizens and their families, who became victims trapped in crime infested neighborhoods.

Drug problems have existed in our nation for a long time. Most people don't realize that the height of drug addiction in this country occurred just after the Civil War when 1 in 200 Americans were addicted to drugs. During our lifetime, drug use peaked during the late 1970's. Since the height of the crack epidemic, drug use – particularly cocaine use – has declined dramatically. I don't think we hear this enough. If the incidents of AIDS or diabetes decreased as dramatically as drug use has, someone would be getting a Nobel Prize.

Yes, we continue to have a significant drug problem in this country. But we have made a huge difference in the past 20 years, due in part, to tough criminal sanctions that both prevent drug use and compel cooperation of individuals to take down drug distribution organizations.

Let me be clear - we understand the sensitivities around the issue of the 100:1 crack-powder disparity. We often work in environments where the law and those who enforce it are not respected, whether it's because of perceived racial bias or some other reason. But we need you, our members of Congress, to understand what we as police officers, sheriff's deputies and drug enforcement agents experience and work with every single day of our careers, and to understand that we are dedicated professionals who work hard to protect our citizens, no matter who they are, where they live, or what they believe.

We are caught in the middle on this issue. Our main concern is public safety – that is what we are hired and trained to do. But it is difficult to protect the citizens, especially those in the drug- infested, high crime areas who need us most, when we cannot rid those neighborhoods of the ones who abuse them the most – drug dealers and gangs. We are criticized by some for not doing enough, and by others for being too aggressive in our prosecution of drug violators.

I can tell you that we view tough drug sentences as a very effective way of getting predators off the streets – we are talking about the dealers and profiteers, ***not*** the addicts and low-end users. As a matter of fact, many crack dealers do not use crack – they know the dangers of the drug. Mandatory sentences punish the dealers - the people who do the most damage to our communities.

As we talk about the violence associated with the crack cocaine trade, I ask you to remember that it isn't just driven by the dealer's desire to make money or the user's need to get money to purchase crack. Many violent crimes are committed by people who are under the influence of the drug itself, and unable to act rationally. Domestic violence and child abuse are common in crack riddled neighborhoods. Many police officers and I have spent our own money to purchase food to feed hungry kids who we found living in crack houses. And, as for those who label drug use or addiction as a "victimless crime", I still haven't found anyone who can explain to me how a crack baby isn't a victim.

We have been asked, repeatedly, over the past few years about our views on legislative proposals to reduce the crack-powder disparity. While we believe that the existing law has been a valuable tool in reducing the impact of crack on communities, we realize that it has also had a negative impact on some people's perception of law enforcement. So, while we agree that it is appropriate for Congress to review the law, we also believe that Congress should consider a solution to narrow the disparity between crack and powder cocaine that includes lowering the threshold quantity for powder cocaine. We do not believe the best approach is to dramatically increase the threshold amount of crack that triggers the minimum penalty.

Why should we continue to maintain tougher sentences for crack than for cocaine powder?

- Smoking crack leads to a sudden, short-lived high, causing an intense, immediate desire for more of it. Addiction to crack is quick – and powerful. Just last month, the director of the National Institute on Drug Abuse, Dr. Nora Volkow, testified before the Senate Judiciary Committee that "research consistently shows that the form of the drug is not the crucial variable; rather it is the route of administration that accounts for the differences in its behavioral effects."
- The violence associated with the crack trade and perpetrated by crack users is more prevalent than that associated with the cocaine trade; public safety is compromised. We have seen this happen in community after community. Part of it has to do with the turf wars – drug dealers and urban drug gangs fighting for control of an area and the customers it contains. Although much of the violence is dealer-on-dealer, innocent bystanders and, sometimes even entire neighborhoods, are often caught in the cross-fire. These are the citizens that we, as law enforcement officers, are sworn to protect. It's difficult to protect our communities if we can't remove those who are responsible for the crime and violence.
- Selling crack is more profitable than selling powder cocaine. If crack cocaine penalties are made equal to that of powder, there will be more incentive to sell crack and make bigger profits. While it is true that crack and powder cocaine have the same physiological effect on the brain, the negative impact on public safety, due to the violence associated with the crack cocaine trade alone, justifies a difference in penalties.

We often hear from advocates of drug decriminalization and legalization that "valuable law enforcement resources" are wasted on low-level drug offenders, and that the low thresholds for crack encourage this. I can assure you that state and local law enforcement across the country are not sitting around plotting how to go after users and addicts – we don't have the time or resources to do that. Most of our anti-drug operations in the communities are in direct response to citizens' pleas for help with problems that affect their daily lives and routines – quality of life issues. To the extent that we are dealing with low-level offenders, it is because they are committing other crimes to support their habit or because their actions, while they are under the influence of drugs, threaten the safety of the citizens in our neighborhoods.

As law enforcement professionals, we value the important roles that prevention and education programs play in helping people to avoid immersion into the criminal justice system in the first place. The NNOAC supports, and is involved with, prevention and education programs around the country. But those who do become drug users or addicts need help and, in many cases, the criminal justice system is a gateway to their recovery. We are strong advocates of Drug Court Programs and we believe that they ought to be strengthened and expanded to mitigate the problems caused by drugs in our communities. In fact, our president, Ron Brooks, was just asked to join the board of the National Association of Drug Court Professionals.

We realize we cannot arrest our way out of the drug problem. But the threat of arrest, prosecution, and imprisonment are important components in deterring drug use, reducing crime and protecting our citizens from falling victim to violent and dangerous, predatory criminals.

I thank you again, Mr. Chairman and Congressman Gohmert for the opportunity to share our views. We look forward to working with this committee and Congress as we attempt to resolve the ongoing problems associated with drug trafficking, abuse and addiction. Just like you, we, too, hope to enhance the vitality of our communities and provide safe streets and stable neighborhoods for America's families in the years ahead.

In: An Examination of Sentencing Levels and Mandatory... ISBN: 978-1-61209-563-9
Editor: Catherine N. Bates

Chapter 17

STATEMENT OF VERONICA F. COLEMAN-DAVIS, FORMER UNITED STATES ATTORNEY FOR THE WESTERN DISTRICT OF TENNESSEE, BEFORE THE SUBCOMMITTEE ON CRIME, TERRORISM AND HOMELAND SECURITY, HEARING ON "UNFAIRNESS IN FEDERAL COCAINE SENTENCING: IS IT TIME TO CRACK THE 100 TO 1 DISPARITY?"

To Chairmen Conyers and Scott, and the distinguished members of this Subcommittee — thank you for giving me the opportunity to appear before you today to share my view on the important issue of the disparities in our federal cocaine sentencing laws.

I practiced law for over 30 years, 25 of those years in the criminal justice system. I have served as an assistant public defender, private defense attorney, assistant district attorney general, juvenile court referee judge and as United States Attorney for the Western District of Tennessee (1993-2001). In 2001 along with 12 of my former U.S. Attorney colleagues as my board of directors, I founded the National Institute for Law and Equity (NILE), a public policy institute whose mission is raising discussion and understanding of our criminal and juvenile justice systems and their impact on us as a society. Given the knowledge that we have today about crack and powder cocaine it is our belief that the current disparity in sentencing should be reduced to a 1:1 ratio. This is not only consistent with good policy, but also good politics.

I recognize that this committee has received substantial data and anecdotal information about the impact of the sentencing disparity between crack and powder cocaine. But, not much has been said about the impact on the African American community and I hope that through these hearings we will begin to understand how devastating this has been on generations of children in the African American community and that too many now view incarceration as a normative rite of passage. We not only need to end the disparate sentences but we also need to ensure some means of prevention, intervention and healing for those affected by incarcerated parents. Having said that, my remarks here today are limited to my experiences in the criminal justice system and not the juvenile justice system.

Prior to leaving the U.S. Attorney's Office, I was invited to participate in a Department of Justice National Institute of Justice think tank on "Why people don't trust the justice system?" I was the only U.S. Attorney in the session and the majority of participants were from the education and civic communities. On the subject of drug prosecutions, the think tank participants discussed the disparity in crack and powder cocaine cases as posing a major reason for the lack of trust in the justice system within the minority community. When it was pointed out that there appeared to be two separate paradigms in drug prosecutions: a law enforcement paradigm for African Americans and other minorities and a health care paradigm for whites, a senior researcher for the group, not only agreed that our system of justice is based upon those two separate paradigms in drug prosecutions, but generally for all crimes.

It is unfortunate that it is in the minority communities where crime generally and low level sales particularly are a plague on the law abiding citizens. As a result, while residents did not like the criminal activity in their neighborhoods they were often reluctant to call upon the police because they knew that the enforcement of the laws were unfairly focused on minorities, especially when it came to cocaine. And we ask "Why don't people trust the justice system?" We all agreed that systemic distrust is unhealthy for a safe and just society.

I have worked with many law enforcement officers over the years who are dedicated to protecting and serving their communities. But, let's look at the practical side of the life of a police officer or federal agent assigned to drug task forces. They want to do their jobs and if they are measured by the numbers of arrests they make, they will make a lot of arrests. There are strong incentives for cops to make large numbers of arrests to demonstrate that they are doing what the citizenry demands, knowing that these efforts will do little or nothing to stop drug trafficking.

I have witnessed drug stings that were solely focused on housing projects where sales were to people driving up in cars from outside of that community. And, arresting low level street dealers selling crack is like shooting fish in a barrel. On the other hand, going after major sellers and users of powder cocaine often means taking the time to develop leads in order to obtain search warrants for upscale homes and then face long drawn out court battles with highly paid attorneys which meant lower arrest stats and questions from the citizenry about not going after the really bad guys...a euphemism for blacks... instead of those afflicted with addiction...a euphemism for whites.

The joint task forces also had the added leverage of giving the low level dealer a choice between state and federal prosecution if he/she were willing to lead them to the "kingpin". The problem with this strategy was that low level street dealers seldom knew the top dealers, so, the lowest level dealers received some of the harshest sentences. If they could give up someone above them in the food chain, then they would likely receive consideration on their sentence. Most could not and the harsh sentence in the federal system sent first offenders with 5 grams of crack to 5 years in prison instead of probation...the likely sentence in the state system for a first offender with the same quantity of drugs.

As U.S. Attorney and chief law enforcement officer for 22 counties, I worked with all of the law enforcement agencies, local, state and federal, to ensure that our limited federal resources were focused on the most pressing problems in our communities. I recognized early in my tenure, that we were spending considerable attorney resources on street drug crimes that I prosecuted as an Assistant District Attorney and not the serious and major drug traffickers that were the intended targets under the Federal Anti-Drug Abuse Act of 1986 and 1988. After reviewing the issues with the Chief Assistant United States Attorney of our drug task force, some of our judges and our district's DEA's Special Agent in Charge, I made the decision that our office would not take 5 gram crack cases that were prosecutable in state courts. We increased our minimum prosecution guidelines of crack cases to 50 grams Notwithstanding the fact that our efforts focused on major drug dealers including cartels, even the 50 gram guideline paled in comparison to the large quantity of drugs that is shipped into our country on a daily basis.

And, yes, I was challenged by one reporter of not prosecuting as many cases as some of my predecessors: I pointed out to him the number of defendants on a single indictment demonstrated reaching the organization as opposed to pursuing ten indictments against low level individuals. As an Assistant District Attorney and as the U.S. Attorney I was known as being both tough and fair. I firmly believe that it is not the duty of a prosecutor to simply obtain convictions by the numbers, but to do justice. As U.S. Supreme Court Justice Sutherland, in *Berger v. United States,* 295 U.S. 78, 88 (1935) said:

> The United States Attorney is the representative not of an ordinary party to a controversy, but of a sovereignty whose obligation to govern impartially is as compelling as its obligation to govern at all; and whose interest, therefore, in a criminal prosecution is not that it shall win a case, but that justice shall be done. As such, he is in a peculiar and very definite sense the servant of the law, the twofold aim of which is that guilt shall not escape or innocence suffer. He may prosecute with earnestness and vigor — indeed, he should do so. But, while he may strike hard blows, he is not at liberty to strike foul ones. It is as much his duty to refrain from improper methods calculated to produce a wrongful conviction as it is to use every legitimate means to bring about a just one.

The pressure to obtain convictions in order to appear to be tough on crime is not doing justice. It may be good politics to stand before the public and parade a hundred defendants who possessed 5 grams of crack cocaine and claim that their 5 year mandatory minimum sentence was going to make the community safer. But, it is not good public policy when you know that the average defendant is poor, black, undereducated, and unskilled and will return to the community angry at the obvious disparity in the prison and jails and unable to get a job no matter how much he/she wishes to earn a living by legal means.

And to add insult to injury, we no longer forgive people who have "paid their debt to society". So, what exactly do we expect them to do?

To those citizens in our communities who are unsympathetic with the fact that someone goes to jail for a crime, let me be clear, I was never called soft on crime. I am the first to say that people who commit crimes should be punished for their criminal activity. But, bringing criminals to the bar of justice also means treating them fairly and equally. Therefore, I do not believe that the average citizen, given what we know today, would agree that there is equal justice in sending one person to prison for 5 years for possessing 5 grams of crack cocaine and another receiving the same sentence for possessing 500 grams of powder cocaine.

How much longer will it take to correct a by now well known and understood mistake in our system of justice? After more than 20 years, multiple studies debunking the myths, 'recommendations from the United States Sentencing Commission and at least two generations of families and children torn by the systemic imposition of imprisonment for one 100th the amount of cocaine than their white counterparts, it is surely not only good policy but also good politics to correct this injustice.

Or, from a former prosecutor's perspective the elimination of this unjust disparity is what Truth dictates and Justice demands.

Thank you for conducting these hearings and allowing me to speak to this important issue.

In: An Examination of Sentencing Levels and Mandatory… ISBN: 978-1-61209-563-9
Editor: Catherine N. Bates

Chapter 18

Testimony of Marc Mauer, Executive Director, The Sentencing Project, before the Subcommittee on Crime, Terrorism and Homeland Security, Hearing on "Unfairness in Federal Cocaine Sentencing: Is It Time to Crack the 100 to 1 Disparity?"

Thank you for the opportunity to testify on the issue of the sentencing disparity between crack cocaine and powder cocaine. I am Marc Mauer, Executive Director of The Sentencing Project, a national non-profit organization engaged in research and advocacy on criminal and juvenile justice policy issues. In the area of drug and sentencing policy, I have published broadly, engaged with policymakers nationally, and have frequently presented testimony before Congress and state legislative bodies.

The Sentencing Project has long been engaged in research and policy advocacy regarding federal cocaine sentencing. Our organization has published a series of policy analyses on the issue, delivered testimony before the United States Sentencing Commission ("Commission"), and submitted two amicus briefs to the United States Supreme Court on issues of sentencing in crack cocaine cases. I would like to take the opportunity in this written testimony to identify the fundamental inequities that uniquely exist within the federal drug laws for crack cocaine, as well as the inefficiencies in enforcement operations that result from these laws. I urge the members of this Committee and Congress to pass legislation to restore faith and fairness to a sentencing policy that has garnered near universal condemnation for more than two decades.

Prison Population Expands with Changes in Drug Policy

For more than a quarter century the "war on drugs" has exerted a profound impact on the structure and scale of the criminal justice system. The changes in sentencing and enforcement for drug offenses have been a major contributing factor to the historic rise in the prison population. From a figure of about 40,000 people incarcerated in prison or jail for a drug offense in 1980, there has since been an 1100% increase to a total of 500,000 today. To place some perspective on that change, the number of people incarcerated for a drug offense is now greater than the number incarcerated for *all* offenses in 1980.

The increase in incarceration for drug offenses has been fueled by sharply escalated law enforcement targeting of drug law violations, often accompanied by enhanced penalties for such offenses. Many of the mandatory sentencing provisions adopted in both state and federal law have been focused on drug offenses. At the federal level, the most notorious of these are the penalties for crack cocaine violations, whereby low-level crack offenses are punished far more severely than powder cocaine offenses, even though the two substances are pharmacologically identical. Despite changes in federal sentencing guidelines, the mandatory provisions still in place require that anyone convicted of possessing as little as five grams of crack cocaine (the weight of two sugar packets) receive a five-year prison term for a first-time offense.

The dramatic escalation of incarceration for drug offenses has been accompanied by profound racial and ethnic disparities. African Americans comprise 13 percent of the United States' population and 14 percent of monthly illegal drug users, but represent 37 percent of persons arrested for a drug offense and 56 percent of persons in state prison for a drug conviction.

Despite the recent findings in The Sentencing Project's report, "The Changing Racial Dynamics of the War on Drugs," that between 1999 and 2005 state incarceration of African Americans for drug offenses declined 21.6 percent, perhaps due to a decline in the crack cocaine market, the same is not true for the federal system. Indeed, the number of federal prosecutions for crack offenses remains substantial, and the overall number of people in federal prison for a drug offense rose by 32.7% from 1999 to 2005. Racial disparities persist, with African Americans constituting more than 80% of the people convicted of a federal crack cocaine offense.

The Case of Crack Cocaine

In 1986 when Congress passed the Anti-Drug Abuse Act, the stated intent of the cocaine sentencing structure was to ensure mandatory sentences for major and serious traffickers – heads of drug organizations and those involved in preparing and packaging crack cocaine in "substantial street quantities." Congress calibrated the sentencing structure based on drug quantities that were believed to reflect the different roles in the drug trade, but in its effort to swiftly address rising concern over crack cocaine, the penalty structure became dramatically skewed. The rationale voiced at the time was that the smokable form of cocaine was more addictive, presented greater long-term consequences of use, and had a stronger association with violence in its distribution than the powder cocaine market. History has proven these concerns to be unfounded, yet Congress has remained silent.

Indeed, the actual differences between the two substances are far more subtle. Crack and powder cocaine share the same pharmacological roots, but crack cocaine is cooked with water and baking soda to create a smokable, rock-like substance. Crack cocaine is sold in small quantities and is a cheaper alternative to powder cocaine. However, crack and powder are both part of the same distribution continuum. Crack is, by definition, at the lower-level end of the distribution spectrum where small batches of powder cocaine are processed and sold in an inexpensive, smokable form.

The emergence of the crack cocaine market in the 1980s in a number of major urban areas was accompanied by massive media attention paid toward the drug's meteoric rise and its associated dangers. A core component of the media coverage was the thinly-veiled (and unfounded) link between the drug's use and low-income communities of color. In a matter of weeks, crack cocaine was widely believed by the American public to be a drug that was sold and used exclusively by poor African Americans. This framing of the drug in class and race-based terms provides important context when evaluating the legislative response.

The resulting federal legislation punished crack cocaine with historically punitive sanctions. Crack cocaine is the only drug in which simple possession can result in a mandatory sentence to prison. A defendant convicted with five grams of crack cocaine – between 10 and 50 doses – will receive a five-year mandatory minimum sentence. To receive the same sentence for a powder cocaine violation, a defendant would have to have been involved in an offense involving 500 grams – between 2,500 and 5,000 doses. This is commonly referred to as the "100-to-1 sentencing disparity." In order to trigger a 10-year mandatory sentence, a defendant would need to be charged with 50 grams of crack cocaine – between 100 and 500 doses – or 5,000 grams of powder cocaine – up to 50,000 doses. The quantity levels associated with the two drugs codify an equivalency of punishment for low-level crack cocaine sellers and high-level powder cocaine traffickers.

On average, crack cocaine defendants do not play a sophisticated role in the drug trade. Nearly two-thirds (61.5 percent) of crack cocaine defendants were identified as a street-level dealer, courier, lookout, or user. Among powder cocaine defendants, this proportion was 53.1 percent. Although the distribution of offender roles is similar between the two substances, the median quantity and applicable mandatory minimum are vastly different. The median quantity for a crack cocaine street-level dealer is 52 grams, which triggers a ten-year mandatory sentence. For a powder cocaine street-level dealer, the median quantity is 340 grams, which would not even expose a defendant to a five-year mandatory sentence. This disparity has led the Sentencing Commission to conclude that crack cocaine penalties "apply most often to offenders who perform low-level trafficking functions, wield little decision-making authority, and have limited responsibility." The Commission has further remarked that "[r] evising the crack cocaine thresholds would better reduce the [sentencing] gap than any other single policy change, and it would dramatically improve the fairness of the federal sentencing system."

Harsher penalties for crack cocaine offenses are sometimes supported because of the perception that crack is more likely to be associated with violence than powder cocaine. However, this is not supported by the evidence and subverts the goal of proportionality in sentencing. While there was a significant level of violence associated with crack after its introduction to urban areas in the 1 980s, that violence was a function of the new drug markets and "turf battles," rather than any effect of the drug itself. Additionally, because of inappropriate assumptions about crack cocaine and violence being implicit in the statute, crack cocaine defendants are essentially sentenced for conduct in which they did not engage or face a penalty that takes into consideration the same conduct twice.

Data from the Sentencing Commission now document that a majority of both crack and powder cocaine offenders do not engage in any associated violence, such as bodily injury or threats, and any distinction between the two drugs is not sufficient to warrant additional penalties. An analysis of federal cocaine cases for 2005 demonstrates that 73% of powder cocaine offenses and 57.3% of crack cocaine offenses did not involve a weapon, and that only in a small number of cases (0.8% for powder and 2.9% for crack) were weapons used by the offender.

Violent behavior by drug offenders should be treated seriously, but the sentencing guidelines already provide sufficient opportunity for judges to penalize such conduct. By making the inappropriate assumption that a crack cocaine offense is categorically linked with violent behavior, the statutory penalty leads to one of two key errors. First, individuals who have not engaged in any associated violent conduct are subjected to a penalty structure that presumes uncommitted conduct. Second, for persons who have been charged with a concurrent violent offense, the 100:1 ratio is tantamount to a "double counting" of the charged conduct, thereby exposing defendants to disproportionately severe punishments. The federal criminal code already has a wide range of penalties and enhancements for violent conduct at the disposal of prosecutors and the circumstances of the individual case should govern their applicability.

Crack Cocaine and the African American Community

The impact of crack cocaine policy on the African American community has been devastating. While two-thirds of regular crack cocaine users in the United States are either white or Latino, 80 percent of persons sentenced in federal court for a crack cocaine offense are African American. Thus, African Americans disproportionately face the most severe drug penalties in the federal system.

These racial inequities have come as the result of deliberate decisions by policymakers and practitioners. When crafting mandatory minimum sentences, Congress had sought to establish generalized equivalencies in punishment across drug types by controlling for the perceived severity of the drug via the adjustment of quantity thresholds. However, in practice, sentences are frequently disproportionately severe relative to the conduct for which a person has been convicted because mandatory minimum sentences rely upon the quantity of the charged substance as a proxy for the degree of involvement of a defendant in the drug offense. Thus, the sentencing statutes function as blunt instruments of punishment that are ineffective at appropriately assessing and calibrating sentences based on the specific circumstances of the charged crime.

Since their introduction, mandatory minimum sentences have consistently been shown to have a disproportionately severe impact on African Americans. A study by the Sentencing Commission found that African Americans were 21 percent more likely to receive a mandatory minimum sentence than white defendants facing an eligible charge. A separate study by the Federal Judicial Center also concluded that African Americans faced an elevated likelihood of receiving a mandatory minimum sentence relative to whites. More recently, the Commission, in a 15-year overview of the federal sentencing system, concluded that "mandatory penalty statutes are used inconsistently" and disproportionately affect African

American defendants. As a result, African American drug defendants are 20 percent more likely to be sentenced to prison than white drug defendants.

The Commission observed that federal sentencing changes in the 1980s, notably in the guise of mandatory minimum sentencing and sentencing guidelines, have had "a greater adverse impact on Black offenders than did the factors taken into account by judges in the discretionary system immediately prior to guidelines implementation" and that there is some question as to "whether these new policies are necessary to achieve any legitimate purpose of sentencing." In other words, the cure has proven to be worse than the disease.

CONCLUSION

Although federal crack cocaine laws were forged with the intent of targeting high- level traffickers engaged in international and interstate drug distribution, an enterprise ill-suited for state and local law enforcement for obvious jurisdictional reasons, more than two decades of practice have clearly demonstrated that the laws are excessive and ineffective. The small quantity triggers for crack cocaine mandatory sentences subject street-level sellers of crack cocaine to sentences similar to those for interstate powder cocaine dealers. And those convicted with slightly higher quantities of crack cocaine, although still considered local sellers, receive average sentences longer than international powder cocaine traffickers.

Restoring fairness to the cocaine sentencing structure requires Congress to equalize the penalties for crack and powder offenses without increasing the current mandatory sentences. Harsh mandatory drug penalties have not protected communities or stopped drug addiction. Moreover, the Commission cautioned Congress in 2007 against any reduction in the quantity trigger for the powder cocaine mandatory minimum, "as there is no evidence to justify such an increase in quantity-based penalties for powder cocaine offenses." Legislative efforts to address sentencing reform with incremental approaches that do not root out the fundamental unfairness of the cocaine disparity will fall short of justice. I urge this Committee and the entire Congress to support elimination of the 100 to 1 sentencing disparity and to end the harsh mandatory minimum penalties for low-level crack cocaine offenses.

CHAPTER SOURCES

The following chapters have been previously published:

Chapter 1 – This is an edited reformatted and augmented version of a Congressional Research Service publication, report, RL33318, dated August 5, 2010.

Chapter 2 - This is an edited reformatted and augmented version of a Congressional Research Service publication, report, R41412, dated September 14, 2010.

Chapter 3 - This is an edited reformatted and augmented version of a Congressional Research Service publication, report, dated July 14, 2010.

Chapter 4 - This is an edited reformatted and augmented version of a Congressional Research Service publication, report, dated October 22, 2010.

Chapter 5 - This is an edited reformatted and augmented version of a Congressional Research Service publication, report, dated October 13, 2010.

Chapter 6 - This is an edited reformatted and augmented version of a Congressional Research Service publication, report, dated August 5, 2010.

Chapter 7 – This statement was delivered as testimony on July 14, 2009. Judge Julie E. Carnes, Chair of the Criminal Law Committee on behalf of the Judicial Conference, before the United States House of Representatives, Committee on the Judiciary, Subcommittee on Crime, Terrorism and Homeland Security.

Chapter 8 - This statement was delivered as testimony on July 14, 2009. Julie Stewart, President, Families Against Mandatory Minimum, submitted to the Subcommittee on Crime, Terrorism, and Homeland Security, of the Committee on the Judiciary, United States House of Representatives.

Chapter 9 - This statement was delivered as testimony on July 14, 2009. Michael J. Sullivan, Partner, Ashcroft Sulliva, before the Subcommittee on Crime, terrorism, and Homeland Security, Committee on the Judiciary, United States House of Representatives.

Chapter 10 - This statement was delivered as testimony on July 14, 2009. National Border Patrol Council of the American Federation of Government Employees, before the Subcommittee on Crime, Terrorism and Homeland Security, Committee on the Judiciary, United States House of Representatives.

Chapter 11 - This statement was delivered as testimony on July 14, 2009. Grover G. Norquist, President, Americans for Tax Reform, Subcommittee on Crime, Terrorism, and Homeland Security, House Committee on the Judiciary.

Chapter 12 - This statement was delivered as testimony on May 21, 2009. Lanny A. Breuer, Assistant Attorney General, Criminal Division, United States Department of Justice, before the United States House of Representatives, Committee on the Judiciary, Subcommittee on Crime, Terrorism and Homeland Security.

Chapter 13 - This statement was delivered as testimony on May 21, 2009. Ricardo H. Hinojosa, Acting Chair, United States Sentencing Commission, before the House Committee on the Judiciary, Subcommittee on Crime, Terrorism, and Homeland Security.

Chapter 14 - This statement was delivered as testimony on May 21, 2009. Joseph I. Cassilly, State's Attorney Harford County, Bel Air, Maryland, and President, national District Attorneys Association, House Judiciary Committee, Subcommittee on Crime, Terrorism, and Homeland Security, United States House of Representatives.

Chapter 15 - This statement was delivered as testimony on May 21, 2009. Willie M. Aikens, before the Subcommittee on Crime, terrorism, and Homeland Security of the House Judiciary Committee.

Chapter 16 - This statement was delivered as testimony on May 21, 2009. Bob Bushman, Vice President, National Narcotic Officers' Associations' Coalition, before the Subcommittee on Crime, Terrorism, and Homeland Security, Committee on Judiciary, United States House of Representatives.

Chapter 17 - This statement was delivered as testimony on May 21, 2009. Veronica F. Coleman-Davis, former United States Attorney for the Western District of Tennessee, before the United States house of Representatives, Committee on the Judiciary, Subcommittee on Crime, Terrorism, and Homeland Security.

Chapter 18 - This statement was delivered as testimony on May 21, 2009. Marc Mauer, Executive Director, The Sentencing Project, prepared for the House Judiciary, Subcommittee on Crime, Terrorism, and Homeland Security.

INDEX

D

E

F

G

H

I

E

F

G

H

I

O

P

Q

R

S

T

U

V

W

Y